Claudius Buchanan Patten

England as Seen by an American Banker

Notes of a pedestrian tour

Claudius Buchanan Patten

England as Seen by an American Banker
Notes of a pedestrian tour

ISBN/EAN: 9783337329006

Printed in Europe, USA, Canada, Australia, Japan

Cover: Foto ©Andreas Hilbeck / pixelio.de

More available books at **www.hansebooks.com**

ENGLAND

SEEN BY AN AMERICAN BANKER

NOTES OF A PEDESTRIAN TOUR

BOSTON
D. LOTHROP AND COMPANY
FRANKLIN AND HAWLEY STREETS

TO THE

English People,

IN HALL AND COTTAGE, IN CITY OR COUNTRY,

WHO SO CHEERFULLY RESPONDED TO ALL MY INQUIRIES;

AND TO

My Twelve-Year-Old Son,

THE COMPANION OF MY TRAVELS,

WHOSE FAMILIAR PRESENCE MADE ALL LANDS HOME TO ME,

THIS WORK IS CORDIALLY INSCRIBED.

ENGLAND AS SEEN BY AN AMERICAN BANKER.

WALKING AS A FINE ART.

OUR notes on this point shall be English notes, and our walks in view shall be walks in England in the spring-time. And first, what of the climate then and there? I may have been the luckiest of men, but I found it the loveliest imaginable. Now I am not going to devote pages to descriptions of the varying aspects of English skies and clouds in spring, but I simply note the fact that I found rural England in April and May a perfect paradise in regard to what I may term a walking climate. There was little rain; or, at any rate, not rain enough to interfere the slightest with my walking. There was no heat, no cold, no scorching suns, no biting winds.

I repeat only what many other pedestrians have said when I say that there was something in the atmosphere of the island that was more inspiriting, — more stimulating to out-of-door travelling, than I have noticed elsewhere. I am not a great walker; yet I often made my thirty miles a day in England with ease, without the slightest overweariness.

The glory of the walker is his independence, his perfect freedom, and *abandon.* He can go anywhere, stop anywhere, and do as he pleases. He can make closer observation, more completely "do" a place, and altogether become better acquainted with countries, cities, or towns, by walking through them, than by seeing them in any other way.

I to-day count no places visited by me in England that I did not walk into, walk through, and walk out of; and, in these rambling notes, I have only fully written of places that I so visited.

In my many long and most interesting pedestrian excursions in lovely rural England, I often found myself travelling broad highways that had been laid out by the Romans in the days when they held sway from the shores of the Mediterranean to the Pictish wall in ancient Britain. The Romans built five great arterial routes across Europe. I came upon one of these which crossed the channel to Richborough, and, passing onward from London to York, is now known as the Watling Street Road; and I walked many a mile over its well macadamized and perfectly straight bed.

Over these Roman roads in the old days, travel,

not only for business, but for health and pleasure, coursed as it does to-day; and then, as now, there was no lack of commodious carriages, and comfortable inns or taverns.

As dead as possible are some of the rural English villages through which I passed, and the air of dreamy quietude that hung over them impressed me most forcibly. Lords, squires, and parsons rule over their population; and these servile villagers hardly dare speak, think, or act, without finding out, in advance, the will and wishes of the ruling magnates named.

I present, as a typical illustration of the village life I have in mind, — a sort of life with which I made close acquaintance, — Brigstock, a place five miles away from any railway-station, and under the rule of three noblemen, who own all the land in the village and thereabouts, and who will not sell a yard of the same for love or gold. Commons were once numerous in Brigstock, but these great landed proprietors have gradually stolen them all. The laborers living here are enduring a sort of hand-to-mouth existence. When they are old and helpless, they go to the "union."

I have entered the cottages of such villagers, have sat by their hearth-stones, and talked over with them their way of life and prospects. I have found them servile, stupid, without hope or ambition, and living upon the plainest fare amid the plainest surroundings. Countries beyond the sea, of which they had faintly heard, seem immensely far away to them; and emigration to such was a thought that seldom entered their minds.

* * *

I shall never forget the long stretch across country which I took in an early walk from the suburbs of London to ancient Oxford, nor how that city dawned upon me, for the first time, as I entered it on foot. Nor am I willing to allow that my walk from Liverpool to Chester and into London was not a sufficient compensation for a voyage across the north Atlantic.

On a bright May morning I have tramped to Abbotsford, visited fair Melrose Abbey, and, following the winding Tweed, stood by the grave of Scott in Dryburgh Abbey. I have walked up and down and across the lake district of England, pausing at every point of particular interest, and shall never forget my sensations, as, at the close of a spring day, I entered the old graveyard at Grasmere, and stood by the grave of Wordsworth and Hartley Coleridge; or my first view of the home of Southey, and the mountains round about it; or of the homes and haunts of poets and scholars, who had made the lake district their abiding places; or my entry into old Coventry, over the very bridge where Tennyson stood and saw the three tall spires, and wove again the legend of

Godiva; or my rambles over the Cheviot Hills of Scotland, among the peaks of Derbyshire, and over the moorlands about the home of Charlotte Brontë. But there is no end to this. I must cut the thread, leaving it hanging on this little suggestive incident in pedestrianism.

I was among the hills about Melrose when I found myself opposite an old land-worker's cottage, the door of which stood invitingly open; and, upon invitation, I entered. The old man of the cottage had become too infirm for work, but he was by no means too infirm to talk. And nothing seemed to please him more than an opportunity to "run on" with me, in a chat about matters and things round about him, and about the times long past. I had been traversing the Bermecide road, that leads from the grave of Scott in Dryburgh Abbey to Abbotsford, — the very road over which the long procession passed that followed the poet's remains to their burial. The old man fired up when I spoke of that remarkable funeral, and said he remembered it well. He had never seen so large an one before or since. He gave me the number of carriages, and said the procession was surely a mile long. I have read again since then — read for the twentieth time — Lockhart's touching account of those obsequies; and Lockhart tells how the procession of "a mile in length," made up of distinguished representatives from almost every Christian land, wound its way over those Cheviot Hills, among which I was wandering. A half-hour after I reached the highest point of the funeral route, — the very spot which had been a favorite point of view of Sir Walter's, and the point where on that sad day, says Lockhart, the long procession almost involuntarily halted, to gaze afar over the valley of the Tweed, and upon a distant view of the towers and battlements of Abbotsford.

"England Within and Without," by the scholarly Richard Grant White, is a pleasant volume of essays; but the pedestrian in England need not feel obliged to carry it in his pocket as a guide-book. When home again in his study, the returned traveller may be glad to turn over White's pages, if he is a judicious skipper, to see what the author has said about places now familiar to his eyes and to his thoughts. I believe, with Mr. Hawthorne, that one only really enjoys books of travels that lead him again to places he has "done" for himself.

I once hunted long for a volume by that learned and good man, Elihu Burritt, which had attracted my attention by a most alluring title, — "A Walk from Land's End to John O'Groat's." It has not been republished here; and, on reading it, I found why no American publisher has had the courage to tackle it. The frontispiece is a picture of the venerable author as he walked that long walk.

His tall, thin form is crowned with a "high hat;" he wears a long-skirted black coat, and carries a large black carpet-bag and cane. Verily some Rev. Jonathan Edwards of a former generation going forth on an exchange. Just one thousand and nine miles is his walk. It gave me nothing.

In wandering over the beautiful highways and byways of England, where every thing was new and strange to me, and where my entire acquaintance with roads and routes was confined to the knowledge I had previously gathered from maps, it may readily be surmised that I had to do very much in the matter of inquiring the way as I passed along. And, as I asked my way from city to city, and from town to town, two things surprised me very much. One was the amount of ignorance that prevailed among otherwise intelligent English people regarding the highway routes which were out of their every-day circle of observation; and the other was, that a people having the reputation of possessing out-of-door habits, and of being, in particular, great walkers, should evince so much surprise at seeing me planning to walk across country to some point twenty or thirty miles away.

Astonishment over this latter idea would sometimes so fully take possession of the staring man whom I was interrogating about the roads, that he would seem to forget my questions, or allow them to be obscured in his mind by the wonder that was absorbing him. Why, in the name of common sense, should a gentleman want to tramp all the way to the town or city so distant, when, for a shilling or two, he could fly there by rail in an hour or less? So, instead of getting the information I asked for, I would often be directed most persistently to the nearest station on the railway.

I had always heard much in praise of the rugged and vigorous out-of-door habits of the young men of England. But my ideas in this regard received rather a set-back when I studied the habits, and observed the physiques, of English students at the famous school towns and university towns. I remember being somewhat astonished when I was starting out one morning to walk from Rugby to London, to find that none of the crowd of rather delicate-looking boys — "spindle-shanks," Grant White has the temerity to call them — who were walking about the town, or gliding over its streets on bicycles or tricycles, seemed to know much about the highway that would take them to London; and this famous Tom Brown school town is, if I remember correctly, only about seventy miles from the mighty metropolis of England over highways the finest and pleasantest in the world. These young men were very much astonished to hear me talk of *walking* to London. When I told them I should think some of them would like such a pleasant ramble in such a mag nificent walking climate as they were blessed with, found no hearty response.

It did not seem to me that the boys at Rugby, the boys I saw at Eton, Harrow, Oxford, and other educational towns in England, where young men and boys most do congregate, and those whom I met in London, home in vast swarms for the holidays, often dressed in a most amusingly antique, high-hatted, and wide-collared style, were as " ruddy and white, and strong on their legs," as American boys of the same age and class.

And my observation of the boys of England of an older growth, both in town and country, in all parts of the kingdom, also led me to the conclusion that the boasted superior muscularity of Englishmen, as compared with their cousins in the United States, did not exist. But, returning to the subject of finding one's way over the splendid roads of England, I note that I found the country generously supplied with guide-posts of a somewhat peculiar character. They stood trim and erect, wherever diverging roads presented themselves, well lettered with the names of the towns, cities, and hamlets not far on the roads along which their index fingers pointed. Yet, singularly enough, I do not remember to have seen a single guide-post in all my wanderings in England which bore upon its boards any figures showing the distances to any of the places to which the hands upon the boards pointed, — or, I might more properly say, to which the boards themselves pointed; for they have a general style in England of making their guide-post boards with one end shaped into the form of a hand, with the index finger pointed towards the town to which they direct.

I have never seen guide-boards of this fashion in America; but, in other respects, they were precisely like those seen in our own country. And as I often lingered by the roadside, and studied the various names that appeared on these my roadway guides, their familiar appearance would, for a moment, make me think I was once more wandering among the hills and valleys of Massachusetts or New Hampshire. Yet would this illusion be quickly dispelled, when I read upon these guide-boards such names as Banbury Cross, Olney, Lichfield, Stoke Pogis, Eton, Harrow, Slough, London, etc., — names that had all my life been familiar to me in connection with nursery ballads, English biography, and English classic prose and poetry, but which were now no longer mere names, but actual places, through which I was wending my way, or upon which I was gazing from some gentle rise in the road which gave me a chance to cast my eyes afar over the lovely English country about me. It sometimes seemed to me as if the towns, villages, and hamlets were so closely crowded together in England, — took up, individually, so small a space, — that I was out of one locality and into another before I had time to find out the names of the various precincts through which I was wandering.

In walking from Barnet to Oxford, — a charming cross-country ramble over a route which I have set down in my note-book as being as pleasant as any I have ever travelled, — I made my first acquaintance with that genuine old-fashioned tramp-house, an English round-house.

Its shape, location, and general character were a perfect poser to me; and I came at once to a halt, for the purpose of making an immediate investigation.

A round-house is, in plain old English, a sort of prison in use by the nightly watch to secure drunken and disorderly prisoners till they can be brought before a magistrate, and fined, or sent to jail. An English gentleman, driving a horse and gig slowly up the hill, reading, as his horse walked, "The London Daily Times," which he had just procured at the station where the morning train from London had a moment before halted, paused in his reading, to tell me that the curious little building I was staring at was an English round-house.

They may not always be of the shape of the one I am describing. This was perfectly round, with a diameter at the base of about a dozen feet. It was only of one story, and contained but one room, which occupied the entire space within its walls, which tapered till they came to a point perhaps fifteen feet from the ground. It was made of brick, and had one door, and two little, well-secured windows. The accommodations for the stragglers and tramps who might be thrust within its walls to spend the night were of the rudest and most uncomfortable character.

I have been thus particular in describing this specimen of an old English tramp-house for two reasons. One is, that it is an institution which my readers may not, in all probability, ever have seen, and may never see, although frequent references to it may be found in English classic prose and poetry; and the other, because in our New England, within a few years past, tramp-houses, that are in many points close imitations of the obsolete and barbarous old round-house of England, have been set up in many towns to meet the exigencies arising under the administration of our modern over-severe tramp laws.

The round-houses of England, like those public instruments of torture the stocks, which an old citizen of Bedford, England, told me he could well remember seeing in use in John Bunyan's town, have become a thing of the past.

While talking with a bent and grizzled old English cobbler, who described himself as a man who had fourteen children, — seven of a sort; that is, seven boys and seven girls,— who all considered him an old fool, he told me the following story of an old English round-house: A poor drunken man, in his after-dark reelings, staggered up against a round-house, and began to feel his way along its brick sides. And this he kept on doing for a very, very long time, going around and around, feeling his way by the bricks, muttering to himself that it was the longest wall he ever saw in his life.

Ancient rights of way, or supposed rights of way, over fields and grazing lands, across lawns and baronial parks, are institutions of which I had often read in English history, song, and story; so that I felt myself familiar with these long-trodden short cuts and by-ways before I had planted my feet on English soil, and traversed these old paths myself. Yet, after all, I found that I had had little idea of the extent of the ramifications of this English by-path system till I made a close personal acquaintance with rural England. Neither had I had much idea of the nature of the tenure which the public held on many of these old foot-paths across lots, nor of the bitter warfare about them being waged between nobles and peasants, great landed proprietors, and the towns-people at large.

One of my earliest acquaintances with this internecine path-war was made during my first protracted stay at an old English inn, rented by our landlord from the rich Earl of ——, who owned nearly the whole town. My nearest railway-station was two miles away by the public roads, and only a mile by way of one of these old disputed paths across the parks of the earl. My landlord, a timid man, hardly dared to tell me of this short path; yet the public was taking it, and I followed suit. Another ancient foot-path near us led right across the grand lawn in front of the earl's great mansion, and over this there was a contest brewing; yet hind and tradesman, tramping cockney and tourist, mounted the stile, and walked the disputed path.

There was less reason in former times for the nobleman to be jealous of these rights of way. But now that population has become more dense, and horrid shops and factories hem in and flood him with a tide of humanity with which he is not particularly enamored, he struggles to keep up a seclusion which is sadly interfered with by the old foot-paths. I have heard of what Englishmen termed an extraordinary scene in connection with a right of foot-way across a park,—Knole Park, the property of Lord Sackville. For sixty years the inhabitants of Seven Oaks had had unobstructed foot-path right over it, when the lord suddenly closed it. An indignation meeting was held. At its close a vast crowd marched to the entrance of the park, wrenched from the ground the posts and chains with which the path was obstructed, and deposited them in front of the main entrance of the mansion, singing the while, " Rule Britannia " and the " National Anthem."

* * *

A ramble by the Wye is a pleasant memory. From the famous old " Peacock " inn, so near to stately Chatsworth, I had taken an early morning walk to Haddon Hall, and had been guided through that grand old baronial home by the young girl who carries the keys to the buildings, and makes her home in a rustic cottage which stands near them.

This young guide was a courteous, attractive person. Mr. Wills, the successful London dramatist, in describing to an interviewer his method of working up his last successful play, the " Docks of London," tells how the plot of this drama came into his mind as he followed the sweet-faced girl who was his guide in a ramble through the romantic old rooms and pleasant grounds of Haddon Hall.

In the play in question, the scenery and action of which are all most realistic, he manages to introduce a splendid view of Haddon, and a garden-scene in its grounds, where the girl he met there is to be seen parting from her lover. After my tarry at Haddon, I turned to the banks of the Wye, and followed its windings for many a mile, tramping through bushes, briers, and meadows, and over rocky paths.

The scenery along my route was very lovely. My walk was a solitary one. From first to last I met not a single person, and had full opportunity to enjoy undisturbed the views of the beautiful surroundings amid which I was for the first time in my life sauntering. At times, particularly in the spring, and at the Easter season, the Wye is thronged with fishermen, who pay the lordly owner of the estate through which the Wye crosses a half crown a day for a license to cast their hooks. And these sportsmen may sometimes be seen ranged along the river in vast numbers. Occupying every available point on its banks, they angle most persistently, though the results are apt to be very meagre.

Said an English Wye fisherman: "I saw the windward bank studded with fishermen as thick as telegraph-poles as far as the eye could see. I walked on for a mile, and finding the outlook a little better, I put up a cast of a blue upright and an iron gray, and set to work. I worked from twelve to four without hooking a fish. Still I plodded on through the meadows, till I found myself far away from all fishing companions; and just at sunset I hooked my first fish. For a half-hour I had lively sport. The seventh fish was in my basket. I had just hooked another pounder under an old willow stump, when a man in velveteen said, 'Allow me;' and took my landing net, and in a half minute had my fish out.

"'A very nice fish,' said he; 'but let me look at your ticket,' he added. He eyed it, and remarked, 'Just as I supposed. Your permit ends at the lower water, which ends where the wood ends. You are in the upper water which his Grace keeps for himself, and don't give leave for to no one whatsoever.' Although I explained I was a stranger, and had no idea that I was poaching, he smiled incredulously; but, after further explanations, offered to show me my way back where I belonged."

Wherever I wandered in rural England in the springtime, I found myself often falling in with the tents and vans of its touring gypsies. Moving through England, over its highways and by-ways, in something of a gypsy way myself, I very naturally made the close acquaintance of the brown tribes of these "separate people,"—these wonderful wanderers who came into England four hundred years ago, and who are still continually on the road, the most persistent of all commercial travellers.

Just two gypsy institutions must here receive a passing notice,—two, and no more. I have in mind the gypsy baby and the gypsy wedding as they are to be seen in the English gypsy tents of to-day, and as I have somewhere seen them photographed by an English journalist.

The child of gypsy parents is born into the

world as poor a child as there is on the face of the earth. It comes into life in a tent or van by the roadside; it has no home; it is clothed in rags, and nurtured under the open sky. Yet it grows up healthy, ruddy, and strong. In due time it is the habit of the English gypsy to bring the baby to the church in the village where his tribe is tarrying, for the purpose of having it baptized.

When it is to be brought to receive the blessing of the Church, the mother endeavors to deepen its brownness, and to enhance its beauty, by rubbing its little body with a dark liquid concocted of roots of wild plants and leaves of various sorts. When the little vagrant has been christened, it is passed back to the arms of the tramping mother, who moves on her way once more; and neither child nor mother will probably ever be seen again within the walls of a church for any religious purpose.

There may come a time when the sturdy infant shall be grown into a stony, dark-faced girl with black and glossy hair, and ornaments of gold in her ears,— a girl with a gown of many colors, and an abundance of rings, chains, and bracelets. And when this maiden is married, a most fantastic wedding ceremony is witnessed. The gypsy wedding is apt to take place in a sand-pit. The tribe arranges itself in two long rows fronting each other. In the middle of the path between them is a broomstick, which is carefully held a little way from the ground in a horizontal position.

The bridegroom walks down the path and over the broomstick, and stops, awaiting the bride. She then comes tripping down the same long path from an opposite direction, and also steps over the broomstick. The couple join hands. The wedding is ended with this simple and speedy ceremony. A little feasting is indulged in. The new couple resume their wandering life with the tribe as before.

The difficulty of finding any one to direct me, while walking in England, was partially obviated by the use of excellent pocket-maps which are in such abundant supply there. I suppose, in fact I know, that there is no country on the face of the earth so thoroughly mapped as is the United Kingdom. As long ago as 1790, the British government determined to make a map of Great Britain, for military purposes, on a scale of one inch to the square mile; and, as a foundation for this work, it began what has been termed the "big-trig," which was an expensive system of triangulation which was not completed till 1852. The preparation of this map was commenced soon after the completion of this survey, and it was finished about ten years ago. But the maps of England now generally in use are those based on a scale of one square inch to the acre. I found these maps able to show me, by their shadings, hills, and valleys, every topographical feature of the country; and also clearly placing before me, not only all the roads, rivers, towns, etc., but all the conspicuous houses of the country.

Inquiring the way of anybody one meets is one of the divine rights of the pedestrian in America; but I shall not soon forget the cold, vacant stare I received as I plodded along between Liverpool and London, when, by stress of circumstances, I was forced to stop the carriage of a stout lady — who may have been, for all I know, the proud wife of an earl — as it was rolling along in stately dignity, to tell her I was a lost traveller, and ask of her my way out of the maze into which I had fallen. As soon as the lady had recovered her composure, she signed to Jeames, on the box, to give me some information. I doubt not the English pedestrian of the humbler class, in which category she undoubtedly placed me, would have continued to be lost forever before he would have had the temerity to ask his way of my lady in her carriage.

English roads are almost invariably a comfort to the traveller, whether he plods over them on foot, gallops along their smooth bed in saddle, or rides over them in carriage. Under a system inaugurated by Macadam and Telford, they have been brought to a degree of perfection that surprised me. A word must be said of English inns, particularly those in the rural districts, since upon the accommodations there to be obtained depends much of the comfort of the person travelling upon the highways. I can assure my reader that he will find plenty of them in his way, if he travels in almost any direction in the rural districts of England. And their fare is wholesome and abundant, though not of great variety; their rooms and beds neat and comfortable, and attendants courteous.

A genuine old English inn that I visited was built of brick, and is three hundred years old. It stands near the roadside under ancient elms; and on every hand are old oaks, beeches, and larches, and hedges of hawthorn. It bears the sign of the Wheat Sheaf, and a sheaf of wheat is rudely painted on its swinging sign and over its old oaken main entrance. In front, outside of its walls, are a few rude seats, upon which wayfarers rest as they drink the ale they have paused there to buy. The roof is either thatched, covered with red tile, or made of huge slabs of slate-stone. Within are no carpeted rooms, but well-worn floors of oak, very old, but white and clean.

On the right, on the first floor, is the tap-room, presided over by a neat bar-maid. On the left, a simply furnished apartment where travellers can sit at rude benches, and drink the beer, and eat bread and cheese. In the rear of both is a wide kitchen, with a stone floor and huge open fireplace, after the ancient New England pattern, pot-hooks and trannels, andirons and singing teakettles, included. All around this room are ranged shelves for cooking-utensils and food; and overhead pots and kettles and flitches of pork and bacon may be swinging, and sometimes bannocks of barley meal. But I have not space to go in detail through all the house. The chambers are neatly furnished, the old style of sinks, wash-bowls, and high-posted beds being there, having windows that open at full length like doors, the glass in them having the smallest of panes, and fireplaces that insure a good ventilation. The beds I always found of extra width, and of extremely comfortable character.

Through an arched passage in the centre of the house, over the top of which are to be observed legs of mutton hanging to ripen for the table, the stable is entered. It stands in a sort of courtyard, and generally has connected with it various storerooms, sculleries, etc., and a room which is the headquarters of *boots*, and where he may be found when he is not on duty, or "Coming, sir." It is made of brick or stone, and the floors of the stalls for the horses are almost invariably made of the same material. One would think such a bed hard for the animal; but the English jockeys claim they are much healthier and cleaner than wooden floors, and that the horses like them better. They give horses most generous beds of wheat straw in England, piling the straw knee-deep. In cities and large towns, large quantities of sawdust are used for bedding cows and horses. Peat is also sometimes used for this purpose. I saw no narrow stalls for horses in England. The stable people there never tolerate such cramped stalls as are common with us. All the old stables have one department set off for "loose boxes for hunters." And this inscription, painted in large letters on the outer doors of the stables as an attraction to sporting patrons, vividly reminded me, when I first strayed among English inn stables, that I was in a country where field sports were still a prominent institution. Another equally vivid reminder of the same fact was the common sight of horse-vans, attached to express passenger-trains, for the conveyance of hunters and race-horses from meet to meet, or from stables to meets.

Split beans, split peas and oats, chopped hay and chopped straw, are the standard stable feed for horses. In addition, American corn — an article not often used in any shape for human food in England — is being introduced into the stable diet of the country. Though beans and barley are given to English horses, neither of the articles appear on English tables, except in cases where green table beans are served. No Boston brown bread nor baked beans on English bills of fares.

And now a few words regarding prices in rural inns for entertainment for man and horse. I can drive from Land's End to John O'Groat's without expending over two dollars a day on the journey; two dollars for self, horse and trap. Early in my wanderings in England I came to this conclusion.

On showing this statement to experienced Englishmen of the humbler class, who had as artisans travelled a deal over England, they said I was extravagant in my estimate; and I found they did travel, and travel comfortably, in the country in England, at far less expense.

Honest, respectable, steady English artisans allow themselves 2s 6d a day for travelling expenses when walking through the country. And their scale is this: 6d for supper, 6d for lodging, 6d for breakfast, 8d for dinner, 4d for fees. The teamster gets his pair of horses breakfasted for 12d; dinner for them, the same. In each case he gives the hostler a tip of a penny-half-penny. I have tried the accommodations in small English inns where the prices all around were those I have named, and found myself very comfortable there. From these figures a very high upward range can be made. For instance, drive ten miles out of London, stop at Star and Garter, Richmond, and pay eight shillings for a lunch of cold corned beef, and be waited upon by servants in livery; and, as you eat your lunch, sit in the most splendid of dining-rooms, and look out over Richmond Park with its eight hundred acres of field and forest.

On the other hand, take this for an illustration. You will find well scattered over England very neat and well-kept cocoa-rooms. These are established to displace beer-shops, and are in the hands of the best people in England. I often visited them, and never found a poor one. They offer a great variety of food and temperance beverages, as well as accommodations for the night. What will show what the modern English cocoa-rooms are so well as one of their own bills? I begged it of the superintendent as I chatted with him in his attractive room at Waltham Cross, eighteen miles from London. Waltham there is always pronounced *Walt-ham*. Here is the bill in full:—

WALTHAM CROSS READING-ROOMS.

Lodging rooms, 1 person per night . . . 1s, 1s 6d, and 2s.
" " 2 persons " . . . 1s 6d, 2s 6d, and 3s.
" " 1 person per week . . . 4s 6d, 7s, and 10s.
" " 2 persons " . . . 7s, 10s 6d, and 12s 6d.
Hire of Club-room for meetings, etc., 2 hours or under, 2s.

☞ *Special terms for longer hiring.*

Refreshments served in rooms other than the coffee and smoking rooms, per each person, 3d.

Beefsteak, small, 8d. Large, 10d.
Cold beef, per plate . . 2d. | Mutton Chop . . . . . 10d.
Coffee, per large cup, 1d. Pint, 2d.
Coffee, per small pot, 3d. Large, 5d.
Tea, per large cup, 1½d. Pint, 3d.
Tea, per small pot, 4d. Large, 6d and 9d.
Cocoa per large cup, 1½d. Pint, 3d.
New milk, per glass, 1½d.

Roll, 1d.   Butter, 1d.
   Bread and butter, per slice, ½d.
      Bread and ham, per slice, ½d.
Bread and cheese . . . . 2d. | Cake, per slice . . . . 1d.
Milk scones, per slice, 1½d.
   Egg (fried or boiled), 2d.
      Rasher of bacon (fried), 2½d.
Compressed beef, per ¼ lb., 3d.
   Peppermint water, per glass, 1d.
      Fruit syrups, per glass, 1½d.
Hariot's bine, per bottle, 2d.
   Lime juice, per glass, 1d.
      Ginger beer, per bottle, 1d.
Gingerade, per bottle . . 2d. | Lemonade, per bottle . . 3d.
   Reading, smoking, and private rooms.
Daily papers supplied, and time-tables of all the principal railways taken here.

All here are good but the temperance substitutes for beer. Those are vile. I refer to the bottled articles. And English coffee everywhere — in hotels at five dollars a day, and in modest restaurants, all the same — bad. Too much chiccory. Tea and cocoa the very best almost everywhere.

It should be borne in mind, in reading this specimen bill of an English cocoa-room, that the one I have selected is that of an establishment situated in a populous town near London, where rent and other incidental expenses must be of necessity higher than in the small country towns.

I have in mind a fact or two bearing upon travelling expenses in England, which I gathered from another source. "Bachelor Fellows" at Oxford, a class of cultivated and gentlemanly men, are in the habit of travelling a deal, both in England and on the Continent. Fifteen pounds a month is by them considered ample means to defray their journey and hotel bills. These students claim that they can live handsomely, and travel four months every year, on an annual income of three hundred pounds. The secret of their getting along so economically on the road is found in the fact that, while they mean to be comfortable, and get good accommodations, they invariably avoid guides, carriages and expensive inns.

In some of the suggestions I have made regarding travel in rural England, I have had in view the purchase in England, for the temporary use of the tourist, of a horse and trap, or saddle. A word regarding the disposition of the team or horse when the traveller has no further use for his purchase is now in order. His best method is to fling this "rolling stock" into an auction mart as soon as his journeys are over. This can best be done either in London or Liverpool.

In walking across country I have had occasion to walk upon the track of a railway; but this is something strictly forbidden in England, and I was quickly warned off the rail. But I noted then, and afterwards observed, the extremely solid and substantial character of the road-beds of the leading English lines. Their steel rails are very heavy, about eighty pounds per lineal yard, and twenty-four feet long. The sleepers are laid about three feet apart. Heavy iron chairs are used to support and fix the rail, and at the joints wedges of wood are used to soften the rigid holdings of the rails by the cast-iron chairs.

I noticed that they have a way in England of covering the sleepers between the rails with earth, cinders, etc.; so that, in walking upon the track, I found my forbidden path a smooth and attractive one, over which I could have wandered from village to village as comfortably as over the macadamized highways, had it not been for the locomotive dangers and the legal restrictions.

The sleepers were formerly made almost entirely of the English larch, and the nobility and gentry of England, who own the vast, heavily wooded parks of the land, have made quite a business of selling sleepers from their timber plantations. I often saw gangs of wood-cutters "getting out" railroad-sleepers under the shadows of the splendid trees on the great home parks in rural England.

Of late years large quantities of timber for railway-sleepers, as well as timber for all sorts of English use, have been brought from Baltic ports. And now a movement is being made to substitute steel sleepers for wooden ones, which latter are accused of splitting long before they decay, and of soon being crushed under the weight of the enormous traffic which burdens English roads.

A FINE ENGLISH RAILWAY.

SUCH I term the London and Northwestern line, upon which I often travelled. The road-bed is excellent; the coaches, especially those of the first class, exceedingly neat and comfortable; and the servants of the road, as all its "help" are termed, courteous and intelligent. The road is seventeen hundred miles in length. It binds together Liverpool, London, Carlisle, Holyhead, Edinburgh, and Glasgow; and I have a very pleasant recollection of being myself whirled into all these interesting localities behind the modest looking but powerful locomotives of the London and Northwestern.

I found its "best trains," to use a favorite English expression, would sweep me across a two-hundred mile stretch in just about four hours. A mile a minute was considered very fair time on these express trains; and I have often and often seen my fellow passengers checking off the miles at this speed, remarking the while, as they flew along, that we were doing very well. The capital of the road is five hundred millions of dollars. Its employés number forty thousand. Every thing connected with the management of this road seemed to be administered upon the most admirable system.

I remember hearing it stated that such a thing as a hot-box was never heard of on this road.

Under the "block system" of signals, the trains are directed with such success that accidents and delays are most infrequent. The stations are models of neatness, and often picturesque in their architecture, location, and surroundings. I can testify that there were to be seen along the fine track of this splendid road, over which I so often travelled, no unsightly banks left at the building of the line, gashed and torn, but everywhere well sodded and neatly terraced slopes.

The traveller coming from a country like ours, where dust, noise and smoke are quite apt to be prominent features of a ride by rail, finds himself on this London and Northwestern road gliding like magic — silently, smoothly, clearly — through a garden-like country, hearing, as he dashes through farm-lands, parks and grazing-fields, little of ringing bells, or screeching whistles, and seeing little of dust, smoke, or cinders.

I found that England had a great many tunnels. When, on a pleasant morning in April, I first set my foot in an English railway-coach, and made therein a dash into the heart of the island, I noticed the porters placing lamps in the roofs of every coach of the train, — lamps which were lighted in the broad day, their flame being sheltered by a curtain that was drawn beneath each hanging burner. My curiosity was excited by this novel equipment, yet it was soon made clear to me why this preparation was made. The flying train had not travelled many miles before its locomotive gave a short, sharp shriek, and dashed into a long, dark tunnel which might have steeped us in blank night had not the little curtain above us been withdrawn to let down upon us the cheerful rays of the roof-lantern. As the train sped on this experience was continually repeated. Tunnel after tunnel was reached and passed in that first journey of a hundred miles, and many of them were quite long. And in subsequent English rail experiences, it seems to me I never made a trip without a deal of tunnel travel.

In the construction of English railways the engineers appear to have adopted the theory that it was much cheaper to run under a gentleman's broad home-park than to cut through it, though, in many cases, the cutting would not have seemed at all deep to an American railroad contractor. Without doubt, the question of land damages and disfigurement of rural scenery on great estates had a large influence in the premises.

I stayed for weeks in one of the most lovely rural districts in England, a locality full of noble parks and plantations, in the heart of which were the halls of great numbers of the nobility and gentry on the line of the great London and Northwestern Railway, which had in that section five separate tracks on its main route, and branches leaping out into the country in all directions. Yet, though near the lines, I heard little and saw little of the railway, for it burrowed its way along by us through a series of tunnels under the gently rolling hills, into the heart of which it entered; but I would occasionally catch a glimpse of a long train as it plunged on and buried itself.

When the metals were first laid down in England, there was a great hue-and-cry against the rails, on the ground that they would greatly disfigure the rural scenery of the country.

The owners of lordly parks which were to be entered by the lines insisted in many instances that the tracks should not be laid on them, or through them, but under them. By thus boring and burrowing their way through great show places, the dreaded disfigurement was avoided, and the lords partially pacified.

But there is certainly one rural and romantic English district from which the iron track has so far been debarred; and debarred largely through the influence of the poetic, esthetic, and cultured taste of the day. Leaving the railway-coaches at Kendal, I walked forty miles through the lake district, without at any point crossing a railway-track, or even coming in sight of one.

To-day, whenever a new line is projected in England, a powerful society, whose mission is to protect and preserve the natural beauties of England, directs its eye at once upon the movements of the builders. The name of this society is "The Commons and Open Spaces Preservation Society." This organization has recently been opposing the plans to build a railway through Epping Forest and the Lake region. The road proposed among the lakes is named the Braithwaite and Buthmere line, and lovers of lake scenery have been greatly excited by what they deem its very objectionable character.

I found a railway line taking me as far into the beautiful lake country as I wished to travel by steam, and was glad enough to be able to leave the line behind me, and walk the thirty or forty miles which will cover the whole stretch of that romantic country. But, without doubt, the time is not far distant when those beautiful hills and valleys will re-echo to the whistle of the locomotive. Great changes are taking place there. Costly villas are being built on the desirable points along the shores of the lakes, and among the romantic hills in their vicinity; and the entire region is taking on an artificial, town-like character, quite disappointing to those familiar with the early rural sweetness of the locality.

While looking down from old Helvellyn upon one of the most romantic of the lakes of Westmoreland, I was told that it had been purchased by the great city of Manchester for use as a water-supply, and that plans for conveying it there by tunnels through Helvellyn, etc., had already been matured.

* * *

I had many opportunities for observing the character and methods of railway employés, a class always termed "railway servants" in English circles. It appeared to me that they were, from the general superintendent down to the humblest plate-layer, of a lower grade in respect to social position, personal ideas regarding self-respect, general intelligence and individual ambition, than the corresponding class in the United States. Their pay is very moderate, their hours of labor long, and their work arduous. The very fact that these workers, high and low, are there merely termed railway servants, seems to me to have a tendency to degrade them in the social scale.

Their uniforms are furnished by the corporations which employ them, and often the companies furnish them their tenements. The rules which govern them in their daily routine of work upon the line are a curious specimen of iron-clad minuteness, governing most rigidly in every detail the duties of their position. From the highest to the lowest they are a fee-taking class. It seemed to me a pity that the fine appearing, even dashing, guards of a splendid flying mail-train, drawn by the most perfect locomotive in the world, and made up of coaches which were a perfect model of comfort, should take your shilling as a matter of course, and, in recognition of the tip, should render you attentions taking on no little servility of character.

There is one point in English railroading that pleased me much, and which might, it appeared to me, be wisely copied in the United States. I found the great London and Northwestern Railway had established orders of merit for their employés. For the various degrees of merit and length of faithful service this road gave money tokens, and badges of honor, that were worn upon the sleeves of the coat.

* *
*

I had been educated into the idea that England's "best hold" was manufacturing. My books had told me that England was the workshop of the world; and when I turned my steps towards the United Kingdom, I expected to find there a nation almost entirely engaged in hammering out implements of iron and of steel, and weaving fabrics of cotton and of wool for home consumption and an export trade, whose range extended around the belted globe. The great manufacturing cities and towns of England are certainly hives of industry, such as are equalled nowhere in the world; and I came out from smoky Birmingham, from noisy and grimy Glasgow and Sheffield, and the great spinning and weaving cities of Manchester, Bradford and Leeds, with the impression that in their shops and factories the world could be easily equipped and clothed.

But there is another side to this question; and I obtained a full view of it when I extended my wanderings into rural England, and became somewhat closely acquainted with the aspects of her farming interests, and had an opportunity to study English agriculture. I have never seen anywhere such fine specimens of farming. But this is a point that is generally well understood, and need not, therefore, be dwelt upon. Every one is supposed to know that England's wheat-fields are like garden-beds, her mowing-fields like untrimmed lawns, her pastures — where I saw such fine specimens of cattle grazing up to their eyes in grass — better than the average hay-lands in the best part of New England. But there are few, however, who know how extensive and overtopping the farming interest is to-day in fertile England.

I have many times heard very intelligent Englishmen say that England would soon starve to death if it were not for the United States; and, in advance, I had had no doubt that such was the fact. As I rambled up and down the farming districts of England, I heard one cry of distress going up from all the farmers, and that was the cry that America was tearing all her produce markets to pieces. And when, in the great dock warehouses of Liverpool and London, I saw mountains of wheat, corn, oats, ham, butter, cheese, etc., that had been pitched out of the holds of the western ships, I felt that the solid facts, corroborating the food theories I have named, were right before me. But now what are, after all, the real facts in the premises? Here we have them: —

Professor Tanner of England — one of those industrious men whose figures, believed in everywhere, are of the kind that don't lie — said, in a recent address at Edinburgh, that England's farming interest was her *leading* interest; that the annual value of her agricultural produce was two hundred and sixty million pounds; that England paid away forty million pounds annually for foreign produce, which she might, if she paid proper attention to farming at home, herself raise. These facts must be a revelation to most readers.

The cultivation of wheat now reaches even to the extreme north of Scotland. Ireland never did raise much wheat, or largely consume wheat; and I found her at the present time everywhere narrowing her furrows, and widening her grazing-fields, thereby reducing her demand for land workers, and so adding to the terrible embarrassment of the labor situation in Ireland. But England proper is a great wheat garden still, though the area of even her wheat-fields is decreasing, while her grazing-grounds are growing in extent.

We deem England the workshop of the world; yet, after all, her best hold to-day is agriculture, and her best hold always has been agriculture. At the period of the revolution of 1689, she was raising annually fourteen million bushels of wheat. In 1872 the United Kingdom raised a hundred millions.

Travelling through the agricultural districts of England in May, I had the chance to see her broad and beautiful fields of young wheat; and such perfection of cultivation I have never elsewhere seen. Costly lands, an abundance of fertilizers, plenty of labor, and an immense demand for every product of the farm at the very gate of the farm, are reasons enough for making the most of every foot of England's farming-lands. And if to-day she is turning wheat-lands into grass-lands and hay-lands, it is not because her wheat is not in pressing demand at high prices, but because the hay and grass products — in the form of beef, butter, etc. — will pay her even better.

It is an interesting fact that England raises annually just about as many bushels of wheat as she imports from the United States; namely, a hundred millions. But England raises a greater number of bushels of wheat per acre than any land on the globe. Her average, during the last nineteen years, has been twenty-three bushels per acre, while ours has been eleven and a half.

I had little idea, previous to my walks and talks in England, of the enormous extent to which machinery of the finest and most modern type is used upon the farms and gardens in the farm-houses and farm-yards of the United Kingdom.

A mere list of the names of the leading articles in this line with which I became familiar will be better than any attempt at detailed description of them, since their simple titles will give quite an idea of what the farmers of England have adopted as aids to handwork in field and farm-yard. There are steam-engines, stationary traction and compound in movement, thus making an immense saving in fuel; huge steam road-rollers of the best pattern, and in use everywhere; ploughs on the wire-rope system, by which a series of ploughs are attached and moved on a single wire-rope; threshing-machines of an endless variety; locomotives for common roads; bone mills, and mills for grinding and cutting all the things that a farmer is likely to wish to grind or cut, from turnips to wheat; reaping-machines; straw-trussing machines; garden ploughs for use in contracted spaces; draining ploughs; thatch or straw yealming machines; straw thatch weaving machines; water drills; manure drills; and sheaf binders.

But I might as well give up the attempt to catalogue England's farm and garden machinery. I saw enough of it to convince me that the English farmers are fully up with the times in their machinery as well as their methods. The smoothness and beauty of their farm fields astonished and delighted me. Their ploughed lands are made as level and as free from all stones as the finest gardens are with us. And, in planting, the English farmers so put in the rows and hills that the fields seem as regularly laid out as the squares on a checker-board. Some of the farms are very large, and many of them are carried on with scientific and business skill and precision.

Many gentlemen of wealth and high social position appear to go into the business of farming for the purpose of advancing the farming interests of their country, by placing before those who are in the same occupation, but who have fewer advantages, examples of the highest art in farming. The Duke of Edinburgh, son of the Queen, carries on an immense model farm. The American visitor to England is likely to become interested in the immense seed farms, some of which I had an opportunity of glancing at.

One of the most famous of these is owned by the great Stourbridge firm of G. Webb & Sons, who use thirteen thousand acres of land for growing seeds, and who have won in prizes for their seeds seventeen thousand pounds.

English farm-work is carried on in a heavy but extremely thorough manner. The English farmer's plough is heavier than ours; his farm-wagon stouter, all his farm implements made more substantially than ours, and expected to last longer. And, of necessity, he uses more force in his work than do we: larger horses, and more of them to the plough, the wagon, the roller; and more stout men, and fewer boys, are managing the machines on his farming-fields.

A significant illustration of this point comes to mind. Intelligent correspondent writes the inevitable letter to "The London Times," setting forth how alarming it was to find that farmers in his neighborhood were actually permitting boys of the tender age of fourteen to handle and drive farm-horses; and how one poor boy of that age had, while driving a horse and cart, been run over. The writer ends up by calling for immediate legislation in the premises, closing in the stereotyped "Times" correspondents' style, "I enclose my card, and beg to subscribe myself your most obedient servant, Bishops Stortford." As I have been used to seeing American farmers manage quite a farm with no other force than themselves, a light-weight horse, and two or three small boys, I was, of course, amused by this panic over the dangers of allowing English boys of fourteen to go near horses.

Having been, from youth, accustomed to a method of farming in New England that is, upon the whole, of a character just the opposite of that which I have in mind when using the words compact farming, the style of cultivating the soil which came under my observation in England seemed, in comparison, to be thorough, systematic, and in most points well-nigh perfect. I have often walked through long stretches of English country where, on every hand, were to be seen pastures that were better than the average of New England hay-lands, and where the hay-fields were like the finest lawns; while the portions of the soil under the plough were like garden-beds, and were growing crops likely to yield per acre an average overtopping the most special crop successes of New England.

Yet, as I have intimated, these things are only matters of comparison; and so I was called upon even in England to hear much talk in condemnation of the faulty methods of her farmers in cultivating the soil, particularly in the matter of spreading their labor and their fertilizers over too much area. It was not uncommon to hear such expressions as "milking the land dry" applied to English farmers; and, in proof of their mistaken methods in this regard, I was pointed to the vast acreage of English land that had been worn out and had become waste, as a consequence of this short-sighted method of its treatment. I have found that there is a word of Continental extraction — the word "intensive" as applied to farming — which happily describes the methods of the agriculturalists of such a country as Holland, whose style of farm management is held up by English writers on agriculture as a model for English farmers. "Intensive farming" is the opposite of what the English term extensive farming, or farming that spreads itself over too much land, gathering from a broad acre a product that might more easily have been harvested from narrower fields. I did not find time to make an exploration of Holland; but wherever I wandered in England, I fell in with specimens of its dairy products, and cattle that had been driven from its fertile fields; for Holland is England's great dairy farm, and one of her chief sources of reliance for live meat. In illustration of Holland's "intensive farming," a few trustworthy figures from one of her snug farms will best serve our purpose. In one of those districts of Holland, which in years gone by was a bog, upon a tract of three hundred and twenty-two acres was found a farmer who was keeping thirty cows, and feeding for the shambles ten cattle, which were made fat, disposed of, and replaced three times a year. In comparison with this statement, I set alongside of it an average of "extensive farming" in New Hampshire. Our New Hampshire man was the slave of a hundred and twenty acres of land, much of which he had already milked thoroughly dry. In toil, and wellnigh hopeless over the prospect, he was keeping three cows, fattening two pigs, and one pair of oxen, keeping fifteen sheep and an over-worked horse, and gathering from a wide stretch of wellnigh exhausted fields a small variety of the thinnest crops.

The hay crop of England is mainly stacked in the fields; and these picturesque cones of hay, ranged in tent-like villages about the farm-yards, are a novel and pleasant sight to the traveller from a country of hay-barns. The hay sometimes remains out several years, and the climate is such that it is often but little injured by the long exposure. To meet whatever injury weather may inflict upon the barnless hay, the farmers often buy a "hay spice," warranted to improve all hay in flavor, smell, and quality, and to give rough, coarse hay attractive flavor and aromatic smell, restoring damaged hay to a feeding value, even when it is black and rotten. This is certainly an idea not adopted in America.

English farmers are much given to the use of composition foods for cattle, sheep, etc. Thus I have seen widely advertised in English farming-papers calf meals, cream of milk, and meal substitutes, by which calves may be reared without expenditure of milk. Mixtures called lambs' foods, rice-meal, feeding cakes, and other curious food compositions for animals, are also largely sold to English farmers.

County agricultural shows are very popular in England, and from them we have copied our farming exhibition customs. But in old England these are held in June, July, and August; and not in autumn, as with us. The great men of the English shows are their patrons,— members of the royal families and nobles of high degree, whose names head the handbills which I saw posted in the farming regions in letters of big size.

Straw for litter is costly in England; and so I found the farmers buying a "moss litter,"— a litter which is largely used in place of straw by the British army. Portable "wooden houses" are advertised and sold in England, and are often bought by farmers. English farmers are quite in the habit of patronizing a public registry, where, on making a small payment, farm servants, implements, horses, cattle, dogs, etc., can be entered under the heads of "wanted," or "for sale."

Splendid crops of oats are raised in England. In some instances, harvests of seventy bushels to the acre are obtained. Very few oats are used upon the Englishman's table in any shape. I had expected to find oatmeal popular with English housekeepers, but they use very little of it.

* *
*

English market terms are decidedly different

from ours. Beasts and sheep, for instance, are terms I often heard, meaning neat cattle and sheep, — as if sheep were not beasts.

Here are some of the names I heard flying around markets where beasts and sheep were dealt in: Home-bred short-horns, Hereford bullocks, hoggetts, fat sheep out of their wool, stirks, barreners, grazing ewes, keeping-hogs, in-calves, cross-bred heifers.

I found sheep abundant wherever I travelled in England, Scotland, Ireland, or Wales; and I soon came to the conclusion that a live-mutton census of the United Kingdom would show that she had a vast number of wool producers. But I was not prepared for the following sheep figures which I obtained from trustworthy English sources:—

June 1, 1882, there existed in the United Kingdom 15,573,884 sheep above one year; sheep under one year old, 8,745,884, — a total of 24,319,768. In all the vast area of the the United States and territories, there are about 45,000,000 of sheep; and it should be remembered that England, Scotland, and Ireland contain together one half as many square miles as our single state of Texas.

I found sheep, under the care of shepherds, browsing in the parks of London. They were large and handsome sheep, loaded heavily with wool, when I saw them feeding in the tall grass of Hyde Park in the early spring; and their presence in the heart of the smoky and thronged city gave a bucolic, pastoral aspect to the scenery, and much gratification to the romping children who were fond of watching the sheep, shepherds, and the wonderful collie dogs which herded the sheep. The sheep in the parks of the towns and cities, and those in the broad pastures of the great mining and manufacturing districts, were blackened in their coats by the dust and smoke of the black country in which they moved; while, on the Cheviot hills of Scotland, the very same species of sheep and lambs were snow-white and clean.

I saw sheep-washings occasionally. They were conducted as with us in America; but proper watering-places for the work seemed scarce in some parts of England, for I have seen a gang of farm laborers washing sheep by the roadside, in a dirty goose-pond sort of water-basin, and have wondered whether the sheep would not come out of the stagnant mud-hole dirtier than when they went in.

In Scotland I rambled considerably among the Cheviot hills and valleys, and there made quite a close acquaintance with the fine breed of sheep that graze upon the heather-covered pastures of the region, and give their woolly coats to make the Cheviot fabrics. In these broad pastures I often saw little circular pens made of stone, standing alone far from the homes of the farmers; and

I found that these walled places in the fields were shelters for the sheep in stormy winter weather. Here they cluster when the snow drives hard and fast, and piles high on the bleak hillsides, plains, and valleys; and, nestling close together, manage to keep life and warmth in each other until the shepherds come to their relief. I was told by shepherds that they had often dug their sheep out from under great depths of snow that had suddenly fallen upon their flocks while they were huddled in these places of refuge from the weather.

In travelling in the farming districts of England, I often saw large flocks of sheep in the early spring penned in the fields near the farmers' homes, where they were fed night and morning from great piles of turnips that had been kept in the open air under a slight covering of straw and earth all winter, and which were fed out to the sheep sliced by a hand machine running somewhat on the hay-cutter principle.

I also often saw the little shelter houses on wheels standing amid the "sheeperies," which are used by the shepherds who are caring for the ewes in lambing-time, and which Thomas Hardy has something to say about in "Far from the Madding Crowd."

Though England grows a huge pile of good wool, it is a small pile compared to that which is brought to her shores from her distant colonial possessions, and periodically sold under the hammer, thousands of bales at a time, in that greatest wool centre in the world, London, and subsequently scattered widely in weaving lands.

I know something of the magnitude of the purchases of wool for American account that have been made through London agencies of Australian and other foreign houses; and it is a constant matter of wonder to me that the United States, with all its vast area, is obliged to go across such wide waters, at such costs in the way of duties, freight, etc., for wool that might be raised here.

* * *

The cow and the pump in England, as with us, are often found working together to supply a trusting public with "pure milk." A vast number of cows are kept in the city of London, but the bulk of the milk there consumed is brought in by rail from points often far back in the interior. I often fell in with the milk contractors of the rural districts. No use is made by them of our own style of milk-can. Wooden tubs and casks are favorite English receptacles of milk, and their general use of wood for this purpose is a custom which deserves to be copied. Another milk holder in use by the wholesale and retail dealers is a vessel of tin holding ten or fifteen gallons, and shaped something like an old-fashioned American churn. In the cities there is more or less difficulty experienced in getting pure "straight milk." Inspection is close, and many arrests for adulteration are constantly made in London. The most common London sin against milk is its adulteration with water. And, as London water is poor, the resulting mixture makes an unattractive fluid. In noting some of the cases where milk dealers were summoned before the petty session for selling adulterated milk, I was interested by accounts of their methods, and amused by the various defences made by the offenders. They were always presenting some excuse or another, which they seemed to expect would relieve them from the fines they feared, — fines which often touched as high as seven pounds for a single offence.

D. Barker, dairy farmer, of Oaks Farm, Chigwell, — in England they always have a name for their farms, — was summoned for putting fifty per cent of water into his milk. An inspector, under the food and drugs act, — by this avenue the law watches the London milkman, — met the defendant at Chigwell Lane station with one of these large churns of milk which I have described, from which he purchased a pint, and sent it to the public analyst with the watering result I have named. Defendant pleaded guilty in fact but innocent in mind, since the water got in through a bad boy who did the milking. He had a cow that was a kicker, and upset the pails. The boy had been directed to tie the cow's legs, which he neglected to do ; and, having some more milk upset, he was afraid of master, and flung into the churn a pail of water which he got from one of the pumps which were "all over the yard."

The Bench thought it a very bad case, and levied a fine of 7£ 10s, and costs. The expression "straight milk," which I have used in describing the watering of London's milk supply, recalls to me the fact that I first heard it used by an American milkman, who told me that, while a beginner in the retail milk business, he was told by a young man, who was foreman for a neighboring milk dealer, that he could never keep his customers if he supplied them with "straight milk." He explained himself by telling the new milkman his experience with the adulteration business.

* * *

Judging from my own experience and observation in England, I should say that many of the sweetest and finest strawberries found upon British tables were brought there from the Continent, particularly from France. But in the gardens of the United Kingdom there are certainly cultivated strawberries of enormous size and splendid appearance. Yet the flavor of these, as well as that of most of the table fruits which are grown on English soil and under English suns, is quite disappointing to one used to the quality of American grown fruits of the same class. It is not uncommon to find upon a London table strawberries of which a dozen will weigh a pound, and whose length will nearly equal that of your finger; yet these magnificent berries are far inferior in taste to the smaller ones which you have picked in the pastures of your American home.

I found many English housekeepers had a dietetic prejudice against strawberries and cream, — one of the sweetest and most healthful dishes ever placed upon a table; and so served the berry with sugar and the juice of the lemon, — an English notion which I have not the slightest wish to Americanize.

The native strawberry (*fragaria*) is really a North American production, though it has been naturalized in many lands. Its cultivation is most largely carried on in Europe. In English gardens strawberries are generally grown in rows, with straw paths between, — hence, say some, the name strawberry; though more likely the name comes from Anglo-Saxon *strae*, from which we have the English verb stray, the strawberry-vine being pre-eminently a wanderer.

Great Britain grows a delicious wild strawberry, called there the wood-strawberry, since it is mainly found in woods and thickets. But it is, like all other wild fruits of Britain, not abundant, and yearly growing less so. Its flavor gives the lie to Voltaire's well-known saying, that "the only fruit that ripens in England is a baked apple."

* *
*

I was interested, while in England, in visits which I occasionally made to the fashionable fruit-shops of the great cities, and was astonished at the prices which were paid by the nobility and gentry — or, rather, by the wealthy classes — for fruits that had been raised under glass for table use. Take the pineapple for an illustration. On sale at all seasons of the year, it is in constant use by those who can afford to pay for it such prices as five and six dollars each, figures I saw it marked at in the fruit-shops. But these pines were of magnificent size and flavor.

This fruit, which is a native of tropical America, and which has been naturalized in other tropical countries, is very largely raised in England in hot-houses, or pineries, as they are there termed; and a pinery is a very common feature of the gardens on large estates. It is quite a general practice to grow the plants in pots plunged in tanner's bark, or other fermenting matter, the plants being transferred from one house to another as they progress. A three-years' culture of this sort will produce fruit of great perfection. And such I saw in the pineries of the Marquis of Westminster at Eaton Hall. The pineapple is also often planted in beds under the glass, and forced forward to fruit in fifteen months. A pine which has once borne fruit is thrown away as useless.

*
 * *

PIGEON-FLYING IN THE NORTH OF ENGLAND.

I CANNOT say that this old-fashioned and very innocent amusement is not common in other parts of England; but I happened to observe it and hear it talked about in the northern counties among the miners and mill-workers. These laborers (men, of course, in a very humble condition of life) I have seen on Sunday (a day among these people little devoted to church-going, and largely given over to out-of-door amusements) clustered in the little back-yards of their lowly cottages, watching and cooing over their pet pigeons, their ruddy and strong and very extensive flock of little children in the group with them.

The Princess of Wales, and many other noble people in England, have set their faces against trap pigeon-shooting, — a brutal sport which I found in great favor in many parts of England; and Parliament is being petitioned to put it down. But nothing can be urged against the lively and exciting game of pigeon-flying stronger than that named to me by a good Wesleyan engine-driver of Lancashire, which was that the poor miners, and others who were given to it, broke Sunday all to pieces with the sport.

But as I had, in my wanderings in the black country of England, seen much of the sad, grimy life of its under-ground and above-ground workers, I could not feel like condemning their Sunday home-play with their beautiful pigeons, — a white and open-air sport which tended to keep the workers out of the beer-shops, and away from dog-fights, cock-fights, and prize-fights, "amusements" all too common among the working classes in "merry England."

The traveller through this hard-working portion of England of which I am writing will sometimes catch a glimpse of a scene something like this: A group of miners, clad in moleskin mufflers around their necks in place of cravats and collars, clustered around a couple of their number, one of whom holds a basketful of pigeons, and the other holds in his hands a watch, and is termed a timer, — a very important character. One by one the pretty little pigeons are let out of the basket, from which they dart aloft swift as an arrow; and, as each one dashes into the open air, his time is taken, and his rapid flight watched with breathless interest by the group of workers, every man of whom knows each separate pigeon. The birds fly away to the home goal, some miles from the point of starting, where their time of arrival is carefully taken. This is the time-honored game of pigeon-flying in old England.

* * *

A Lancashire miner graphically described to me the process of coal-mining. He did it well, for he had spent years sixteen hundred feet under ground. England mines half the coal that is mined in the world, and Lancashire is one of England's heaviest contributors to her coal-heap. All about him were men and boys who had never known any other employment than that of winning coal. He liked the work; they all liked it; preferred it, with all its dangers, and what I should deem its disagreeable features, to any sort of above-ground employment that presented itself. He had known the time when women and little children went down into the mines.

For a long time after they stopped working under ground they were employed on the pit hills — that is, on the mounds at the mouths of the pits — in handling coal. But even that was not now allowed. Boys of fourteen worked by his side. They began with light occupation, such as leading the ponies, loading the coal after it had been taken out by the picks, the blasts, and the coal-getting machines. Yes; the little boys also seemed to like their occupation.

The "shifts" were eight hours; yet he had sometimes, in time of danger in the mine, worked forty-eight hours without sleep or rest. No ; they never went to sleep down there, no matter how long they might remain there, for they would not dare to do this. In his long stretches of work, he had labored at helping the carpenters and masons shore up, and set brick supports, where there was danger from falling earth, rocks, and coal.

The miner, in descending into the mines for his eight-hours' shift, takes with him as food a most simple little lunch which he terms his "jackbit." Sometimes he finds the water that springs out of the earth about him, as he delves in his deep cut, fit to drink ; but this is seldom the case, and so he is always supplied with water from above ground. But the water from the deep cutting generally answers for the ponies. These animals, when once taken down, are never brought up again until they are dead or disabled. No ; they never seem timid or skittish when once they are down below, though they often kick about "like thunder" when first brought to the mouth of the mine, and led to the cages which are to bear them to the bottom. The most wild and fractious ponies become mild and patient as soon as they went to work down in the mine. It seemed to my mining man, who had spent his life with them in this coal depth, as if they were overwhelmed by the awful surroundings to which they were so suddenly introduced, and had all their spirit and courage crushed out of them. Hay, grain and bedding went down the cages after them; and the bottom of the pit became forever after their stable, pasture, and field of work.

He thought the occupation of a miner was not an unhealthful one, — was, in fact, sure, from his own experience and observation, that such was the case. But he knew it was one of the most dangerous occupations followed. Down they went, a thousand yards in some cases, leaving all sunshine behind them. The descent was made most rapidly. He was just a minute and a half in going his sixteen hundred feet. His cage was a double-decker. A dozen men stepped in. It fell till their heads were out of sight. Another dozen stepped upon the table above them. Then down they spun. Huge engines, furnishing power for lowering men, horses and supplies, stood far from the pit mouth. Always two; so, if one became disabled, another would be ready. His engines were big fellows, a hundred and eighty horse-power each.

In my wanderings in Derbyshire, I had entered the cottages of some of the miners; and I remembered finding some of the men off work, and hovering over the fire in the chimney corner, doubled up with rheumatism, which they said they had caught from exposure to draughts in cuttings in the mines; and these invalids told me mining was very apt to bring on rheumatic troubles. The miner now talking with me, who was strong and healthy, still averred he had never heard of mining being unhealthful in any respect. But he remarked that the business was cramping to the limbs, and that, after long service, miners were apt to become more or less deformed in shape. He could always tell a miner above ground by his cramped gait.

The great wheel at the mouth of the pit I was looking at was thirty feet in diameter, the shaft eighteen feet in diameter. Though eight hours was the regular day's work with the miner, he had six-hours' shifts, where his labors were of unusual severity, and under extremely disadvantageous circumstances. Extreme wetness was one of his worst mining troubles.

I saw and heard a deal of the miner's home-life, and I found his home more attractive and comfortable than I had expected. His cottage was often a model of neatness. The little muslin curtain was in the window; and there were flowers in the windows, and, in summer, in front of his house. His little children were in good schools. Himself and family attended the Wesleyan Church. Where there were no small children, the wife and daughters went to work in the factory, while the husband and sons were delving in the mine.

In estimating the limit of England's coal supply, it should be borne in mind that the volume of the coming demand may be materially reduced by increased economy as the price increases, and by the introduction of coal-saving appliances, — inventions which shall make the most of every pound of coal used. London, in 1882, consumed 10,500,000 tons of coal, upon which the city duty was about £600,000. But her consumption would have been far greater had not this modern economy, and these coal-saving inventions, come in play to reduce it. In fixing the time when England shall be coalless, scientists agree that this date will depend, not upon the exhaustion of the beds, but upon the time when the depth and narrowness of the seams shall render their working impossible. Leading authorities have generally held that the coal imbedded in the United Kingdom must be abandoned when it could not be reached without going below a depth of 4,000 feet. Below 4,000 feet the heat of the mines becomes, they say, unendurable by the miners. The temperature sinks one degree Fahrenheit for every 60 feet descent into those coal-mines, and at a depth of 4,000 feet reaches 116°. There are, however, some English theorizers upon this point who contend that a high-priced demand for coal will induce miners to work in hotter temperature than this; and one eminent professor, who has seen men working in John Brown's Sheffield steel works, where the temperature was 140° in the Bessemer pits, with a radiated heat quite sufficient to roast a sirloin, argues that men will dig out coal in heat like this if paid well. The philosopher doubles the 4,000 feet limit, and believes coal will be mined in England in the far future at a depth of 8,000 feet, in a temperature of 183°.

Another difficulty about mining coal at great depths comes from the narrowness and hardness of the seams consequent upon the tremendous pressure. But still there are those who believe an English miner will crouch and dig a seam of less than three feet in height, at a depth of 8,000 or 10,000 feet, if he is paid high wages. But England may, in time, find it cheaper to import her coal, than to dig it out of her soil at the extreme depth, and under the extreme disadvantages, I have described. North America has seventy times as many square miles of coal area as has Great Britain; and when it costs more to move coal into England vertically than to bring it there horizontally, then it will not be mined, but imported. And there are other countries than America from which it may, in time, be profitably brought to England,— from China, for instance, which has 4,000 square miles of coal-fields.

Coal panics are engineered over the question of the probabilities of an early giving-out of the coal-supply of the kingdom. Royal commissions, and other authorities, have given forth any amount of statistics relative to this question. The student may take his choice from a wide range of figures in the premises, — a range running from an official statement that the unmined coal in the kingdom foots up 146,480,000 of tons, and will last, at a fair estimate of current consumption, for 1186 years, to another scientific report which takes the ground that England will be out of coal in a hundred years. The judicious reader may plant himself at will anywhere in this field of figures.

The London prices for coal delivered range from twenty-four to eighteen shillings per ton. The very common London habit of delivering coals in large sacks is not a universal practice, for I saw many deliveries going on in about the style usual in the United States. Many of the great coal-mining companies advertise in the leading cities their readiness to deliver coal to direct consumers in any quantities wanted. They also advertise to deliver coal by the car-load to any railway-station in the kingdom. These cars, or trucks, as they are termed in England, carry from five to eight tons.

They have novel names in London for the different sizes of coals; for instance, cobbles, strong kitchen, hard cobbles, and also an endless number of names indicating the mines from which they have been dug, some of which are familiar well-nigh the world over, for they are names of mines of immense productiveness. In this class are the Clay Cross, Walls End, Wigan, Thorncliffe Main, Seaham and Derby.

During some of England's great wars the tax on coal rose as high as nine shillings a chaldron. These national taxes have long been abolished; and the only tax upon the article that remains is the local tax now levied by London, and a few other large towns. At one time the city of London weighed all the coal consumed by the city, and fixed the prices at which it should be sold.

All about the coal regions of England I found coal-mines that had been exhausted and deserted. Other mines which I saw had been driven deeper and deeper into the earth, the supply nearer the surface having been exhausted, and mining at this great depth was very costly. This is one of the reasons why coal has been steadily increasing in price during the last quarter of a century. As I travelled through the coal-mining districts of England, I had pointed out to me districts where the coal-diggings led under villages, hamlets and the estates of noblemen. And it was no uncommon thing for me to be shown places where the operations of the miners had undermined the very railroads over which I was being whirled, — literally undermined; for my attention was frequently called to instances where the coal companies had inflicted such serious injuries on lines by their excavations under the tracks that they had been sued for heavy damages, and some of these cases were in court while I was in England.

In towns and villages not too far from the shafts of coal-mines, the supply of coal is taken in carts direct from the mouths of the coal-mines to the bins of the consumers. I very frequently saw in such vicinities the stout horses and heavy carts of these local coal-carriers toiling over the roads with their big loads of coal. The long and rapidly flying coal-trains that I saw whirling towards London so thickly, and from so many directions, shunt their coal-vans into the great coal-yards of the city.

From these vast coal-yards, which have, as a general thing, water as well as rail avenues leading to them, coal is delivered to consumers in the following manner: Such purchasers as prefer so to receive it have it delivered to them in enormous blocks which they pile up as one piles wood, and from which they get their daily supply by splitting the blocks. A majority prefer it shall be delivered to them in sacks made of Liverpool bagging, each sack containing two hundred pounds.

Deliveries of coal in this style were constantly being observed by me during my stay in London and other English towns and cities; and I could not fail to note the many advantages of the method. The obstruction and soiling of sidewalks and doorways was, by this mode of handling the coal, entirely obviated; and the delivery was accomplished more speedily and more handily than it is with us. Here, again, I raised the question, why do we not, in our large towns and cities, at least, give the English coal-sacks a trial.

Besides the delivery of coal by the quantity in the ways I have described, coal peddlers do a retail business in the streets of London from horse and pony wagons, and sometimes even from little carts drawn by themselves. These retailers sell in the smallest lots, if so requested; and touchingly little parcels of coal are often taken by their poorer customers. All coal sellers in England are obliged, by the laws of the realm, to carry weighing apparatus on their carts; and they are thus in readiness to satisfy the careful or doubting customer by weighing all purchases under the eye and on the premises of the purchaser. How would it answer to have such a legal requirement as this in the United States?

* * *

While walking over the highways and by-ways of England, I often fell in with artisans of various classes who were travelling from town to town in search of a "job;" and with them I had many interesting talks respecting their different occupations, and the condition and prospects of English mechanics.

As a class, these wanderers were a badly discouraged and well-nigh penniless set of men. Many of them had been stranded, as it were, by the changes in methods of manufacture that had taken place since they learned their trades. For illustration, many and many a shoemaker that I met on the road told me that the various modern inventions in the way of cable screw and other wire fastenings, that were taking the place of the old-time hand-sewing with thread, had nearly ruined his trade, which was that of making sewed shoes. These artisans had, for the most part, learned their trades under the old-style apprentice system; and one and all they united in a severe and most decided condemnation of this system. They felt that the long and tedious apprenticeship had been an injury to them, and they had a bitter grudge against the laws and customs which forced them into the servitude. In old times in England there were statues (enacted in reign of Elizabeth) providing that an apprenticeship of seven years must positively be served before one could work as a journeyman at a trade; and heavy fines were imposed upon any man found violating this law. In those days trades were held to be secrets; and "stealing" them, as now quite often practised in the United States and elsewhere, was deemed an offence against the laws. The term "master of arts," as now used by our colleges, had its origin in those old days; and was applied to those who, by seven years' service, had made themselves master of some mechanical art.

These apprentice laws are relics of a semi-barbarous age. An old English shoemaker, who was on the verge of starvation, though he had served seven long years in Bedford to master the art which now would not support him, bewailed to me bitterly that the apprentice laws of England had been far less favorable than those of the Continent, of which, in some points, they were copies. In this unfavorable comparison, he instanced that pleasant feature of the German trade laws which provided that the apprentice shall have the privilege of wide travel after he had served his seven years, and before he settled down as a journeyman. Said the poor old English mechanic: "I worked like a slave sixteen hours a day during my apprenticeship, and never got a bit of a chance to see my own country. But it used to be a saying among us apprentices, '*See London, or die a fool;*' and I thank my stars that I have, once at least, seen mighty London."

While walking from Liverpool to London, I had, on one portion of my route, the companionship of a young mechanic who had served out a long indentured apprenticeship with a London master. By the terms of his indentureship his parents surrendered the entire control of the son to the master; and, the master being a bad one, his condition became worse than that of a slave.

His food and bed were mean; his hours extremely long; he had no amusements; much of his time was spent on work that had no relation to a trade. Other English artisans have told me stories similar to this that I learned as I walked through Epping Forest with the wandering English mechanic who was travelling to London in search of a "job." An old English artisan, who had never been to school a day in his life, and who had been hard at work ever since he was six years old, told me that he served seven years' apprenticeship with a perfectly honest but very poor and much overworked man; and his condition, during that seven years, was that of an underfed and overworked slave. This man had never read that wonderful book for the times in which it was written, Adam Smith's "Wealth of Nations," for he had just barely taught himself to read the simplest words, and to little more than write his own name; yet he expressed precisely the ideas laid down by Adam Smith, when he told me that he thought every man ought to have a chance to learn any trade in the quickest time he could; and that every man working at a trade ought to receive pay for what he did, if what he did was of any value.

This man had been apprenticed to a shoemaker; and his account of the way of life, while an apprentice, was a sad one. He worked sixteen hours a day, and lived almost entirely on bread and water served up in various simple styles. For instance, his breakfast was usually teakettle broth, prepared by mixing hot water with crumbs of stale bread. The result, a broth to be eaten with a spoon. His supper was plain bread washed down with cold water. His dinner, bread, potatoes and pork. Did not remember ever having any other meat but pork. Master kept pigs.

Caste in trades is quickly observable in England. That castes exist will be readily apprehended by American readers, since caste in trades exists, to a certain extent, in the United States. In illustration of the English situation in such matters, I may state that I found in England that such trades as watch-making, and maker of other classes of fine machinery, were deemed high caste trades; while the trade of shoemaking may be named as an instance of a low caste trade. The somewhat anomalous position of this trade arises in part from the old-time English custom of generally apprenticing paupers' sons to the shoemaking trade.

* *
*

Not long ago an enthusiastic English lady, who was "doing" Athens for the first time, was shocked by hearing her guide exclaim, on her entrance upon sight-seeing in this ancient city, "Behold the new gas-works!" Just as I was coming in sight of the ivy-mantled towers of the picturesque ruins of the castle of Kenilworth, after a beautiful cross-country walk from the charming Spa city of Leamington, a brisk young Englishman asked me if I would not like to look into his tannery. I was at that moment lingering at the gate of his tan-yard, looking up at the immense chimneys belonging to it. English laws require that all her steam factories shall have very tall chimneys. The tanner seemed to know at once that I was from the United States; and, pointing out his tall stacks, he asked me if we had any finer chimneys than those in America. One word led to another, and I was soon up to my eyes in tanpits, though almost within a stone's throw of one of the finest bits of ruins in all England. The proprietor said that he had been much troubled by American competition. Leather from United States tanneries had been pouring into the London and Liverpool markets, depressing the prices for his product.

Old-fashioned tanning has also been suffering in England, during recent years, from the introduction of short processes of turning out leather by the use of various substitutes for oak bark. Tawing had also encroached upon tanning. There have been many large failures of tanners who had clung tenaciously to the old methods which kept the hides so long in the vats. The whole business is now in a transition state throughout the entire kingdom. Tanners must adopt all the modern improvements, or go to the wall. England imports annually one and a half million hundred weight of hides, and her home crop of the same is large. These are food for her own tanneries. But every year witnesses an increase of importations of leather into the kingdom. The United States is a heavy shipper. Many an American who buys a sole-leather trunk in London, because he wishes to possess a genuine oak-tanned article of English origin, gets a trunk made of good American-tanned leather. And many of the boots and shoes bought in England by American travellers, who suppose they are buying goods made entirely of leather tanned in England, are deceived in the same way as the trunk buyers.

These are some points that came out as I chatted with the man of leather. All about me were methods and machinery, and an aroma that carried me by association three thousand miles New Englandward; for I was standing in the midst of tan-pits, curriers' shops, and bark-mills that were precisely like those so common fifty years ago in almost every New England town.

Like so many English institutions and methods which our fathers copied, the original was before me unchanged; while the copies had gone down before the march of American improvements. The small back-country tanning and currying establishments of the New England of old times have, to a great extent, been consolidated into great tanneries in other localities, where all the modern accelerating processes have introduced aromas other than those of oak and hemlock bark. The laborers about me in the English tannery were, in appearance, very like those of the same occupation in the old New England tannery; and it is a coincidence that their hours of labor, habits of eating and wages, were of the kind common in the United States in the old days.

The oak used in the old-fashioned tanneries of England comes mostly from the oaks on the estates of the kingdom. I found that the nobility and gentry very generally counted on getting quite a revenue from sales of this product of their forests. I have several times lingered by the roadside, and talked with the bark men as they were slowly (they do most things slowly in agricultural England) stacking the bark under the shadow of the magnificent old trees on some gentleman's home park, or piling it upon some heavy, lumbering old cart for conveyance to neighboring tanneries.

An apt illustration of the stupidity of the average English laborer comes to mind in connection with these bark recollections. I was never quite able to find out just what good merchantable oak bark was worth in England, for the reason that these "chaw-bacons" could tell me only that they believed it brought so much a "load." And they could give me no idea of how much in cord quantity a load was. I struck the same snag of English stupidity in many other premises which I endeavored to investigate.

* * *

Canals are very numerous in England; and, though they have fallen behind in the race in which steam has been a competitor, it is a curious fact that, in the see-saw of time, canals are again in England coming up, while steam is actually getting depressed. After having been in England for a long time partially eclipsed, the canal shows signs of reaching its former importance and usefulness. There are to-day 20,000 canal-boats plying on English canals, many of them being in the hands of share companies which farm them out of the canal corporations. Only 8,000 of these 20,000 boats are registered, for the registration act is not compulsory in its requirements. And it is loudly complained by the canal philanthropists of England that on these 12,000 unregistered canal-boats 50,000 men, women and children spend their lives in gypsy-like ignorance and filth. On English canals, says George Smith of Coalville, the great canal-boat missionary-in-chief, are 30,000 children, growing up in ignorance of every thing except steering a canal-boat, and driving its horses.

It has been said that one cannot get over fifteen

miles from navigable water in any part of England. There are in the kingdom about 2,200 miles of canal proper, and over 1,300 miles of rivers that have been improved into a canal sort of navigation. In regard to the small, slow-moving rivers of England that have, as it were, been partially turned into canals, I must remark that, in many cases, I found it difficult to distinguish the rivers that are used as canals from the canals themselves.

At the close of a long walk across country of forty miles, in a ramble in one of the midland counties, in the lovely English month of May, I found myself, as the sun went down, approaching a remarkably quiet old village, built mostly upon a hillside along the banks of a canal that had once been one of England's great inland water routes, but which had now nearly fallen into disuse. There were all about the decrepit old town signs of better and busier days. Here were long rows of store-houses unoccupied and going to ruin, wharves rotten and half fallen, skeletons of old canal-boats stranded along the water-side, and dwelling-houses that had once been the homes of merchants who had transacted a canal business, and lonely houses that had once been inns to which the canal traffic had brought large custom. Over all the village there hung an air of desertion and decay, forming a picture of desolation and hopelessness such as I have never elsewhere seen.

* *
*

England is a great place for bee-keeping. The mild, equable climate of the country, and the luxurious growth of both wild and cultivated flowers everywhere observable in the growing seasons of the year, favor the life and labors of the honey-bee. I shall ever carry with me, as one of the sweetest and sunniest recollections of my early summer rambles in rural England, a simple breakfast, and a subsequent garden walk and talk I had with a venerable cottager, the wife of a farm laborer, near Stratford-on-Avon. She was a tenant upon the estates of the Lucys, — the Lucys of Shakespeare's time, whose descendants still occupy the broad lands over which Shakespeare wandered in his young days, — and she was a keeper of many hives of bees, which she showed me with a deal of pleasure as we strayed about the flower-crowned southern slope of her fields which stretched Stratfordward behind her cottage. And at her table I was offered bread of her own make, honey, and milk and eggs from her own hired farm; and, in the end, beer from Stratford-on-Avon, — a town which was more famous among the laborers in its vicinity for the beer brewed there than for the Shakespeare born and buried there. The beer drinkers of the country about Stratford claim that Stratford has water wonderfully well adapted for the production of excellent beer.

But though beehives — particularly the conical hive of straw made familiar to us by many an English picture — are a common sight in England, the habit of placing honey upon the table to be eaten with bread seemed less common than in America, where honey has well-nigh become an exotic. Bee-keeping, like many other domestic productive interests, receives systematic and organized encouragement from associations established for that purpose. That wonderfully lively and public-spirited lady, the Baroness Burdett-Coutts, is president of the British Bee-keepers' Association, — a society which annually holds, at the Duke of Wellington Riding School in London, a great exhibition of bees, honey, hives, etc., at which is given, at stated intervals, instructions in the art of bee-keeping. It is a curious fact that the honey-bee ("the white man's fly," the American Indians used to call it) was never known in this country till brought here from England; and, though they are now found in all parts of the country, they did not reach California till 1850, and South America till 1845.

I found a practice in bee-keeping prevalent in Scotland which seemed novel to me. Early in August they transport the hives to the heath-covered tracts, and there let them remain while the heath flower is in bloom. Honey is on sale in Edinburgh known as heath-flower honey. Collections of forty or fifty hives may sometimes be seen in Edinburgh under the care of a single person, who is superintending their transportation in spring-carts to the heath-fields.

I have mentioned the common use in England of the old-fashioned conical straw hive. I shall not soon forget the first time I saw a little stock of these hives ranged for sale at the door of a small shop in an old market town in rural England. The sight carried me back to the English story-reading days of my childhood; and I lingered a while with the old beehive maker, and learned his trade and his prices. The sweet white clover abounds in England, and the bees among it make the sweetest honey. I found that the old-time idea, that bees will not travel much over a mile from their hives, prevails in England; and the hives themselves are made to travel, as I have described, on easy-going tip-carts, somewhat as in Egypt they are to-day floated along the Nile from flower-field to flower-field. While riding in a dog-cart with an Englishman in Chester, I was surprised to see him stop at an inn, and order beer for his horse, which beer the horse drank from a pail. I was afterwards more surprised to learn that the Englishman's everlasting beer was fed, with boiled sugar, to his bees.

* * *

Any one who has been a constant reader of

"Punch," has no need to travel up and down England with me to discover that the traditional, ingrained, agricultural laborer of the country is, in very many cases, so stupid, so ignorant, so devoid of all ambition to get out of the plough-ruts in which he and his progenitors have been travelling like cattle for many hundred years, as to rank, in the mind of the careful observer, only a shade above the domestic beasts among which his life has all been spent.

I walked and talked with these English hinds, and can testify that I never met, in my own country, outside of the imbecile asylums, so stupid, so stolid and stunted a class of human beings. They have a dialect of their own, which the stranger can hardly understand; a smock-frock sort of an attire which has been in fashion for a hundred years; and a way of life, as regards work and play, and general home habits, that is the same as was their fathers' and grandfathers'.

There are, however, lower depths of human unintellectuality in England than this. Underneath this last-named class is to be found a set of men and women that is the natural outgrowth (downward) of the stupid hind class. These are a sort of "innocents," who wander about the country roads in a state bordering upon complete imbecility, and are saved from starvation by the charity of those who have pity for these unfortunates.

IMBECILE ASYLUMS. 79

Downright imbeciles are cared for in England, to a large extent, in her immense imbecile asylums. And these institutions have to be large and numerous to accommodate the stunted imbeciles abounding in crowded old England. I call to mind, in illustration of the character of these establishments, one of the largest of them located in Watford, — a town which I passed through on my pedestrian excursion from London to Oxford. It contains two thousand chronic imbeciles who are under the charge of Dr. Case, an eminent medical man, and who are maintained at a net expense of twenty cents a day.

* * *

Wandering theatres are a marked feature in English rural life. I have many times happened upon little companies of humble travelling actors and actresses, with their modest stocks of properties, wardrobes, etc., prepared to set up, in some cases, a temporary theatre in those hamlets and villages which seemed to promise them paying patronage.

This extemporized exhibition-room was sometimes a tent which they carried with them; and sometimes a house on wheels, in which they travelled and lived, simply extended a little when made to serve as show-room. A still more humble class of strolling performers are those jugglers, acrobats, and sleight-of-hand artists, whose home at night is the cheapest inn to be had, and whose stage and audience-room is any available patch of ground they may seize upon, in a locality likely to call around them a paying group of spectators.

I was standing in a crowd which was waiting in Epping Forest for the coming of the Queen, when a sad-looking man, accompanied by a little boy about twelve, appeared upon the scene, and, spreading upon the ground an old threadbare piece of carpet, opened his exhibition. It was the same old story,—a phase of the life of the strolling performer which has so often been pictured in English tales, and which I saw again and again at fairs, horse-races and market-gatherings.

I was struck by the real professional merit of the little exhibition, by the dreary and sad aspect of the performers, and by the apparently meagre receipts when the cap went its round among the spectators.

The entertainment was of the usual type. The funny boy was kicked and banged about, and made to perform wonderful feats in balancing and tumbling; and, when the man had exhausted the acrobatic part of his resources, he gave some wonderful individual exhibitions in the way of fire-eating, sleight-of-hand, etc.

In 1879 Parliament enacted that no child under fourteen should be allowed to go through any performance whereby life or limb could be endangered. But this law has not, in the opinion of its friends, answered the purpose for which it was intended. And now, under the lead of that venerable philanthropist, the Earl of Shaftesbury, they are moving for a passage of a more stringent enactment of the same general character, which has, among other additional safeguards, a restriction placing the prohibited age at under sixteen, and obliging these youthful performers to attend school a portion of their time.

At the parliamentary committee hearings on this proposed bill, a mass of the most painful testimony has been presented, showing that the old-time methods and machinery of this business are still in full blast; taking wretched children of a tender age and treating them in the most inhuman manner, inasmuch as one who had been conversant with the system for a lifetime testified that eighteen out of twenty of these performers who escape fatal accidents are obliged to wear pads and bandages, the result of sprains or falls, and that every accident that occurs is, if possible, hushed up, and kept from the public.

*   *
*

The United Kingdom is giving a deal of attention, at the present time, to the matter of forestry. And well it may. From being one of the best wooded countries of Europe, it has come into the condition of being, with a single exception, more thinly clad than any of them. Reafforesting is now being entered upon in many parts of England with vigor and system. It has been sharply said by an able writer, that humanity signalized its sudden leap of material progress in the nineteenth century by springing, axe in hand, at the throats of the forests throughout the globe. And in no land was there more rapid and more severe gashing than in Great Britain. In my long and extensive rambles in rural England, my observations fully convinced me of this. I found few, very few, natural forests there. The woods that crowned the hills, and ornamented the parks of the great estates of the nobility and gentry, were woods that had been planted, — were not natural forests, but plantations. And in these private parks great care is often taken to keep up the artificial groves.

I saw the portable steam saw-mill at work in many a park, but wherever it mowed a path through the woods, that path was likely soon to become a nursery of young saplings that were to be carefully trained to fill the gaps made by the saws.

I can remember seeing few more beautiful sights in Scotland than the views I had in springtime of the forest-crowned hills round about Melrose. These forests were plantations, and in the work of reafforesting Scotland, Sir Walter did more than any man of his time. He made his power in the matter felt by means of his social influence and his literary labors, and he also did a deal to help along the business of tree-planting by his own practical example. The traveller finds Ireland, whose log-packed bogs show her to have once been a thickly-wooded land, now well denuded of forests. An earnest effort is to-day being made there, by many of Ireland's best friends, to replant her waste and well-nigh worthless lands with forest trees. Of the twenty millions of acres of land in Ireland, at least five millions of acres are waste lands, which might, it is claimed, be profitably planted with trees, — planted, says that high authority, Dr. Lyons, with conifers, deciduous and hard-wood trees, and many sorts of bushes.

There are yet nearly three-quarters of a million of acres of land in Scotland under forest growth, though Scotland has allowed her tree-lands to be reduced. India has to-day seventy-five thousand square miles of forests, and it is a singular fact that the forestry of that distant possession of the British empire is placed upon a better basis than that of any European country.

More than twenty-five thousand square miles of forests in India have been placed directly under the care of the most scientific system of forest management. This advanced and most sagacious care of one of India's greatest sources of wealth is owing to the fact that England has sent to that country the most accomplished of administrators, and given them the widest sweep of power over a people whose ignorant prejudices they are not obliged to consult or yield to.

One of the most successful instrumentalities in this work of preservation of the trees has been the Society for the Preservation of Open Spaces for the enjoyment of the people. Aided by private contributions, and grants from public sources, this society has wrested from the hands of greedy speculators and land-hungry noblemen, some of the finest fields and forests, and set them apart to be forever the pleasure-grounds of the people.

One of their latest and most valuable acquisitions has been that of those grand old Burnham Beeches, near Stoke-Pogis, whose venerable branches have so often sheltered the scholars and poets whose names have been associated with them, and whose curious old hollow trunks and gnarled limbs have been such objects of interest to the many Americans who have visited them.

The work of preservation in question has also been greatly aided by an act of Parliament, passed in 1872, to run thirty years, which levied a duty of three-sixteenths of a penny per hundred weight on all grain brought into the port of London, and enacted that the duty so raised should be used for the preservation of open spaces in the neighborhood of London.

London has, out of the tax thus raised, paid for Epping Forest, containing 5300 acres; Wanstead Park, 183 acres; Burnham Beeches, 373 acres; Coulson Common, 347 acres; West Ham Park, 76 acres; and also maintained St Paul's churchyard in a condition adapting it for public use.

England's consumption of timber, especially of the harder woods, is immense. I found that its greatest source of foreign supply was the northern countries of Europe, which were separated by only narrow waters from the shores of the British Isles. It is a far cry to the timber lands of America, yet vast quantities of American oak are brought across the North Atlantic to supply English demands.

At those immense repair and construction shops of the Midland Railway, a road that has in its rolling stock fourteen hundred locomotives, the American traveller can notice, with satisfaction, great piles of American oak in store for use in car and locomotive building. I made many a timber note as I wandered about England. Among the lakes I talked with woodmen who, in those romantic regions, were busy getting out of coppice stock-bobbins, etc., for the cotton-spinners of Manchester and Bradford.

In the black country I chatted with mill-men who were turning out, by the cord, from English oak, handles for picks to be used by the miners.

I asked them why they did not import these handles ready made from America.

They replied, in the tone of genuine English prejudice, that they had tried invoices of them at the mines, and found they were not good for any thing. At Hatfield House, the baronial hall of Lord Salisbury, I saw fireplaces of the largest size, where the tall andirons were loaded with big sticks of wood which had been cut in Hatfield parks, and which were all ready to be set ablaze as soon as my lord came up from London and the House of Lords.

On the Thames at London, and on its branch at Oxford, I took a look at the woods that went into the constructions of the boats in use there, and found cedar and mahogany the favorite materials.

While wandering about rural old England, I often saw a sight that reminded me of the primitive days of New England. It was that of a couple of stalwart men, sawing logs into planks and boards by hand. One man stood above the log; the other, in a saw-pit below it. So they would work hard at this slow, wearisome business day after day; and I sometimes saw, as I passed by the houses of laborers of this kind, where they had left their task for the day, the saw resting in the partly-sawed log, the finishing of which would take many days.

The most of this tedious and old-fashioned sawing was done upon the hard-wood logs that had been obtained from the plantations of the nobility and gentry; for these two classes, who own most of the wood land in England, sell from their parks all the trees they can spare, planting a new tree whenever an old one is cut down and removed. The trees most frequently made subject to this home-sawing are oak and elm; and the uses to which the boards, etc., which were the result of the sawing, were put, were in the making of carts and wagons, and the construction of coffins.

The elm is the hard-wood of England that is the most used for this coffin work; and so often did I see, as I walked the rural highways and by-ways, huge elm logs prone by the roadside, that had been selected for the coffin-maker, and so often did I see coffin-makers at work sawing these logs into boards for coffins, that I began to think that in rural England coffin-making was one of the leading mechanical industries.

The dense population on every hand, and the even more densely populated graveyards all about me as I travelled, very naturally tended to confirm this impression. I have never anywhere, if I make an exception of some portions of Paris's great cemetery of Pere le Chaise, seen such crowded graveyards as I have seen in the oldest portions of rural England.

Perhaps the best illustration of the way the

graveyards of the old villages of England are actually crammed with graves may be seen in the burial ground at Haworth, where the family of the Brontës lie buried,—a graveyard which has been occupied as such for hundreds of years, and where every foot of land has been over and over appropriated for graves. And, at times, it seemed to me, as I reflected on the great age and populousness of England, as if it was all one vast graveyard. In London alone, about twelve hundred persons are borne to the graveyards every week. These country-made coffins of old English elm of which I have made mention are made of the shape and by the same class of mechanics, that they were made in old New England before the advent of the modern factory-made coffin and casket.

In the rural districts in many parts of England to-day the village carpenter comes and measures the body of the dead, and then bends speedily to the work of making by hand the old-patterned coffin of elm. One old English village carpenter told me how he had measured and coffined hundreds of his departed neighbors. The price paid for a plain elm coffin of the style and shape I have described is about twenty shillings. From this style and price, there is an indefinite range upwards; for many of these coffins of elm are richly covered with cloth, and adorned with plate.

And while speaking of the fact that the old

fashioned English coffin is of that peculiar shape, — that is, long and narrow, with a swelling width near the head, — I am reminded that I saw, in the church-yard at Dryburgh Abbey in Scotland, a gravestone, upon which were the usual inscriptions, which was made in the precise shape of one of these coffins. Standing upright at the head of the grave, it appeared as if the actual coffin of the dead had been planted there in that erect position, instead of being buried; and the effect was very startling.

There have been shipments made to Great Britain of American caskets and coffins in nests, but these shipments have not been at all successful. Not if the Englishman knows himself will he be buried in such a new-fangled notion as a factory-made American coffin or casket, and these mortuary goods found no sale in his country.

A London undertaker, who has lately been visiting the United States, has expressed himself as very much surprised at the great improvements that had here been made in goods in his line, and was also surprised that his countrymen do not better appreciate these American products. A Boston dealer in mortuary goods not long ago imported from Sheffield, England, quite a quantity of adornments and trimmings for coffins that had been made there, and he found them so clumsy and tasteless that they could not be sold.

OSIER HOLTS.

In going from Barnet to Epping Forest, whither I went to see the good Queen throw open that vast common, — throw it open for the perpetual use of the laboring classes of England, who had been gradually deprived of their privileges in it by the encroachments of the nobility and gentry, — I for the first time passed through a series of fields devoted to a sort of farming with which I had had no previous acquaintance. This was the cultivation of osier beds. These beds are not so extensive in England as in Germany and France, but the same methods are used in England, and about the same product obtained.

An osier bed is simply a bed of small willows, but the willow grown for osiers is of a different class from our common willow. There are, said an old willow-cultivator to me, more than one hundred and twenty-five different kinds of willows. I leave this unendorsed statement for the consideration of botanists. What he denominated the red willow, he deemed the best osier. The osier grows best in fenny places, and flourishes well where the ground is a part of the time submerged. I saw little islands in the Thames devoted to the culture of the osier. Osier holts is the name given in England to the osier plots.

These osier holts are started by putting down

little cuttings of the willow quite near together. The first year the growth of the osier does not amount to much. But afterwards they are good for a crop, with no cultivation of any account, for from ten to twenty years. Planted thus closely, in moist places, this little red osier sends up its delicate shoots to the height of from five to ten feet. These shoots are cut from November to April, when the sap has descended to the roots, and they are equally good when cut in any of these months. After cutting, the twigs are placed under water till May or June, in which situation they throw out leaves, at the foliage season, the same as if they still clung to the parent roots. Then they are carefully peeled by a small hand-machine, dried, and packed away in bundles, such as we see in the hands of the osier-dealers in London and New York, and which weigh about fifty pounds each. Out of these delicate little white rods — comely, clean, and tough — an almost endless variety of things have been made, and are to-day being made.

Extraordinary attention is being paid to-day in England to the subject of burials; and the earnest opponents of intramural interments, and interments in tombs, and brick graves, who have from the first been firm advocates of simple burial in plain graves in the earth, have, in some instances, gone a step further, and proclaimed themselves in favor of the use in these burials of wicker coffins.

A company which has been formed in London for the purpose of introducing these wicker coffins advertises them in "The London Times" as the only coffin in which the dead in populous lands can be buried without detriment or danger to the living. "Bury me," said a ruddy and strong man, with whom I was discussing the subject of wicker coffins, — "when I am dead, bury me in an earth-to-earth wicker coffin, so that I may get out again into God's pure air just as soon as possible."

An aged German basket-maker, who worked mainly upon the willow osier, showed me a fine, large wicker coffin he had made. Nothing entered into its construction but willow rods. It was of regular coffin shape, but, in all other points, it reminded one of a basket, — and simply a basket-coffin it was. Neat, sweet, and attractive was this casket made of the fragrant willow osier, and as I looked upon it I felt like re-echoing the sentiment of its impulsive advocate whom I have just quoted. And I also thought well of the suggestion made by the maker of this willow basket-coffin, that when put to actual use no cloth of silk or woollen, no mortuary ornaments of any sort be added to it, but that the mortal remains laid to rest within it be supplied only with a pure, soft pillow of shavings of the white willow or fragrant pine.

Willow caskets, of the sort I have described, have been used in a few instances in American burials; and there are here mechanics in wicker-work who are ready to make a willow coffin comely and perfect in construction as any on sale in London. And the osiers themselves, out of which such a variety of pretty things can be made, can be grown most successfully in this country. I have seen beds of them here in a flourishing condition, grown from cuttings brought from England.

Our American wicker-workers have also sometimes gathered from the wild willows growing on our farms, and in the moist places by the roadside, the slender roots that shoot out from these trees in such luxuriance and beauty; but, though some use may be made of them, they are far too brittle for the nicest work.

The finest osiers I have seen in use in this country were imported from Germany and France. In those countries great attention is given to their production, and out of willow a vast variety of articles are made. One can see, on the Continent, carriages made entirely of wicker-work, with the exception of the wheels.

The use of the willow rods dates back to the very earliest days. They have, in old times, been used in architecture, and shields for the soldier have been made of them. In some countries the osier has been woven so deftly and closely as to make water-tight vessels for domestic use; and boats, gates, hats, sledges and shoes have been made of them.

But it is only in our own days that these supple and tough little twigs have been called upon to make a house for the dead.

* *
*

THE LICH-GATE.

The old English name of the main or principal gate to the church-yard is the lich-gate. The word lich, which is of Anglo-Saxon origin, signifies a dead body or corpse, and the lich gate-way of the graveyard is that through which the body of the dead is borne for burial.

In one of those disgraceful contests which have of late years so often taken place between English vicars and nonconformists in regard to burial rights, this word lich-gate has been called into English courts. It was my habit, wherever I wandered in old England, to enter the old church-yards that fell in my way, if time permitted me to linger by the way-side. And I never found the lich-gate fastened. In fact, the lich-gate was generally no gate at all, but an ever-open passage-way. But it seems this way is often shut, by the ruling vicar, in the face of that awful modern heretic, the Dissenter. The new burial laws endeavor to forbid this, but, somehow or other, these bigoted vicars fly in the face of these statutes, or evade them In the sad case I have in mind, the nearest relative of a deceased Nonconformist gave notice to the vicar of Harlow that she should claim the right to bury her mother within the gray old walls of the parish church-yard, without the use of the rites of the Established Church. The grave was dug, but the vicar said the body should not be taken through the lich-gate, but must enter by some other way. And by one of these minor gate-ways the dead body was finally borne to its last resting-place.

* * *

The term steeple-jack is applied to men who make a trade of ascending tall chimneys and spires, for the purpose of repairing them, or to prepare the way for the ascent to their summits of mechanics who can do the needful work in the high places. The professional steeple-jack's usual mode of getting to the top of a tall chimney is by the kite method. Taking advantage of desirable wind and weather, he skilfully sends up his large kite by the side of the chimney, and coaxes it over its top. Then it is allowed to descend to the ground on the opposite side, carrying behind it, all the time, a small string. When a ground connection is made with the small cord, the principal work is done. A large rope is then attached to the little line, and drawn over the chimney, and made fast at both ends to the ground. On this the steeple-jack climbs to the top of the chimney as best he can, — perhaps hand-over-hand, or with blocks. And, when there, he either does the necessary repairs himself, or brings up an artisan to help him. The occupation is necessarily a hazardous one, and I have heard of several instances where these climbers had been killed by falling from great heights. An English brick-layer, who had often worked at the top of tall chimneys, said the steeple-jack often took weeks in getting his kite and strings over a tall chimney.

These tall factory chimneys are always built up from the inside, without the use of any staging. I was told by a Lancashire man, who had worked on many of them, that there was a regulation in his country, which is one of the greatest manufacturing districts in the world, that no factory chimney should be less than ninety yards in height.

* * *

One of the sweetest of my memories of England — rural England, in particular — is the memory of its chiming bells. How often, at the close of a long ramble, have I, on entering some quiet village, whose long single street and ancient ivy-crowned stone church I was seeing for the first time, been charmed and well-nigh spell-bound as the sound of the chimes came to my ear. In this country nearly all our churches in town and country have bells. In England all churches have chimes of bells. In English country churches these chimes are rung, as a side occupation, by some artisan, or other laboring man; and for his musical work he receives what we should here deem a very light remuneration. He chimes his bells for church services on Sunday; for jubilation service on gala-days and holidays. His chimes are also called for when weddings occur, and on special occasions; as, for instance, when the rector has a party. And in preparation for these duties, and also in preparation for chiming-matches, the bell-ringer does a deal of practising. And this practising was what oftenest struck my ear as, at close of day, I lingered under the shadow of the gray old churches.

The bell-matches of which I have spoken, and which are a very common thing in England, are conducted just like any other contests of skill. After due preparation, the competing belfries ring out their notes upon the listening ears of the duly elected judges, and the best chimes and chimers win the prize. I have said all English churches have chimes. All rules have exceptions. I suppose some of the meeting-houses must be without them, for I have heard a curious Lincolnshire story of this sort: A traveller, once passing through Messingham on Sunday, saw three men sitting on the stile in the church-yard, shouting,

"Come to church, Thompson; come to church, Jones; come to church, Brown;" and so on. And he was informed that, having no bell on their church, that way of calling together a Sunday congregation was the regular Sunday programme.

Scripture readers are a great institution in England. They constitute a regular, recognized religious organization which is patronized by some of the most prominent laymen belonging to the nobility and gentry, and, with the other great religious bodies, hold great anniversary meetings in London in May. I used to fall in with many of these patient laborers as I wandered about the United Kingdom, and I had many a talk with them about their ways of work. They dress in a plain suit of black, and resemble, in their dress and address, the regular clergy.

As I travelled about England, I discovered many peculiar features in the Englishman's way of observing the Sabbath. Good society is supposed to attend the Established Church. But I am confident that not more than one-tenth of the people attend any church. Church accommodations abound; but I seldom entered an Episcopal place of worship, in city or country, that was not thinly attended.

The phantom congregations of the old churches in London made such an impression on my mind that my Sunday visits to those places of worship seem now like ghostly dreams. I have before me the authority of an English bishop for the statement that many of these London churches only secure a "quorum" of hearers by paying them a dole to attend, just as London boards of bank and insurance direction pay the ornamental lords of their management a guinea a time for attendance.

"The London Times" says that there is not in existence a business, social, or political organization that so completely fails of reaching the ends aimed at as the Church of England. And in the many church congresses of England whose discussions I have studied, this declaration of "The Times" has been endorsed by advanced thinkers in the clergy. All sorts of measures of reform in church methods have been broached. But the most curious plan I have noted, and one that gives a vivid insight into the average English idea of Sunday, is that described by Archdeacon Denison as having been operated by him with complete success. He said he had gotten up a Sunday cricket club, the object of which was to give his worshippers a chance to have a game of cricket on grounds near the church between the services on Sunday. One is reminded, by this scheme, of the story told of the muscular cricket-playing English preacher who closed one division of his morning church-service with, "Here endeth the second innings."

The great mass of the English people do not go to church. The attendance among the well-to-do classes is greater than among the agricultural laborers, artisans, etc. I gave some little attention to the church-going question while travelling about England. At home I heard a great variety of opinions on the matter, and I wished to see for myself.

In city and country in England, as in the United States, a very small percentage of the people attend public religious worship on Sunday, — attend one service, and that a morning one. There, as well as here, there is a general abstention from work on Sunday. And it seemed to me that in England there was more thoughtfulness on the part of employers of household servants of all types in the matter of giving them Sunday for rest than there is here. Good society does not go to drive on Sunday in England. It is there deemed a very improper thing to deprive the coachmen and the other stable employés of their Sunday, — or, at least, to deprive them of more of it than is absolutely necessary for service in the matter of getting the families to church in the morning. There is an active society in London called the "Lord's Day Observance Society."

The drift of its teachings and labors is illustrated in the following interesting advertisement: —

SUNDAY POST.—In order that deserving letter-carriers and other postal officers may not be deprived of their birthright of a weekly rest-day, please neither to receive letters nor to post letters for delivery on the Lord's Day. If living in the country, give orders to the Postmaster not to deliver your letters on Sunday.— *Vide* Post-office Guide, pp. 18, 19.

Lord's Day Observance Society, 20, Bedford Street.

On Sundays, particularly in the after part of the day, the roads leading out of London that are the highways to places of popular resort in the suburbs are thronged with pedestrians belonging to the class of tradesmen's clerks, shop-keepers and mechanics of the better order.

And on that day the costermonger, who keeps a horse and gig, takes it out of the treadmill of week-day shop-work, puts his wife and children into it, and makes a dash into the rural districts. In the manufacturing districts the average artisan dons his best clothes, and goes to church or to the beer-shop, the latter being open on other than church hours. And in many country localities out-of-door sports of various characters are indulged in quite freely on Sunday afternoons.

* * *

Cheshire County, England, is a small county. I walked across it in going from Liverpool to London. Greatest length, fifty-two miles; greatest breadth, thirty-eight miles. But it is a very productive district. It is rich in coal and salt. It is a rich dairy and grazing country. It keeps a hundred and fifty thousand cows, and annually makes about twenty thousand tons of cheese. Cheese is a great food staple in England. I can go through the United Kingdom on a half-crown a day, if I put up with a diet very common there; namely, bread and cheese and beer. In plodding through Cheshire it may be imagined that I found good Cheshire cheese on the tables at all the country inns.

In the heart of Cheshire are the great salt-mines, which have been steadily worked since their discovery in 1670. Here in the little town of Nantwich and vicinity is mined and pumped about all the salt used in Great Britain. The salt lies in great beds below a thick stratum of very hard rock, and a deal of gunpowder is used in blasting the rock and rock-salt.

Vast quantities of the Cheshire salt come to the surface in the form of brine; and, with the assistance of pumps, this natural brine is placed in great evaporating pans, where its progress into solid salt is accelerated by a boiling-point heat from traversing steam-flues. About a hundred and twenty thousand tons a year of Cheshire salt are exported through the Mersey. The United States takes the largest amount of this exported Cheshire product, and it comes to us under the name of Liverpool salt.

We are a salt-loving people. In lunching in

the vicinity of a great English salt-mine I found no salt in my butter; and very little is used in bread, on meats, etc. Yet the beer is salted so as to create a thirst for more beer!

* * *

I was whirled through a town in England whose rapid growth and youthfulness disabuses the American traveller of many of his preconceived ideas of modern English ways of business. The town was Middleborough; which, in 1851, had a population of a hundred and fifty-four, and which to-day has a population of seventy-two thousand. As a village, Middleborough is of very ancient date; for, in the Middle Ages, there were records of transfers of its town-lands to the Abbey of Whitby. But in the early years of the present century, it was simply the home of four farmers.

And the cause of the mighty and swift growth of this town is also a matter of astonishment to me. I had always had the idea that old England had long ago burrowed in its soil in all directions, and knew to a jot just what mineral wealth was underlying there. But it was not till 1851 that John Vaughn of Middleborough, son of a laboring man, and himself an iron-worker, while browsing around the blue hills about Middleborough in company with John Morley, discovered the existence of an iron ore in well-nigh inexhaustible supply, which has been the foundation of the prosperity of Middleborough, and which made Vaughn, the Bocklows, Peases, and others, millionaires. To-day Vaughn's company turns out four thousand tons of steel-rails a week, all made by the Thomas-Gilchrist process from the iron stone of Cleveland, which slept, unknown and undreamed of, till the middle of the present century.

The idea so commonly entertained in the United States that old England is stagnant and rusty will surely get shaken out of the head of any American who will wander, as I have wandered, among the iron, cotton, woollen and steel workers of the north and the heart of the kingdom.

* * *

A HIVE OF HUMAN INDUSTRY.

SUCH is Manchester, England. My stay in this place was short; but I remained there long enough to be convinced that it was the noisest, dirtiest, smokiest city on the face of the earth. It is said that there are in England one and a half million operatives in cotton factories; that she has, humming within her borders, nearly two hundred thousand power-looms; and that there is annually imported into the kingdom three million bales of cotton.

These are figures which astonish one; yet, after a run through the spinning and weaving districts of England, I was ready to believe that they were true. And Manchester, which is the largest cotton city in the world, may be depended upon to consume every year a giant's share of the vast supply of the cotton which flows into England from the United States and the East. It has a population of about four hundred thousand, nearly a hundred thousand of whom are employed in her factories. Although her cotton manufacture is her leading interest, she is largely engaged in other industries, prominent among which are her linen, silk, worsted, paper, iron and chemical establishments.

It seems to me that the factories last named must have a most deleterious effect upon the city, for I saw a most marked absence of growing grass and flowers within her borders. In other parts of England, notably near Liverpool, I have seen whole regions which were under the blight of the fumes from vast works for the production of chemicals, and which presented a scene of blasted vegetable desolation most painful to witness.

There are one or two points of peculiar interest relative to this great factory city, a city which I present as a typical modern manufacturing centre which I cannot pass over, though I willingly leave behind me its history and statistics. Here may be found, in most successful operation, the most perfect machinery — particularly machinery for spinning and weaving — that can be found in the world. The machine-shops of England have, within the last twenty-five years, turned out cotton and worsted machinery which has found favor in all the spinning and weaving world. And in Manchester the last and best products of these engineering establishments are to-day busily humming.

But I think it quite possible that this seemingly perfect and well-nigh automatic machinery is lowering the general standard of intelligence of the operative, and introducing into the mills an increased proportion of women and children. I have seen the finest machines in the best mills tended by laborers of the last-named classes; and if they do it as well, and at the same time at less wages than it can be done by men, the women and children will be employed.

The avarice of parents leads to their pressing their children into service at the earliest possible age, and the consequent neglect of their physical and mental education. In the jails and penitentiaries of Manchester, a great majority of the prisoners are comparatively young persons who cannot read or write at all, or who are only able to do so most imperfectly. Another point noted in our representative manufacturing city of Manchester comes from a glance into its hospitals. Here are found two classes of sufferers, who bear upon their persons marks of the effects of the machinery among which they have lived and moved, — sufferers from pulmonic complaints, caused by the cotton and wool surcharged and overheated air of the power-loom and spinning-rooms ; and sufferers from painful accidents from contact with the ever-whirling, dashing arms of iron and steel of the cloth-making machines among which their lives have been spent. I have statistics by me bearing upon these last points which forcibly illustrate the situation.

* * *

In entering Sheffield for the first time I could think of nothing but steel and cutlery. What a tremendous workshop the place is! But if Sheffield has been famous for any thing, it has been for its razors.

For a very low price, say about four and a half pence, it turns out a scraper — razor is from the Latin *rasus*, to scrape — of the finest steel and the finest temper. It is believed in England that much of the credit of the Sheffield razor is due to the water of the place in which it is tempered. And some razor-makers in this country, who also had this idea, once brought all the way from England some Sheffield water to aid them in turning out the right sort of tool. But I doubt not fine steel, long experience, and great skill has more to do with making the Sheffield razor what it is than has Sheffield water.

In smoky, grimy Sheffield, where I saw the huge steel and iron works whose products have been so largely consumed in the United States, what are termed the limited manufacturing companies, whose shares have been worked off upon too credulous investors by the small army of "promoters" of companies for which Sheffield is quite noted, have had very checkered careers. The Sheffield Red-book, a volume devoted to the manufacturing interests of the city, gives a list of about forty companies connected with the coal, steel and iron interests, whose affairs have been recently wound up under what is termed the Winding-up Act. And these failures were failures of concerns that had largely been promoted by accountants who had left the city, after pocketing heavy profits in the way of commissions for reporting. The losses of share-holders in Sheffield steel and iron companies, which are running without profit, have been very heavy.

There are many instances there where companies have not paid a dividend for many years, and where these shares are as low as twenty pounds on a par value of a hundred pounds. The tall chimneys of the great shops of Joseph Rodgers & Sons, and the River Don Works (Vickers'), called to mind the story of some of the immense successes of Sheffield in the way of steel and iron manipulation of which these two concerns are bright examples. The paid-up capital of River Don Works is £750,000. The company is now worth £1,646,250. The Rodgers' one thousand shares are quoted at £277½ on a par value of £100. While thirty-five limited companies show a depreciation of £3,500,000, only fifteen out of the fifty in the Sheffield district show an appreciation, the aggregate of which is £1,757,625.

* * *

Liverpool is now England's great gate-way to her Western commerce. Her gigantic docks, and the ships of all nations, and the products of all lands which one sees there, make up one of the seven modern wonders of the earth. I made a faithful endeavor to see the docks of Liverpool, and the memory of my long tramps up and down the banks of the Mersey is one of my most interesting recollections of English travel.

Liverpool, said an American captain to me, Liverpool is the cesspool of the world; for into its docks can be brought all the merchandise of the world that has been "left over," and there sold at some price or another, and from thence scattered again to all points, for it is a great point for the redistribution of merchandise. It is one of the dearest ports in the world. American captains are always grumbling to American travellers over the heavy port charges of Liverpool. Its situation is such that it can lay a large export duty on all the out-going products of Manchester, and many other of England's inland cities which have no outlet to the sea. I have been told that sixty per cent of the whole charges for freight on Manchester goods bound to Calcutta are incurred before the merchandise is out of Liverpool harbor.

Such a fact as this has developed a plan for a ship-canal from Manchester to the sea, — a plan which may, if carried out, inflict a most stunning blow upon Liverpool. Mac Iver, member of Parliament for Liverpool, fears that the Mersey will in time be silted up if this canal is built, for he knows that this river requires a most careful and costly treatment in order to keep its channels properly navigable. He and other Liverpool opponents of the canal say that this great Liverpool may in time become another Chester, a city which I found one of the best to sleep in of any in England, if its citizens are not alert enough to head off Manchester's canal plan.

* *
*

In York Minster, in the venerable and most picturesque city of York, on Whit-Monday, May 29, 1882, I attended a meeting of a peculiarly interesting character. It was a meeting of the York Branch of the Royal Society for the Prevention of Cruelty to Animals. It was an annual service for the young, which is held in this magnificent cathedral of York. A great swarm of

English boys, belonging to some charity foundation in York, occupied the body of the audience-room.

They were a ruddy and strong set of little fellows; and, in their neat, becoming uniform, presented an attractive appearance. They sat through the long address in a most demure and quiet manner. If they did not care for it, or listen to it, they appeared as if they did, which made it all right with the speaker. The speaker was the Rev. F. Laurence, one of the secretaries of the society with the long name. His discourse was long, and not particularly interesting. I trust that I, like the great squad of charity boys, maintained a demure and quiet appearance, and so also set myself right with the speaker, to whom I did not closely listen. After the services were over, I made a pretty *close* acquaintance with preacher Laurence's boy audience. It came about in this way: One of the sights of York is to ascend to the top of the great cathedral. From the roof a prospect is obtained, not only of the whole city, but of a vast extent of the interesting but rather level surrounding country. To get to this sightly roof of the minster, one must climb the long, dimly lighted and very narrow winding staircase. I know not the number of the steps of this dark and stuffy passage, but I know that few tourists must ever care to force their way up them a second time. On this Whit-Monday, which is a holiday in England, these hundreds of robust little boys, who had sat through the society's lecture, were given a ticket to go to the top of the cathedral. This ticket actually costs a sixpence, a sum which they could never spare to spend for a luxury of this sort. I doubt not the tickets were given them as a sort of reward for coming to church, and listening so demurely. I was descending from a visit to the roof and towers, in company with quite a delegation of visitors, a large proportion of whom were Yorkshire lads and lasses, workers in the great mills of the region, who were trying to make the most of their holiday by climbing to the top of every thing in old York which could be climbed; and, when about half-way down the narrow spiral stairway, met the crowd of ascending boys. They were forcing their way through the darkness and dust, completely occupying the old stone steps. Gradually they became wedged in with the party which was descending, and a perfect jam was the result. I was in the heart of the throng, and, for a while, actually feared that some of us would be suffocated. As it was, it seemed to me that nothing but the pluck and vigor of the little English rascals, who had got us into the scrape, helped us out of it. They finally butted and bored their way to daylight at the top of the cathedral. I came out of the hole at the bottom, feeling as if I had been dragged through a dirty chimney.

The Royal Society for the Prevention of Cruelty to Animals — the York anniversary of which has recalled this reminiscence — is one of the noblest organizations in England. Its branches and their agents were to be found wherever I travelled. It stretches out a protecting hand over a wide range of domestic and wild animals, and its monthly returns of conviction show the force and success with which it works.

One of these regular returns, a return covering the whole English field, shows that, in the thirty days of April, 1882, there were three hundred and ninety convictions of offenders secured by this society; and that, from January to March, 1882, it had compassed 1089 convictions.

I hastily summarized the details of one of the returns, for the matter is of curious interest to any thoughtful person. Convictions for abusing horses leads the list in numbers, and the offences against these faithful beasts are of about the same character as those commonly noted with us. The donkey outrages come next. I could but note, as I wandered about England, that the "numerous donkey" has a terribly hard time there. Being a tough and cheap beast, he is apt to fall into tough and cheap hands. I myself saw enough instances where he was being maltreated to put any feeling friend of the animal into a state of frantic distress. I saw him beaten, thin from want of food, overloaded, and working when in a generally unfit state. For such abuses as these, the society prosecutes and convicts. Sheep, pigs, dogs, cats, ducks, bears and wild birds follow the donkeys on this list of sufferers; and the crimes against them are, in these cases, much the same as those noted in the United States.

One little case in point will show the sort of cruelty which I have seen many and many a time in London streets.

His name was Henry Suett, and he was a flower-dealer. He was charged in police court, at Guildhall, with driving a pony in barrow up hill on Fleet Street, which pony had sore knees and a sore back. He had a big whip knotted in two places. There were five large men on the barrow, and it was only with great difficulty that Suett could get his pony up the hill to Peel's Hotel, where the men all got down, and went in after some beer. He was given twenty-one days imprisonment with hard labor.

The American traveller in England notices, with pride and satisfaction, the noble philanthropical organizations of his mother-country. And among them all there can be none more deserving of admiration than this Royal Society that I met with in old York Cathedral.

* * *

In many ways I had imbibed the idea that the old days were very saintly days, and that the old-time priests and lay-brothers were fasting, hair-cloth, self-denying sort of men.

But here are some solid, beef-eating facts, copied from the registers of Durham Cathedral, which have never been made very public, that are a curious revelation of the character of the Churchmen of the old days.

The register in question gives a statement of the consumption of provisions in this Cathedral of Durham during Whitsun week in 1747, together with the prices of the articles.

Here are the facts and figures:—

	s.	d.
Six hundred salt herrings	3	0
Four hundred white herrings	2	6
Thirty salted salmon	7	6
Twelve fresh salmon	5	6
Fourteen lings, 55 'keelings,' four turbot	23	1
Two horse-loads of white fish and a "congr"	5	10
'Playe,' 'sparlings,' and eels and fresh-water fish	2	9
Nine carcases of oxen, salted, so bought	26	0
One carcase and a quarter, fresh	6	11¾
A quarter of an ox, fresh, bought in town	3	6
Seven carcases and a half of a swine, in salt	22	2¼
Six carcases, fresh	12	9
Fourteen calves	28	4
Three kids, and twenty-six sucking porkers	9	7½
Fourteen capons, fifty-nine chickens and five dozen pidgeons	10	3
Five stones of hog's lard	4	2
Four stones cheese, butter and milk	6	6

	s.	d.
A pottle of vinegar and a pottle of honey.	0	6½
Fourteen pounds of figs and raisins, sixteen pounds almonds and eight pounds of rice	3	7
Pepper, saffron, cinnamon, and other spices	2	6
One thousand three hundred eggs	5	5
Sum total £10	12	6

Similar "consumptions" occurred during the week of the feast of St. Cuthbert, and other saints among the monks of Durham, for a long period of years.

I hardly know which astonishes me most in this table, — the quantity of provisions eaten, their peculiar character, or the extreme lowness of the prices named.

Of a piece with this Church revelation is a statement I saw in a Lancashire paper made by an old Malton antiquary, that Torgan beer was always the favorite drink of Martin Luther, and that he was in the habit of using vast quantities of it.

* * *

There are many curious names for trades and occupations in England. I often saw, in city and country, the name cow-keeper posted upon houses, barns, etc. The cow-keeper, with us, is a milkman who keeps cows. The man who lays bricks is, in England, often termed a brick-setter. A lumber dealer is called a timber merchant.

While walking over a country road in Hertfordshire, I saw upon a small building the sign "lath-render." This was a poser to me. A little conversation with the man within the shop opened my eyes. Laths in England were formerly made entirely of oak. They were rent or split out of the solid log. In fact, said an old English mechanic to me, the time was, and not so very long ago, when custom demanded in England that all the wood that entered into the construction of a house should be English oak. The English lath-render of to-day splits out of soft wood, by a slow, hand-process, great quantities of the laths that are used in England.

The wood of the lath-render whom I talked with was a clear and straight-grained pine that came, in quarter-sections of the log, from northern Europe. The lath-worker said to me that the sawed laths of America that had been brought to England were just good for nothing. All the builders of his acquaintance rejected them. Those he was making were certainly an excellent article, and the wood he was working was first-class. They were strong and supple laths. Being split with the grain, they could not be otherwise.

* * *

In that humming city of coal and iron, Newcastle-on-Tyne, is an old school called the Royal Jubilee School, which once had for its head-master a man whose fame as a rhymer has gone around the world. His name was C. F. Springman, and he was one of the best teachers the school ever had. Yet millions who have read his rhymes have never heard even the name of their author.

I doubt whether any dictionary of poetical quotations ever gave him a place in its index, yet his lines have buzzed in the heads of more persons than any lines that were ever written.

This schoolmaster introduced into his school the idea of teaching history, geography, and other studies through the medium of rhyme.

Springman of ancient Newcastle was quite successful in many of his rhyming excursions. But he won immortality when he one day hit upon a bit of jingle that had for its object the stamping on the minds of his boys, in an indelible manner, the number of days in the different months of the year, undoubtedly grumbling to himself, as I have often grumbled, over the stupidity of somebody or other in the far past, who, in getting up this monthly arrangement, did not make them all of the same length. And here are the perennial lines, — lines that hum in the head of every interest calculator on the English-speaking globe every day : —

> "Thirty days hath September,
> April, June and November;
> All the rest have thirty-one
> Except poor February alone."

I might say much of Newcastle, upon whose

tall chimneys, rising above the grimy town and strange mixture of ancient and modern objects upon the summit and declivities of the three eminences upon which the town is built, I looked out through the cloud of smoke which seems ever to rest above this heart of the black country. But time is precious, life is short, and only "thirty days hath September, April, June and November;" and so I must leave the ancient city, after having given this "literary allusion," which I am sure, because I got it from an original source, that no one else on this side the water has put on record.

* *
*

I often saw advertisements in the north of England local papers of this description:—

"HIRING FOR SINGLE SERVANTS.— A hiring for single servants will be held in the Corn Market on Monday, the 7th of May next.
(Signed) THOMAS GEORGE GIBSON, *Mayor*."

Sometimes these advertisements would be "hiring for double servants;" that is, for men with their wives. These fairs are, in some localities, held every six months, but the general custom is to hold them once a year. At Carlisle, an ancient city full of historical interest, situated on the southern border of Scotland, I happened to arrive at the time of its great yearly hiring fair.

The huge railway-station in that city, belonging

to the London and Northwestern line, and situated in the heart of the place, was a scene of the most unwonted bustle and confusion on the morning of Whit-Monday, when I was whirled into it in the Scotch mail, for Carlisle's annual hiring fair is always held on that day, and was just then being opened with a rush.

Contracts in the locality of which Carlisle is the busy centre, made between master and man-servant or maid-servant, are made for a year, and begin and end on this Monday. And so on this Monday — a day when all the old labor-contracts are completed — employers, and those who seek employment, come together, and make new arrangements. A hiring fair is a labor-exchange open for a day.

At this semi-annual fair the tariff for male and female single servants was made up as follows: Strong girls, about seven pounds for the six months; women, about eight pounds; for women-servants of an exceptional character, ten pounds. Men were in good demand at from ten to twelve pounds for the half-year, with exceptional payments of fourteen pounds.

I have here given the precise figures and classifications as reported in the local paper. Here we have a hundred dollars a year for some of the right stamp of female servants, and a hundred and forty dollars a year for some men-servants. I had a talk with a Newcastle artisan whose sisters — who were, he said, very capable girls — were out at service; and his figures corresponded with those I have given.

The stations of the railway, on the May morning of which I am writing, were placarded with handbills setting forth the fact that Carlisle's great hiring fair was being held, and offering to carry the employers and the laborers at greatly reduced rates. When, on the next morning, I made a farther plunge into Scotland, flying through to Edinburgh, I saw the highways along the line of the railway full of one-horse "tip-carts," bearing the household goods of laborers' families; while the men, women and children trudged along on foot by the side of the teams. These family flights evidenced a pretty general change of base, the result of the new contracts made at the hiring fairs.

* * *

THE GUN-FLINTS OF OUR GRANDFATHERS.

IT seemed to me that I discovered where they all came from, when, one afternoon in May, I took a long walk in the county of Hertfordshire, from Barnet to St. Alban's Abbey, one of the most magnificent abbeys in all England. My road lay through a region of a chalky formation; and in England that dull, black mineral quartz, which we term flint, abounds wherever the chalky formation exists. And here on every hand I found flint in abundance. Piles of it lined the roadside. Walls and dwelling-houses and ancient churches were to be seen built of it. The bed of the road itself was partially made of it.

Forty or fifty years ago, the old flint-lock guns gave place to the newly discovered percussion-cap guns; and in 1830 matches came into general use, and flint and tinder boxes for raising a fire went out of use forever. Before that time the cutting out of flints for the shooting and firing purposes named was a great industry in the flinty regions of England. A good flint-worker would split out three hundred merchantable flints in a day. They were exported to all parts of the world, and the gun-dealers of America received all their flints from this source.

I found that Birmingham was still making the old-fashioned flint-lock guns for shipment to Africa, and other points where the rude natives would not use any other sort of fire-arms. There are dealers in America who are able to fill a large order for gun-flints from stocks they have had on hand a long while, and who have occasional orders for flint-lock guns for the African trade. England at one time used large quantities of flint in making glass and porcelain, but other articles are now used in its place.

* * *

An American gentleman said to me, when I was landing in England for the first time, that I should be very much disappointed in her rivers. He remarked further, in that contemptuous manner which Americans are apt to display when comparing English scenery with American, that I should find the most famous English rivers little better than ditches and sewers. After no little travel about the United Kingdom by the banks of the best-known rivers of the country, I came to the conclusion that my American critic was nearer the truth than I had anticipated. But there is a more disagreeable fact connected with most English rivers than merely their disappointing character to an American as features of English scenery.

These polluted, muddy rivers, flowing through densely populated cities and towns, which often drain into them, and which always cast into them much filth and garbage from the homes and factories along their banks, are, in many cases, the sources of the domestic water-supply of the country through which they flow. I visited and examined some of the river water-works which supplied drinking-water for many large cities and towns.

Water which no one would consider potable, and which seemed to me little better than raw sewage, and too mean for a fish's home, was drawn from the sluggish streams, and passed into the water-pitchers and teakettles of Englishmen through a series of filtering-beds made, on the most scientific principles, of layers of gravel, coke, shale, sand, charcoal and other substances, which made the water bright, sparkling and perfectly clear, but may not have deprived it of its dangerous qualities.

And now here we reach the gist of this English water question. And the point raised is one of deep interest, and has a close application in this country. And this is the great question. Can dirty, bad water be made really clean and healthful? The judges of the Maidstone (England) County court have lately had before them an important lawsuit, in which this question was a vital issue. It was urged by the defendants, with great force, that the filtration we have described fails to deprive water that has once been polluted by sewage, and other dirty agencies, of any of its more dangerous properties. Very high scientific authority was adduced in support of this position. My own observation leads me to take this ground. Some of the most dangerous water that has ever been used for domestic purposes in America — water that has bred typhoid and other fevers — has presented to the eye the most attractive appearance, and in taste revealed nothing objectionable. Yet it held within it deadly disease, and came from sources that had been terribly contaminated. Passing through veins of gravel and sand, it had been bleached, but had not been purified.

Water is not much used as a beverage in England. It is about the last thing people there think of drinking "straight."

So completely are the English out of the habit of using water as a beverage, that the traveller is not only not offered it when he is expecting it, but finds some difficulty in getting it if he asks for it. I shall not soon forget the astonishment with which a highly intelligent Englishman looked upon my little boy of ten, who, at the Cunard steamer's table, would have his glass of cold water. He said to me he could not see how I dared let the little fellow pour such stuff into his stomach along with his dinner.

* * *

A memory of a long ramble among the gray old college buildings of venerable Oxford is among the pleasantest of my reminiscences of English travel; yet, after all, what I remember most vividly of Oxford, and what was most novel and interesting to me there, relates to the outside life of her students, as I studied it, when I mingled amid the throngs of Oxford's young men, as they watched the great champion games of cricket that were going on between the famous Australian eleven and their own selected team, crowded the banks of the Isis to see the eight-oared races of their crews, which were preparing for the great Oxford and Cambridge contest at Putney, or plunged out into the country about their great university town, on long walks, bicycle runs, and rides in the saddle.

The rage for athletics runs high at Oxford. Years ago, when Mark Pattison went up to Oxford from his quiet Yorkshire home, he was struck by two features of its life. One was the unstudious habits of a large proportion of his fellow-students; the other, the strange character of the Oxford dialect.

To-day far more Oxford men are absorbed in boating than in reading for honors. And, as for dialect, her students have a most marked and peculiar "lingo," as noticeable and characteristic as is their gait and carriage. Pattison said their dialect was as offensive to him as "English is to a Yankee." To-day the travelling American will find Oxford talk (Oxford slang) in many points quite unintelligible to him.

But in the matter of the Oxford craze for boating, etc., let the following amusing incident speak for itself:—

The Oxford eight were out on a training pull on the Isis, under the lead of a stroke oar who was a scholar of Brazenose. The stroke heard one of his crew discussing for a moment with a fellow-oarsman some point about their studies, making some classical allusions. The indignant captain paused; and, while from his uplifted, feathered oar the glittering water was for an instant allowed to drip into the stream, he thundered out to the astonished undergraduate, "No damned intellectuality here!"

This was the bark of a rough bull-dog, yet it well showed the tone prevailing in Oxford boating circles. And I doubt not this terse, sweeping command might stand emblazoned upon the rooms of many a college man in our New England Oxford, without seeming at all inappropriate to the atmosphere there prevailing.

* * *

The fashion, that was brought over here from London with the "Waukenphast" style of shoe, of wearing very heavy walking shoes, I do not believe in. I looked into the "Waukenphast" shoe-store while in London, and noticed that this sort of shoe was now largely made there for the American trade, European walkers having adopted something lighter.

But of all the leg-wearying foot-wear that I ever set my eyes upon, the English laborer's farm-shoe leads the procession. I thought of bringing a pair home to open a shoe museum with, but they were so large and heavy, I gave up the idea. An

Irish gardener said their weight was seven pounds, and I think he under-weighted them. They are made of cow-hide uppers and oak-tanned soles, shod with great iron heels, and a large array of big nails; and as the unfortunate wearer of these high-lows comes tramping towards you over the stones in the streets of some rural hamlet, you may well imagine that one of England's "Suffolk Punches" (heavy shod cart-horses) is coming over the road. These shoes cost the laborer fourteen shillings (three dollars and a half), and afford him at least a year's constant wear. No American farmer would live and move in such clumsy shoes.

It takes the dull, slow-moving, contented English laborer, who has in him the dull blood of many generations of men just like him, to live a happy life in such cumbering foot-wear. They chain him to the soil where his masters wish him to be chained. He has never, perhaps, been twenty miles from home in all his life. Emigration to lands beyond seas is made to seem something frightful to a man born and bred to the wearing of such shoes as these. So he plods through life in them, more stolid in manners than the heavy cattle he drives. "Over Edom will I cast out my shoe" is a scriptural signification of proprietorship. These dull ploughmen cast their broad shoes over a good-sized patch of English soil; but, alas! in their case the shoe does not gain proprietorship in the soil which it covers.

On the Continent I saw and heard the clatter of the *sabot*, or wooden shoe; and in the north of England I saw children wearing shoes with tops of leather and bottoms of wood, and visited shops where such were made. They are a useful, economical shoe, but terribly noisy. At Haworth, all the little children of the working classes wore these shoes, when I saw them on the way to school week-days, but they said they never wore them on Sunday, but had fine leather shoes for that day.

* * *

THE BROAD ARROW.

THE first time I noticed this singular mark of British proprietorship was when it walked past me on the backs of some English convicts under sentence to penal servitude. This last term means a good deal in England; for the authorities there succeed in getting a vast amount of hard labor out of their prisoners, a large proportion of which is done on the great public works, such as the harbor improvements at Portsmouth and Plymouth, and in the great stone quarries, where the tourist often gets glimpses of the branded men as they work under careful supervision.

The next time I met the broad arrow was when, in walking from Liverpool to London, I found in the road, in the town of Daventry, a flat stone under my feet, upon which this sign was plainly marked, and, upon inquiry, I found that the branded stone solidly noted the fact that my feet were planted upon the heart of England,—that I stood in its very centre. And afterwards I found this broad arrow mark, the origin of which has never been discovered, stamped upon the Queen's property of every description, from castle, ships, and huge guns down to a piece of Liverpool bagging, and protected in its position by a statute which fastens a penalty of two hundred pounds upon any person who is detected in removing it.

The mention of English prisoners abroad with this arrow upon them brings to mind that singular Australian idea that has been introduced into English prison discipline,—the plan of sending the criminal who has reduced his term of confinement by good behavior out into the world upon a ticket-of-leave, upon which he must report at stated times until his full term of sentence has expired. This ticket-of-leave system must not be confounded with another peculiar English method of treatment of criminals, known as the police supervision sentence. In England a criminal is often sentenced to seven years of penal servitude, and five years of police supervision; and in all these five years of supervision he must report himself to the prison authorities monthly, or be liable to immediate arrest.

* * *

I was continually seeing in the windows of shops and inns, in England, handbills announcing the existence and meetings of coal-clubs, watch-clubs, clothing-clubs, umbrella-clubs, etc. ; and my curiosity was naturally excited to discover just what these novel institutions were.

I soon obtained an easy explanation of the mystery, and here it is. These clubs are working-people's organizations. A company of artisans, or agricultural laborers, — or, in fact, any set of men who are in receipt of moderate incomes, band themselves together into a watch-club, for instance, the object of which is to supply each member with a watch of a class agreed upon. One of these watch-clubs, which existed in Newcastle-upon-Tyne, had forty members.

Each member paid into the club two shillings a week, and with these eighty shillings the treasurer of the club each week bought a silver watch ; and a very good silver watch can be bought in England for eighty shillings.

The names of all the club were then written upon cards, thrown into a box or bag, shaken up, and one drawn out in lottery fashion, the name drawn entitling its owner to the watch. It will be at once seen that this fortunate proprietor of the early "turnip," who had acquired a watch in a week for two bobs (English for shillings), might, if he were loose in his morals, attend no more meetings of that club, pay no more shillings for watches which were not for him; in fact, think it a good thing for him to "resign." The constitutions of the organizations anticipate this danger, and provide that the drawers must put up bonds that they will remain and pay till the last man of the club is able to parade with an eighty-shilling silver watch in his pocket, and the mission of the ring is ended.

I was told that in Lancashire there was hardly a retail dealer of any description in that county who was not ready to get up one of these clubs, and I should judge that the custom of fostering them was common with most of the retail shopkeepers in all parts of the kingdom.

The artisans and agicultural workers of England are great users of the co-operative principle; and, when they can add to it an element of chance to give a little excitement to the business, and also some social features that shall give them an opportunity to get together often over the inevitable beer, they are supremely happy. The drawings, the assessings, and the general management of these clubs lead to a social gathering once a week, at which no small amount of beer is apt to be drunk, and a good deal of hilarity indulged in.

I believe these people beat the world in getting up supply-clubs, — little rings for supplying themselves with almost every thing, from a ton of coal to an orderly funeral. Burial-clubs are quite common; and when I heard of instances where laborers had been thrust into earth uncoffined, and of other cases where they had been carried to the grave in a cheap coffin which went not beneath the sod with the body, but which was reserved to be used again for transportation purposes, I did not wonder over the application of the benefit-club principle to burials.

But one of the oddest clubs I heard of was termed a "goose-club." The typical English laborer thinks every thing of his Christmas goose. The turkey will not do. He deems this bird dry and unsavory compared with the "royal goose." And in some country localities the people find the goose-club a capital organization. A speculative old lady is apt to be at the head of it. About three months before Christmas she begins collecting her sixpence of each member, so that each one shall be sure of the fat goose when Yuletide arrives.

* * *

English newspapers are quite in the habit of giving the occupation of the man whose death they print. This is particularly the case in the north of England, and from a North-of-England paper I take this record as an illustration: "At Shilbottle, 23d June, aged 93, George Hunter, mole-catcher, much respected."

The expressions "much respected," "deservedly respected," and "dearly beloved" appear often in English death notices.

But in the record of death which I have quoted, I doubt not my readers have been struck, as I was, by the novelty of the occupation followed by the nonagenarian, "A mole-catcher, deeply respected." I had not to go far to find an explanation of the methods and machinery of such a queer English trade as this. I found a man near me who could intelligently answer all my questions about this mole business.

Mole-catching has long been a distinct trade in Britain. There are, curiously enough, no moles in Ireland, but England, Scotland, and Wales are mole-burrowed to an enormous extent. The old English name of the animal is *mouldwarp*, and I found this term still in use in the north of England, and also another mole name which sounded like "wunt." The animal is deemed a great nuisance, for he bores and burrows and throws up his mole-hills in wheat-fields and pastures, doing a deal of damage. He lives upon grubs and insects; yet, though he cares nothing for grains and vegetables as food, he cuts their roots and ruins their growth as he bores his paths under the soil.

The mole-catcher works with traps, clearing fields of the enemy by contract at so much an acre, or at so much a dozen for the moles destroyed. Some of these mole-catchers are sharp fellows, said my laboring friend who was telling me what I am now writing. They will save the moles they have taken from a field cleared at so much an acre, and sell them at so much a dozen to the man they are working for on the dozen plan, pretending they have been taken from *his* land. But this old mole-catcher, dead at ninety, was not one of that sort. He died respected. The moles, whose old enemy he was, got him at last, however; and he was laid to rest under the sod where moles could burrow and bore about him, fearless now of his traps and snares.

* *
*

Of all the antiquated and blind weight and measure terms existing, the English list of these is the champion. I have often endeavored in vain to find out what things cost as I have wandered through the meat-stalls of English markets, because I had not in my head or pocket the key to their cockney way of cutting up things.

But here is a curious table showing those English weights and measures which are so common in England, yet so unfamiliar in America:—

A fodder of lead is	$19\frac{1}{2}$ cwt., or 2,184 lbs.
A firkin of butter	56 lbs.
A stone of butcher's meat (London)	8 lbs.
A stone of horseman's weight	14 lbs.
A stone of iron shot	14 lbs.
A stone of glass	5 lbs.
A seam of glass	24st of 5 lbs., or 120 lbs.
A fagot of steel	120 lbs.
Pig ballast	56 lbs.
Cask of bristles	10 cwt.

A bale of feathers, about	1 cwt.
A pocket of hops	1½ to 2 cwt.
A bag of hops, nearly	2½ cwt.
Hhd. of tobacco	12 to 18 cwt.
A sack of potatoes	168 lbs.
A sack of coals	224 lbs.
A sack of flour	280 lbs.
A dicker of hides	10 skins
A dicker of gloves	10 doz.
A last of hides	20 dckrs.
A last of feathers	17 cwt.
A last of gunpowder	24 bbls.
A roll of vellum	5 doz., or 60 skins
Barrel of butter	224 lbs.
Stone of fish	8 lbs.
Gallon of flour	7 lbs.
Ton of potatoes	40 bush.
Load of hay or straw	37 truss
Truss of straw	86 lbs.
Truss of old hay	56 lbs.
Truss of new hay	60 lbs.

* *
*

I could find but very few wooden houses in England. Brick and stone are the well-nigh universal building materials. I found clay very abundant in England, and brick-yards abounded.

Red bricks are just now very fashionable, and their popularity is steadily increasing. The nobility and gentry, who are, in many cases, giving more attention than ever before to the improvement in tastefulness and in comfort of the dwelling-houses upon their estates, are quite generally erecting for the use of their farmers and other tenants upon their estates, red-brick houses of the Queen Anne and Elizabethan styles of architecture. The great land-owners employ the best London architects. Rural England owes much of its attractiveness to the pains taken, and the advanced ideas held, in the matter of home-building by her nobility and gentry.

I was much pleased by the effect produced in house architecture by use of bricks of various colors. Brick clays contain more or less iron. The hue of a burned brick depends upon the amount of iron in the clay. Clays containing less than one per cent of iron change in the kiln to cream-color and buff. Brick houses of these hues I found abundant. I thought them very attractive on account of their shade. Clay with more iron in it comes from the kiln red. Blue bricks, which I also noticed, are made out of the same clay as are the red.

A peculiar method of supplying air, as they are being burned, and the application of hotter fires to them, turns them out blue. Very fine brick, and terra cotta fancifully enamelled, are used with great effect in English architecture. By their use a great variety of colors is secured.

Brick houses coated with cement, mastic, or something of the sort, and by their outside finish made to resemble houses of stone, are numerous in England. But this is an old style. The present day, which cultivates the "sincere" in architecture, does not favor this sham in building.

I visited several clay-pits where the clay was of a color to turn out bricks of a yellowish hue, and bricks of this color are just now very popular with English builders. I also observe that many of the English bricks were made with a space scooped out on their broad side so that they might catch on a good supply of mortar, when laid, or *set*, as they say in England. The brick-setter's trade is an active one in England; and, since houses are so universally made of stone and brick in England, the outside house-painter has a poor show there. And the inside one likewise; for unpainted, natural wood interiors are very much in vogue in England.

There is a local name in England for artisans who do outside work at coloring. They are termed "smudgers." An Englishman said to me, that when he first saw in America painters at work on the outside of our wooden houses with the large brushes, he thought they were all whitewashing, since painting the outside of the houses was a thing hardly known in his county in England.

I found fireplaces in almost every room in England, but saw no stoves in rural England. And rural Englishmen, when they come over here, often complain that our ever-present stove is about the hardest thing they have to endure. English people do not demand such warm living-rooms as we do. I soon found that out as I travelled in England. I should say that sixty degrees would suit them far better than our customary seventy.

But notwithstanding the fine ventilation afforded their living-rooms by the ever-present fireplace, they have a habit of paying more attention to the ventilation of their houses from the outside than we do. This is the case with houses of high and low degree. Perforated bricks, iron gratings, etc., permit the outside air to circulate freely within the outer walls, and under the floors of laborers' cottages, farmers' houses, and baronial halls.

Intelligent Englishmen were surprised when I told them how little attention the majority of our builders paid to ventilation. Philanthropists and men of science, working individually and in organizations, are doing more in England than in any other country on the face of the earth to improve the conditions and surroundings of the common people.

Solid roofing for houses is that which I saw in parts of England and Wales. Stones from the mountains are split into slabs of about four inches in thickness, and two and three feet square, and used to cover the roofs in place of boards and shingles. The sides of the houses are, in these instances, made of stones, and some of these houses which I visited among the stony peaks of

Derbyshire, not far from Chatsworth, had walls eighteen inches thick. These places were little farm-houses. All their out-buildings, from the barn to the well-house and hen-house, were made of solid stone. And in the farm-yards were watering-troughs, and troughs for the swine, made of the same material. On such home establishments as these time could make little impression.

* * *

To thatch properly is quite an art, — an art usually followed by those who have learned the trade of thatching, just as any other mechanical trade is learned. In the farming districts of England, barns for the storage of hay and straw are not commonly seen. But on every hand I saw huge ricks and stacks of hay which were covered with thatch. I was interested in noting how finely the hay was preserved that had thus been kept out-of-doors. In many towns I saw hay-stacks that had remained out-of-doors for three and four years. Turnips and other vegetables are in England piled in heaps in the fields, and covered with a coating of earth and straw. I saw many of these thatched heaps, most of which were turnip-heaps, which were opened, as the spring came on, for the purpose of feeding out the turnips to the sheep. The universal method was to cut up these turnips by running them through a hand-power cutting-machine.

Rye straw is one of the best and most popular sorts of straw that is used for thatching in Great Britain, but all kinds of straw, as well as rushes and reeds, are used. Wheat and oat straw are very good for the purpose. In Ireland I saw many laborers' huts that were "thatched" with turf. The turf was generally a sort of heather-growing turf, and, after being well laid on, the heather would grow, forming a fine, mat-like covering to the roof. It is not an uncommon sight to see the goats browsing on such roofs, for the huts are so low studded they have little difficulty in mounting to the ridge-pole from the lowest corner of the cabin. In some parts of Ireland there are humble cabins of clay and mud, whose roofs are covered, at least in part, with a thatch made of dried potato-tops.

While wandering in English hamlets, where the straw-thatched cottages were numerous, I often asked why the people living in houses thus covered were not very much in danger from the roofs catching fire, these roofs being apparently of such combustible material. But I could not find that there had been any serious objections entertained against thatched roofs on this ground, though cases of fire in the straw coverings had occasionally been known. But other objections against these straw-thatched roofs were spoken of, and noticed by me as I travelled in the regions where they are common. The birds are fond of building their nests in them, which serves to disarrange them; and they are also quite in the habit of pulling the straw out of them, and carrying it away to use in building their nests in other places.

Thatched roofs belong to the olden times in Great Britain. The red-tiled roof, which is also a very old-fashioned roof, holds its own there better than the straw roof, and I saw many new roofs of these tiles.

* * *

Public libraries abound everywhere in England, and it seemed to me that all classes of people there had better opportunities than we have to supply themselves with reading-matter. It was not uncommon for me to find books from several different free libraries in the hands of one workman's family. And excellent newspapers are so abundant and cheap that few households are without, at the very least, one regular newspaper. The average reader in an English manufacturing town inclines, as with us, to turn to fiction for entertainment; and there, as here, is a complaint against the public libraries on account of the temptations they offer to the omnivorous story reader.

In a humming coal and iron town in the heart of the black country, I found that out of a total of about five thousand books issued by its public library in a week, over three thousand were works of fiction; while of history, biography, works of travels, and geography only about four hundred and fifty are called for. Surely the novel reader abounds abroad, as well as in the United States.

* * *

I doubt not some of my readers will be greatly astonished when I tell them that London has, within its fifteen miles' radius, the enormous population of five millions, and is steadily increasing its numbers with a rapidity rarely excelled in city growth the world over. I travelled every quarter of this vast, teeming metropolis, and can bear personal witness to the fact that on every hand buildings were springing up and new streets being built. Seventy miles of new streets are yearly added to the vast network of London's avenues.

I was, I must confess, overwhelmed by the immensity of London. But I was not so much impressed by what may be termed its material greatness — that is, by the number and size of its buildings, the maze of its streets, and the length of its broad avenues of homes and trade — as by the tide of humanity that ebbed and flowed about me wherever I wandered in the mighty metropolis.

Statistics and descriptions give one no idea of the way the great London hive is packed, and all that I had read relative to the number and density of its population had in no wise prepared me for what I saw and felt as I sauntered hither and thither, day after day, in the busiest and most populous portions of the city.

And still the city keeps on growing with a rapidity that really alarms London thinkers, who are to-day discussing the question, what means shall be undertaken to check the growth of the already unwieldly monster. Suggestions have been made that special efforts be undertaken to promote direct emgration from London to the colonies. But this would do little good, for the aided emigration would be more than out-counted by the immigration from the country to London. General emigration schemes are the only ones which would tend to relieve London. The real *vitality* of London is only maintained by the country immigration, for the country is to-day to be credited with furnishing the metropolis the best of its citizens.

The serious problem which I am discussing is in amusing contrast with an imaginary one of the same kind which came up in London in the sixteenth century. In 1580 London placed a restriction on its extension, forbidding the erection of new buildings, on the ground that such expansion would be likely to increase the plague, create trouble in governing such multitudes, make a dearth of victuals, multiply beggars, bring together more artisans than could live, and impoverish other cities for lack of inhabitants.

Along with this growth goes a struggle, on the

part of London's wisest people, to preserve all the open spaces existing, and to yearly add as many more of these as possible. These commons of the city are used to an enormous extent by the laboring classes. To see vast crowds there, in the full enjoyment of the green fields and forest shades, one should ramble through them, as I did, on a bank holiday.

It has been proved that the immense number of fires steadily burning in London, for household purposes, etc., have the effect to raise the temperature of the atmosphere of the city above that of the surrounding country. And in summer, when this effect, added to the clouds of smoke and dust hanging in and over the city, makes the city air particularly oppressive, the Londoner seeks the magnificent open spaces that lie without the walls — the Epping Forest, Couldon Common, or Burnham Beeches — with a feeling of great relief. The utmost freedom is allowed the visitors to the parks. In Hyde Park young and old walk on the grass everywhere as they please, and "keep off the grass," is a sign unknown in any London park.

No dogs are allowed in these open spaces unless led by their keepers. During the last nine years the corporation of London has acquired, as open spaces, between 6,000 and 7,000 acres at a cost of £312,950; namely, West Ham Park (76 acres), costing £15,000; Epping Forest (5,348 acres),

£275,300; Wanstead Park (783 acres), £7,625; and Couldon Common (347 acres), £7,000. All that has been obtained from the duty on the importation and measurement of foreign grain.

Opponents to the acquirement of these open spaces have sometimes said that the bread of the people was taken from them to purchase the fields, but this seems jargon when one reflects upon the fact that the grain-tax in question is only one seventy-fifth part of a farthing on every quartern loaf.

It was told me that, without doubt, not less than a million people move into and out of the business portions of London every day. I have never anywhere seen such crowds on the wing as I have observed on the lines of suburban rail and other means of public conveyance at the close of the day, and in the early morning hours.

But on holidays the rush and jam of the human tide that sets outward from London is something indescribable. Fares are extremely low on these holidays, both on the railways and steamers. For five shillings passengers are taken from London to Brighton and back (ninety miles); for thirty shillings, from London to Paris and back, if the the tourist is willing to travel by the night service. And in every possible direction London holiday trips, by rail and steamer, are advertised at correspondingly low rates.

I have wandered long and far in the most poverty-stricken districts of London. These are situated at the east end of the city. Of this slum of London, Huxley, president of the Royal Society, who had at one period been a practising physician in this east end, has spoken as follows : " I have several times travelled around the globe, visiting, as I journeyed, the most savage and degraded peoples in barbarous lands ; but I have never anywhere seen such degradation and misery as I have seen in the east end of my own city."

An English archbishop, speaking of this same district before a large London audience, made a profound sensation by exclaiming, "The east end is hell without the fire!"

But pleasanter is it for me to show the sunnier side of the city. Thronged, grimy London is full of the sweetest and noblest charities, and careful study and observation in London convinced me that it was one of the most generous cities in the world. Here are found organizations of an infinite variety for the relief of want, suffering and sickness. And, outside of these organizations, individual charity laborers are more numerous than in any other city in the world. It is nobly fashionable for the nobility and gentry of London to give often. And the poor give their pennies to those poorer, while I have often seen the poorer flinging their farthings to those even more destitute than themselves.

In illustration of London's generosity to its established charities, let me describe the methods and machinery of two of its great charity systems. The city has what it terms its Hospital Saturday and its Hospital Sunday. On Hospital Saturday, the first Saturday in September, a large collection is taken up on behalf of the hospitals of the city, at which time the fifteen thousand different establishments connected with the industrial interests of the city are visited, and all employed therein are solicited to contribute. About twelve hundred stations are also set up in the streets, and attended by ladies belonging to the first circles in London, where hospital collections are also made from the throngs that surge through the streets of the teeming city. The post-offices, all the railway-stations, and other public places, are also included in the swing of this Saturday hospital collection-box. It seemed to me that the Saturday hat was passed around in this open manner to reach the pockets of those who would not be present in church when it was sent around on Sunday.

Over thirty-six thousand subscription sheets, and an immense number of collection-boxes, are in use on this Hospital Saturday; and when the lists are closed, all the money taken in is brought to the central office in Fleet Street, and counted by a volunteer corps of London bank clerks. Hospital Sunday is the Sunday on which collections are taken up in all the churches on behalf of the hospitals of London. And these hospitals are vast in number, and of an almost endless variety. Almost every disease is represented by a large hospital for its treatment, among which are several for the care of incurables suffering from cancer, consumption and other diseases.

I shall not not soon forget the deep impression made upon my mind, as, in the heart of London, I read upon the outer wall of an immense pile of buildings the inscription, "Hospital for strangers who are sick. No recommendation necessary. Strangers in London who are in sickness and poverty will be admitted here to the full extent of the accommodations."

Many of those noble hospitals, and other charitable institutions of London, are in possession of vast funds, accumulations of individual gifts and public grants, that have been bestowed upon them during the past. Many others have very small endowments, and are, therefore, mainly dependent upon current voluntary donations. These they call for in a way not common with us, which is by advertisement appeals in the leading London papers. Here may be found column after column of the cries for help. At the holiday seasons these solicitations for gifts crop out more strongly than ever.

In England, more than with us, resort is had to balls and parties, and entertainments of various kinds, for money to carry on the public charities, which in Paris are supported, in some instances, by a direct tax upon the theatres. And these London entertainments in aid of the great charities are often very fashionable affairs, and under the patronage of the nobility and gentry. Says one young swell to another young swell, "Are you going to the Throat and Ear ball?"

"No," replies swell number two; "I am engaged to the Hospital for Incurable Idiots."

"But I may meet you at the Epileptic dance?"

"Oh, yes! We are sure to be there, the Epileptic stewards will be so delightful."

So the society young men go the rounds of these gay parties in aid of these noble charities. I noted that there has of late been a falling off in the current voluntary subscriptions to the great London charities, and "The London Times" has been urging the necessity of a direct government support for them.

* *
*

If London has a wicked aspect, it has also its attractive side, and I know of nothing more encouraging and inspiring than a glance at its many admirable organizations, which have for their object the care and elevation of the young of both sexes who are thrown upon the city by the country from which they come in search of occupation and fortune.

In illustration of this may be mentioned one of London's organizations for helping young men, which is, without doubt, the most successful society of its class to be found in any city in the world, and also one of the largest young men's associations to be found anywhere. I refer to the London Polytechnic Young Men's Christian Institute of Regent Street. The term Christian, as applied to this association, is used in its noblest and widest sense; for in admitting young men to membership, what is popularly known as a "religious test" is not applied, and the society is entirely unsectarian. This is in happy contrast with some so-called Christian organizations for young men I have known elsewhere, which, announcing that a good moral character is the only qualification for membership, will not really admit to full membership any young man who has not joined some "evangelical" church, no matter how excellent a young man he may otherwise be. The London Polytechnic has already some twenty-two hundred members, all young men of the working-class, and at least five hundred more have booked themselves to join as soon as there is room for them. The institute has its reading-rooms, library, its classes for instruction in a wide range of things, from single-stick to short-hand, its tennis club and bicycle club, bands of music, savings bank, insurance company, ambulance corps, bathing establishment and debating society, and I hardly know what else. Its rooms open at 5.30 A.M., and close at 10.30 P.M. It does not admit the use of cards and dice, and it also makes an announcement, that sounded curiously enough to me, that it had no drinking-bar. The Polytechnic was founded by a most liberal London gentleman by the name of Quentin Hogg, and to it he has devoted a large portion of his time and fortune. I had an opportunity of attending the anniversary meeting of the London Young Men's Christian Association in Exeter Hall, Lord Shaftesbury in the chair, as usual, and learned something of the methods and machinery of this excellent organization; but I am convinced that the Polytechnic is better calculated to reach the poor young men from the country. In a most touching article printed not long ago in a leading London journal entitled, "A Bitter Cry from Outcast London," and which painted in sad colors the poverty and loneliness of the thousands of working young men and women who annually pour into the city from the country, it was proved from English blue-books that whereas, in 1861, for every hundred people who resided in rural districts, there were one hundred and sixty-five living in towns, that in 1881, one hundred and ninety-nine were living in towns against one hundred in country; so that it is claimed that it is accurate to say to-day that there are in England two people living in urban for every one residing in rural districts.

* * *

Fires in England, in country and city, are growing more and more common, and the means of checking or extinguishing them do not appear to be keeping pace with the increase in liabilities to conflagration. It is a singular fact, and one which I found Englishmen ready to concede, that a people famous for their manufacture of fine machinery, and for the perfect discipline of their soldiers, have not turned out such fine steam fire-engines as we have, nor handled them so skilfully and rapidly at fires.

The London fire department, as at present organized and managed, is one of the most interesting and effective institutions of the city. And it is a hard-worked department, for fires are very frequent in the great metropolis, and the character and location of many of its buildings such that the conflagrations are often most difficult to cope with. For proof of this, follow along for a month or two the fire column in "The London Times."

At the great fire in London, in the time of Charles II., more than thirteen thousand wooden houses were burned down. London is to-day a city of brick and stone buildings, yet they are, in many instances, of such vast height, and so closely packed in narrow streets, that they are more difficult to manage, viewed from the fireman's standpoint, than were the low-roofed tinder-boxes of the seventeenth century. And think of the vast ocean of houses in the London of to-day!

Every year now sees at least twenty-five thousand new buildings put up in London, and some of these brand-new edifices, which I saw springing up on every hand, are each big enough to tenement a village. Very familiar landmarks in London are its forty or more fire-towers, — the watch-towers rising at least one hundred and twenty feet from the level of the street, and forming a feature of the stations of the fire-department.

When information of a fire reaches the engine-house, it is the custom of a fireman to ascend the tower and look out over the city for the purpose of locating precisely the conflagration point, and then through a speaking-pipe shouting down his report to the starting engine-company. Travellers have generally had the idea that men were constantly kept on watch in these towers, but I found such was not the case.

* * *

One feature in the management of many of the large fire and life insurance companies of London attracted my particular attention, and, as explained by English friends, both astonished and amused me.

Large numbers of these companies parade, with a good deal of apparent satisfaction, in their advertisements and in their prospectuses, the names of chairmen and directors who bear high-sounding titles. Earls, viscounts and dukes figure in these capacities. In some cases I doubt not the nobility have ability, time and taste for the discharge of such fiduciary duties. But Englishmen told me that, in a majority of instances where the names were paraded as I have here described, the titled directors were not conspicuous for their business talents. It was often said to me that such names might be viewed as baits with which to catch the custom of an English public, which has, as every one knows, a greedy appetite for titles. These baronial managers are supposed to have great attractions in the eyes of a majority of the outside investing public; though the few who are thoroughly posted know well enough that these great names are often used but as baits for the unwary, and give the widest berth to the shares of the companies, laying the greatest stress upon the fact of having earls and marquises on their boards of direction.

Without doubt these noble lords go through the motions expected of them, and serve, in a dummy capacity, in a prompt and proper manner; for it is a curious fact that a guinea a time for prompt attendance at board meetings constitutes no trifling attraction to many of these noble directors.

A thorough business man of London said to me that many an impecunious lord could not live in London during the "season," were it not for the guinea-fees he received for attendance at the various corporation boards of which he was an ornamental member.

There is no country in the world that has a larger class of cultivated and well-born gentlemen who have nothing in particular which they are really obliged to do, though many of this class are voluntary workers of the busiest and most praiseworthy character. Some of these noble gentlemen are in an impecunious condition, and are, therefore, more than willing to receive directors' attendance guinea-fees for services on railway, bank and other corporation boards to which they bring neither the ability nor inclination to do any service of value. When a railway bill was under discussion in the House of Lords, where it happened to meet an undeserved defeat, it leaked out in the press that the bill was killed by lordly railway directors, a list of the same being at the time printed, showing that some of the members of the House of Lords were on as many as five railway boards of directors. The great lords of England are its great land owners; and the railways have cut their way through and under their splendid parks and farms, preserves and plantations. And these large landed proprietors, who have generally been directors in the lines which have been put through their estates, have dictated, somewhat at the expense of the public welfare, locations and land damages. But the blight of the dummy director has often proved worse than the action of the sharp board member. Especially has this proved true in English boards of bank direction, where the *rota* and the *agenda* have borne the names of titled nobodies, who have attempted to perform supervising work about which they know very little. And this incompetent supervision has given swindling managers and subordinates unlimited chances for those stupendous bank defalcations which have been startling all England.

Some idea of the profitableness of the profession of a director of public companies may be gathered from the admission of Sir Henry Tyler, at the meeting of the Anglo-American Brush Electric Light Corporation (Limited). The directors' fees in 1882 amounted to £25,896. Sir Henry Tyler's share as chairman would probably be as much as £4,000; and, as he is on at least fifteen boards, his income as a professional director would be as much as £60,000 a year, on the supposition that he charges each company the same terms.

* * *

I did not cross the Atlantic for the sole purpose of visiting the greatest bank in the world, — the

Bank of England; but, having for the most of my life been up to my eyes in banking business, I fully resolved, when I started Londonward, that one of the first places I would visit on reaching the English capital should be that great banking institution of which I had heard and read so much, and whose methods I had so often studied from afar. Through the kind offices of Hon. Russell Sturgis, a former resident of Boston, I obtained a card of admission to the bank; and, on one of the special days appointed for visiting the institution, I passed within its gates, and handed my card to the first employé of the bank whom I encountered. This person was an old porter, dressed in a green swallow-tailed coat with brass buttons, buff waistcoat and dark trousers, — the official uniform of his corps, and of ancient date. I was by him at once conducted to the room and desk of the chief accountant.

The Bank of England, which is situated in the very heart of London, and which occupies three acres of ground, somewhat resembles, in the number and extent of its departments, the United States Treasury. The different rooms of varying size and style are connected by long public passage-ways, which, in their many windings, assume a labyrinthine character quite confusing to one who seeks to explore the bank without a guide. It was by a winding route through these many halls and passages that my guide now led me to the chief accountant. This officer holds a position very similar to that of the cashier in any large American bank. I found him writing, with several subordinates within easy reach of him, in the small and plainly furnished room which he occupied. Interested in the fact that I was also a bank officer, he readily turned from his work to converse with me; and, after selecting a deputy to pilot me about the institution, he urged me to return for further talk.

I shall not attempt to give a detailed account of all I saw, but shall endeavor merely to present a few instantaneous views of the great institution as I that morning saw it, when all its complicated machinery was in motion. Readers who wish for minuter detail will find what they require in Francis's "History of the Bank of England," in two portly volumes, or "Gilbert on Banking."

A banker by profession, it was but natural that I should look and listen with intense interest as I walked and talked in the central and regulating bank of the world. Merchants, bankers' clerks and messengers were thronging past me, making deposits and drawing checks, dealing over the counters with the receiving and paying cashiers, officials whom we in America term paying and receiving tellers. Members of the great corps of out-tellers — for so the Bank of England styles its regular messengers — were passing in and out in the discharge of their running duties, such as presenting and collecting drafts, and making other outside settlements. In the Rotunda, a large circular room with a lofty dome, persons of all nations and many classes were clustered in groups, or moving about, making the place an exchange where shares and bonds were sold, and financial negotiations of a general character transacted. But I was soon brought face to face with novelties in banking which were of great interest to me, and merit careful description. And in these hasty bank notes of mine, I know of no better way than to begin at the bottom of the bank and work upwards.

The Bank of England lunch-room is situated in the basement of the building, and is a spacious and solidly furnished room of an exceedingly neat and attractive appearance. All its arrangements were of the most substantial and comfortable character; and its bill of fare, which I looked carefully into in search of suggestions for the lunch-rooms of our home banks, was of a thoroughly English type. It offered a limited list of solid, wholesome articles of diet, among which bacon, roast beef, puddings, bread and cheese were prominent. As for liquids, in addition to coffee, tea and cocoa, the Englishman's inevitable bitter beer was plentifully supplied, and almost universally patronized by the bank officers, for London bank officials do not attempt to live without beer any more than do London mechanics. The Bank of England lunch-room is a feature of long standing, and the lunch-rooms of American banks are but copies of the English idea.

* * *

The Bank of England has, in England proper, a monopoly of the business of circulating notes, and the aggregate of its circulation in the hands of the public averages about twenty-five million pounds. The issue and redemption of this immense circulation are managed by the issue department of the Bank of England.

The thin, strong, crisp paper upon which Bank of England notes are all printed is made by the bank's own mills in Kent. It is turned out in long, ingeniously water-marked strips which are of the width of two notes. This paper I saw and handled in the printing-room, where a wonderfully complicated press was turning out, at a stroke, completely finished Bank of England notes, of denominations ranging from five pounds, its smallest issue, to one thousand pounds, its largest. Special issues of Bank of England notes of an enormous value have at various times been made, but the regular denominations are as I have just mentioned. There is nothing hand-made about a note of the Bank of England, not even an autographic mark, number, or signature. The nearest approach to these are the numbers, which are inserted by a marvellous piece of automatic machinery, and the signatures, which are printed fac-similes. An average of about sixty thousand notes are turned out each day. No note is ever reissued, and the average life of these notes is about a week. In a rapid inspection of the assorting and redeeming room, I saw how these notes were received, assorted by their denominations, cancelled, and relegated to the storage-rooms for five years' careful preservation, and final destruction by fire. It is, by the way, a curious fact that these relegated notes are burned in the dead of night, so that the noxious fumes from such vast masses of burning paper may disturb no one. In the assorting-room I saw, behind the bronze lattice-work which enclosed them and their morning receipts of redeemed notes, perhaps a hundred hard-working clerks, mainly young men, at their task of assorting these vast accumulations of paper money. The air was white with the flying notes as, with astonishing rapidity, the assorters scattered into their proper places in the drawers before them the redemptions they had in hand.

The redeemed notes of the Bank of England are cancelled by punching out the words and figures indicating their denominations, and the tearing off their signatures. They are then packed in boxes about a foot square, and stored in a great vault under the bank. An average stock on hand of these dead notes amounts to about fifteen thousand boxes, representing a former value of about two thousand million pounds, and a gross weight of nearly a hundred tons. I have been too long in contact, all my business days, with paper money, to be very much stunned by such figures as these, or to be carried away by the sights of the assorting-room where bright and new thousand-pound notes were rapidly being transformed into waste paper. I was here looking only at the productions of the Bank of England's paper-mills and printing-presses. The reserves upon which this paper money had been issued, the gold and silver coin and bullion of the institution, are what the professional banker looks upon with real interest and respect.

The Bank of England's stock of gold and silver generally amounts to about two million pounds, or, I might more properly say, this is a fair average of its specie reserves. A large proportion of these reserves rests in its strong room in the shape of bullion. Its vaults carry a stock of bullion varying in value from two to three hundred millions sterling. The gold coin of the bank is kept in what is termed the Treasury Department, that division of the institution which has the management of the public debt of the realm, and the administration of the coinage monopoly which it holds under the government. Here it is stored in bags of one thousand pounds sterling each. Every bag weighs two hundred and fifty ounces. A million pounds sterling of gold will weigh not far from a ton. Bullion is gold in bars of about eight and one-half inches in length, three inches in width, and an inch in thickness. These bars are stacked on little wagons.

I have given some figures as the average of the amount of gold coin and gold bullion held by the Bank of England, but it is difficult for any one to know just the state of the bank's reserves, except at the time of its weekly returns. From all lands gold is constantly flowing into the bank. To all lands gold is constantly being shipped from the bank. The ebb and flow of this golden tide are watched with sharp eyes by financiers of all countries, for the Bank of England holds the reserves of all the banks of London, and the banks of London hold a good share of the reserves of many lands. The Bank of England's rate for money rises and falls with the rise and fall of its specie reserves, and operators in money and merchandise, from Manitoba to the Congo, are governed in their movements by the swing of its interest figures.

It is only within a comparatively recent time that the Bank of England has made a practice of publishing weekly public returns of its condition. In former days its internal affairs were kept a profound secret, and even an order of Parliament was powerless to extract from its managers any statement of the amount of gold and silver it was carrying. There are two very interesting machines in the specie departments of the Bank of England, — one in its bullion-room, the other in its coin-room. These are the wonderful instruments for weighing bullion and testing sovereigns. The weighing-machine of the bullion-room is kept in an air-tight glass case, where it rests, over six feet in height, upon a solid bed of concrete. So accurate is this heavy-beamed machine, with its capacity for weighing three hundred and sixty ounces of bullion at a time, that the weight of a penny postage-stamp will easily record itself on the indexed dial. This bullion scale was invented by James Murdock Napier.

The coin-tester of the treasury division of the bank, the invention of Mr. Cotton, a former governor of the bank, and which is one of the greatest curiosities of the institution, may well be likened to a mill. I saw the employés of the bank thrusting sovereigns into its hoppers at the rate of sixty thousand a business day. These testing-mills, of which there are at least a dozen in the bank, are run by a small air-engine. They may be characterized as marvellous automata, which have only to be supplied through their hoppers with the sovereigns and half-sovereigns whose weight is to be tested. When once the coins have come within the embrace of the clock-work-like machinery of these testers, they are not allowed to pass out till all which are deficient in weight are separated from those of full and satisfactory solidity. These coin-testing machines are deemed by ingenious mechanics the most wonderful mechanical achievement of modern times.

* * *

The directors' room is a fine, high-studded hall, plainly but solidly furnished. A prominent feature of the room is an open fireplace, in which, on the cool day of the early spring in which I visited the bank, a cheerful coal-fire was burning. The centre of the room was occupied by a long and wide table, about which were ranged, in stately order, twenty-six capacious mahogany chairs, which, on directors' meeting-days, are supposed to be filled by the governor, deputy-governor, and the twenty-four directors of the bank.

At all times the meetings of the Bank of England are regarded with interest by the business and financial world; and the doings of such meetings, when action of importance is taken, are telegraphed around the globe. But, in times of general disturbance in financial matters, or of extreme panic, the keenest interest centres in these meetings, and the monetary world waits with breathless anxiety for their results.

Let us drop in upon one of these monetary

A DIRECTORS' MEETING.

meetings. The governor of the bank, Mr. J. S. Gilliat, takes the chair. Mr. Hammond Chubb, the secretary of the corporation, who takes a position on his right, reads the minutes of the last court, — that held in September.

This is the March gathering. The governor reports upon the bank's work for the six months which have intervened. He has in hand an immense institution, and the figures he reels off are really gigantic. With a capital of a hundred millions of dollars, deposits of nearly two hundred millions, and a circulation of nearly two hundred millions, the Bank of England can make up a very large slate. Recall one or two significant items from one of these semi-annual statements. This bank, which started in 1695, with fifty clerks working in one room, and paid on an average eighty pounds a year each, now reports a thousand employés, and a pay of a million and one-half dollars a year.

The earnings figures presented at this meeting which we are attending may be considered a fair sample of these usually brought out at these Bank of England stockholders' meetings of modern days.

Here they are: Net profits for the last six months, £710,857, making the amount of the "rest" on the day of the meeting £3,742,923. The chairman proposes a dividend of five per cent, free of income tax, to be paid on the 7th of April. Shareholder Botley, who has in advance been selected as seconder, and duly coached for his part in the play, now rises and seconds the motion for the five per cent dividend. He compliments the managers for their skill and success, praises them because they have shown such persistency in prosecuting the rogues who have within the last six months been defrauding the bank, and wishes that every bank and commercial company would follow the same course; "for," says he, "this course is the only way to stop fraud." He then indulges in some general remarks on the subject of banking, and advises depositors to take very great care of their check-books, and to be very particular in their methods of filling out checks. Mr. Botley is not a brilliant speaker, neither are his remarks highly original, yet they are solid, after the English style, and he is solid himself; and the motion which he seconds is of course the one which is to be unanimously passed, — that appears to be thoroughly understood.

But every thing that is done at one of these general courts of the Bank of England must be done in red-tape style. The bank holds its charter under the crown, and the legislative enactments that hedge it about are many and complicated. Year after year, from the day of its birth, they have been added to, and there is not a passing year in which its representatives, or representatives of the bank-dealing public, do not go before Parliament with prayers for modifications of laws ruling the bank. And now at this meeting it is found that, in order to conform to law, an adjournment must take place, and at the adjourned meeting a ballot will have to be taken on the dividend. All this simply because the last dividend, which was four and three-quarters per cent, must now be increased to five per cent.

But this present meeting is not to break up without some little debate. A certain Mr. Jones rises and "wants to know"—wants to know what are the causes of the present great depression in the banking business, why the directors have done certain things and left others undone, whether the bank has been duly compensated for the work it has been doing in attempting to assist the government in converting its three per cents into two and a half per cents.

He has seen that the bank has paid over to the government during the last year £2,000,000 unclaimed dividends, and he desires to know how long these unclaimed dividends remained with the bank.

This last question brings to mind a curious point relative to the business of the Bank of England. The dividends referred to by Mr. Jones are the interest payment upon the public debt. One department of the bank is devoted to the management of England's debt, — is England's treasury department. All interest due upon the consols which remains unpaid for ten years is paid over to the government — covered into its treasury — from which it may, by certain processes, be reclaimed, if its owners subsequently turn up and prove their ownership.

An immense sum thus stands uncalled for, — ten millions of dollars a year. I had some little talk with an English banker on this, and he gave me these views on the matter. He said Englishmen were quite apt to cultivate the habit of keeping their money matters very much to themselves. This was peculiarly the case where they were married men, and heads of families. Wives and children were often kept in utter ignorance of the financial condition of husband or father. If the "governor" paid the bills and kept up the establishment, they were content, and asked no questions, and neither wished nor expected to know the character or amount of his investments in three per cents, or in any thing else.

With such carelessness in living the outcome must often be financially troublesome. The sons cut loose from the old home, and seek their fortunes in the larger Britain abroad. The daughters get married, and make homes for themselves. And then, if the father die without making a will, there may be no one left behind who knows all about his personal estate, — how much it is, or where it is. Hence such extraordinary accumulations of uncalled-for English consol interest at the Bank of England and in the hands of the government.

But I am getting out of that Bank of England shareholders' meeting. I was speaking of Mr. Jones and his speech and his questions. At all shareholders' meetings, the monetary world over, there is apt to be present the inevitable Mr. Jones. He is generally a retired capitalist, of rather moderate property and immoderate leisure, who owns small lots of stock in many corporations, and who is fond of attending corporation meetings, and of making a few remarks thereat, which are seldom of much account, and which receive only faint attention. Nevertheless Mr. Jones is often a convenience. He may be depended upon to count one in a gathering which needs a certain number to make a quorum; and is often a handy appointee upon a committee to count votes, judge of an election, or prepare resolutions.

The model chairman always listens politely, and rather patronizingly to him; replies courteously, but in effect takes, in fact, very little notice of either his schemes or inquiries. At this meeting the governor in the chair makes a response to Mr. Jones, which may, in many respects, be taken as a model for other governors and chairmen.

In putting the motion, which is in due form to be passed unanimously, — the motion for the dividend, — he states "that Mr. Jones read and thought a great deal, and was, no doubt, as well able as any of the directors to make up his mind as to the reason of the existing depression. He was sure Mr. Jones would forgive him for not detaining the proprietors by entering into the merits of the conversion scheme. As to the payment received by the bank, he would be glad to answer Mr. Jones afterwards in his room. He might make the same remark as to the various loans which the bank had managed in the last few years, before they paid over to the Government unclaimed dividends."

The salary of the governor of the Bank of England is a thousand pounds yearly. The deputy governor is paid at the same rate, while the directors each receive five hundred pounds a year. On the board of directors of the Bank of England are men whose names are known in the walks of trade and finance in the leading cities of all lands, — men who are some of London's most eminent merchants and bankers. Yet there are on this board only two persons whose rank, in respect to titles, is higher than esquire. One of these is a right honorable, and the other is a baronet. The Bank of England selects for its managers men whose merit lies in their real financial ability, not in their social status. To be a director in the

Bank of England is an honor which the most substantial of London's kings of trade and finance may well covet, while the position of governor of the bank is unquestionably the highest financial post in the world. On the list of men who have held this place are the names of London merchants whose reputation and financial position are known on the exchanges of all the great financial centres of the world.

The annual election of Bank of England officers takes place early in April in the directors' room. The governors, directors and proprietors nominally do the electing; but the attendance of shareholders is usually very light, and, on many of these occasions, only a few formal votes are recorded. The directors, in effect, really fill their own vacancies and choose their own successors, as is commonly the case with American bank boards. The directors are always expected to recommend candidates for directorships to the proprietors, and it has rarely happened that the proprietors have not followed these recommendations. In one notable case, that of the introduction of the Hebrew Rothschild into the board, it is said that a very strong outside pressure was successfully brought to bear upon a board which was at first determined that the Jewish banker should not form one of its number.

The directors of the bank are not all drawn

from the mercantile classes, as formerly. Bankers are eligible when not directors of other banks, but all directors must be shareholders in the bank. The directors meet every Thursday.

The bank allows no over-drafts, and makes no advances upon land or real estate of any description. The Bank of England transacts all of the treasury business of the English Government, and manages entirely that seven hundred millions debt. In regard to the matter of the advances made upon paper by the bank, I noted the interesting fact that it was the bank's regular rule to require all persons for whom bills had been discounted to take up at once all unmatured bills which had been discounted for them, whenever it appeared that the acceptors of the bills had suspended payment. This rigid rule of the bank has, like many other of its regulations, been brought before parliamentary committees, from time to time, for investigation and modification. There is in London, at all times, a strong force of financiers who, year after year, attempt to secure, by legislation, all sorts of changes in the bank's management; but these reformers make slow progress. The Bank of England does a large business in receiving deposits of money from persons opening new accounts current, who wish merely to put their money in the safest bank in the world, and have no desire to see it earning interest. The bank also receives and stores in its strong rooms, free of charge, chests of plate and other valuables belonging to heavy depositors.

The Bank of England rarely discounts bills which have more than two months to run. The bank was formerly so encumbered with ancient forms and rules that few ordinary merchants and traders kept accounts with it. But its methods have since been thoroughly reorganized, and it has now all the facilities for doing a modern style of banking business. Neither at its head office nor at its branches does it allow a single penny of interest upon deposits. It looks to the average of the depositors' balance as compensation for receiving his deposits and paying his checks.

It now takes on many very small accounts. At one time it would pay no check under ten pounds, but its customers can now draw upon it checks of any size.

The bank's hours are from nine till five; and, in the matter of time-keeping with its clerks, it is very systematic. If an officer reaches the bank late three times he is called before the directors, and, if their reprimand does not reform him, he is discharged. An arrival book is kept open before the clerks. Those who arrive before nine write their names above the black line which is drawn to separate their signatures from those which are made by late clerks. All the clerks are given annual vacations, and an average of fifty out of its thousand employés are always absent on vacations. These vacations vary in extent, being graduated by the length of time the clerks have been in the bank's employ.

Nine families of bank employés live within the bank, and several of its chief officers live in a court near by. The bank has a pension system for its employés, and keeps a physician in daily attendance at its offices. When officers absent themselves on plea of illness, the physician visits them and reports upon their condition. A very large proportion of its staff are young men. It receives in its employ boys of eighteen at a salary of eighty pounds a year, and these persons either work their way up or down and out.

The bank holidays are Good-Friday, Easter-Monday, Whit-Monday, the first Monday in August, Christmas-Day, and the day following.

This gigantic bank, whose methods we have been endeavoring to explain, was projected by William Paterson, a Scotch speculator of an impecunious kind who had made a bad miscarriage with that great colonization scheme known as the Darien Expedition. It received its charter in 1694. Its original capital was twelve hundred thousand pounds, which sum was lent at a good rate of interest to the sovereigns William and Mary. Its charter has been many times renewed.

To-day the Bank of England has a capital of £14,533,000, deposits of about forty millions sterling, and a circulation of £25,000,000.

My tour through the bank ended in the directors' rooms, and I turned away from the great temple of finance, after tendering my thanks to the chief accountant for his attentions.

A sagacious humorist has said that the natural end of all banks is "to bust up." If this be the fate of the Bank of England, when is it to occur? In what coming time shall some successor of mine, some financial tourist from New Zealand or the Congo, wander over the grass-grown pavements of Lombard Street, Cornhill, Threadneedle Street, and King William Street, and gather from their associations and traditions facts relating not only to the rise and progress, but to the decline and fall, of the Royal Bank of England, which once reigned in that locality with more than regal power?

* * *

"Strong room" is the standard English name for what, in this country, is termed a large vault for storage of valuables, such as cash, bonds, and plate. I like this good old English name of strong room, and will use it as applying to safe deposit vaults the world over. Less than twenty years ago all the strong rooms in this country, which were used for storage of cash, bonds, and so forth, belonged to the banks and bankers, and were a part of their business machinery. Since that time safe deposit companies have been established, and they are now quite numerous in this country, having larger and better strong rooms than the bankers ever had. No one will ever know how many million dollars' worth of valuables are stored in one of these great safe deposit companies, for each customer has his own special lock-up within the great central strong room, and keeps his own keys and counsel. I shall be asked who is responsible to depositors for safe-keeping of all these treasures, and I reply that the company is responsible for the exercise of due care and diligence in the work it has undertaken, and what is demanded of it in these premises would have to be settled in the courts if any dispute in the matter should arise between some loser and the safe company.

But of this I am sure. If one can imagine any contingency by which a great safe deposit company should lose all its valuables, I can, without the exercise of any imagination, see that they could not pay for the stupendous loss. Since the establishment of safe deposit companies the banks of this country have pretty much given up caring for the special deposits of their customers. This they have done for two reasons, — one, that they have become alarmed about the great responsibilty this increasing business was throwing upon them;

and the other, that the banking department at Washington has taken the ground that it is no part of the regular business of a bank to take care of the special deposits of its customers.

I found the banks and bankers of London and Paris still going along in this matter as we used to do. There is only one regular safe deposit company in London, the "National," and that has not been a success. Attached to all great banks of London are strong rooms much larger than any thing of the sort our banks have ever had; and in these the regular customers of the banks are permitted to store their bonds, money, plate, and so forth, without charge. Inside these strong rooms are ranged great numbers of small safes, in which the depositors place their treasures, retaining their keys, and visiting them when they please.

The business we have been describing has of late years so vastly increased in London that its bankers have become greatly alarmed over their responsibilities. This alarm has recently been deepened by the fact that they have met with some large losses from some of these strong rooms by the dishonesty of their clerks. Though they have never acknowledged themselves responsible for the property in their hands, they have so far thought it best to pay for these losses, since they have believed that any other course would injure their reputations and their business. London bankers are now proposing to make a charge for special deposits, and openly assume responsibility for their safety.

In Paris, where I found that the United States type of safe deposit companies has not come into vogue, the bankers make a common custom of receiving special deposits of valuables in their strong rooms, and always charge a commission for the care of these deposits. And the Parisian custom is the one generally followed on the Continent. The modern strong room of this country and Europe is a marvel of ingenuity, strength, and mechanical skill. I have watched the construction of one of the best that ever was made, from the setting of its first foundation-stone to the turning of its last lock. The work began by the deep setting of immense blocks of granite, so that neither burglars nor fire could enter from below, and went on, by the erection on every side of the most invulnerable walls of iron, steel, brick, stone, and cement, and ended by the application to doors of hardened steel of combination locks of the most perfect description. And when the mechanic had finished his work, the whole machinery of protection was placed in the hands of watchmen by night, and tried managers and clerks by day, and connected by burglar electric alarms with military and police departments. But, after all, its most vulnerable point is its danger from an attack from the inside.

Banks and companies of trust have always suffered a hundred times more from dishonest employés than from thieves without.

I have elsewhere mentioned that the safe deposit business had advanced so little in London that there was only one safe deposit company in the city that amounted to any thing; and that that concern had, so far, been lightly patronized, less than a quarter of its thirty thousand safes having so far been rented, and its only dividend having just been reached. Its great vault, which is a strong room within two other strong rooms, is eighty feet long, forty feet wide, and forty-five feet high.

I don't propose to give all the details of its construction; but the reader who may think of putting his bonds within its walls of iron, stone, undrilled steel armor plating, and hard-blue bricks, may be assured that London's safe-builders have done their best here. Here are outer walls of hard brick-work in Portland cement, with a backing of hydraulic concrete, — in all, twenty-one feet thick. Next comes an insulated structure, made of fire-brick, and London's famous hard-blue brick, three feet thick, and coated with four and one-half inches armor-plate. Inside this house within a house are thirty-two corridors of safes, with doors weighing four tons each, which are opened and shut by hydraulic power.

The foundation floors are of concrete twenty feet thick. The whole establishment is guarded by twenty-one years' service men from the corps of commissioners, armed with revolvers, and it can be flooded from the main of the New River Water Company at a moment's notice, "in the extreme event of a social disturbance," as it is all under ground. I was amused at hearing that the committee of the Confederate bondholders had selected this fortress as a place of deposit for their precious rags.

A banker, who has done heavy business with banks both sides the water, concedes that in the matter of vaults and safes the bankers and banks of London are better equipped than any other bankers in the world. All the leading banks of London advertise their willingness to receive and care for the valuables of their depositors without any charge.

I found the banking men of London, as well as those in charge of the country banks of England, intelligent, progressive and courteous. It was natural that I should make pretty close observations in their field of work, and for this purpose I visited many banks in the city and in the interior. The rooms usually occupied by them are exceedingly plain, almost always finished in very dark woods, and often located in retired positions. Tellers, and other bank officials, with whom a person travelling upon a letter of credit is apt to be brought in contact, appeared to be expert in their business, and the head managers were always gentlemen of cultivated manners and pleasant address, who were more than willing to linger a while over a payment to an American for the purpose of discussing the methods and machinery of banking in the United States. They were just as ignorant of our national banking system as we are of the banking system of England, and no more so. There is one little point about the machinery of English banks which I must particularly mention. In the matter of stationery used by them — in the preparation of all their blanks, such as checks, letter-heads, bills of exchange, notices and circulars — they show a taste, accuracy and thoroughness that might well be copied here. The laws and customs governing the details of English banking business are, of course, very like ours, for we have generally copied from them. I was interested in observing, while in London, that "Story on Bills of Exchange" was several times quoted in a banking lawsuit.

I am confident that English bankers, and, in fact, the higher class of English business men generally, are rather more in the habit of living two lives than are the same classes in our country. By this, I mean that they have a habit of quietly sinking the shop, to which they have given during business hours the closest attention, as soon as they are out of it, and of giving themselves over to quite absorbing hobbies of one sort and another. The result is that they often become men of taste, culture and general intelligence.

In London banking, as in English railroading, I found many unfamiliar names standing for very familiar things. The lines have their "metals," "vans," "trucks" and "guards," — terms whose meanings I have elsewhere explained. The banks give to their officers, and to the duties of those officers, titles which I had to have explained to me, though I had supposed, when I came in contact with London bankers, that I was entirely conversant with English as "she is spoken."

What we here call a bank-messenger is, in London banks, termed an out-teller, or collecting clerk. His duties are very much the same as our bank-messenger, though he has some few methods not common here. When he starts out from the bank upon what is there termed his "walk," he leaves behind him a record of the route he is to travel, and the collecting, notifying, and presenting he is to attend to on what the London banks term their "walk-book."

In this way the bank is kept informed of the whereabouts of their absent messenger, a bit of information that must be highly appreciated. In our banks and offices the inquiry "Where is that messenger?" has become a note of interrogation as familiar as "Where are the police?"

The London collecting-clerk, or out-teller, invariably has his wallet strapped to his body with chain and belt, a practice which has in some cases been copied here, and ought to be here more widely in vogue. The drafts which he takes upon his route for presentation for acceptance he always leaves with the drawees, who have twenty-four hours in which to return them to the bank. Next to the collecting-clerks, whose duties I have described, come the bank porters.

The English "bank manager" is an official corresponding quite closely to an American bank cashier or working bank president. The London bank manager is the head man in the bank under the directors. I think the London bank directors are accustomed to take quite an active part in the management of their institutions, for I noticed that the custom of having a director for the week is generally kept up there. English banks have no bank presidents, though the governor of the Bank of England holds a position similar to that of president.

It is an interesting fact that, with the single exception of the old Bank of England, there is not a joint-stock bank in the United Kingdom over fifty years old. Before that time all the banks of England were private banks. There have been times in the history of banking in Great Britain when the most extraordinary reverses were experienced in the business. Notably was this the fact in 1819, when, out of nine hundred and forty private banks in England and Wales, two hundred and forty became hopelessly bankrupt, or were forced by reverses to go out of business. Another panic in the banking business came in 1825.

"Limited" is a word now attached to the title of many an English corporation. The word simply means that the companies have been formed under the "Limited Liability Act" of 1862, which holds each shareholder liable only to the amount of his shares when fully paid up. Joint-stock and private banks throughout the kingdom are quite in the habit of allowing interest upon deposits, but the Bank of England never does this.

"Cash credits" at banks are a great institution in Scotland, and are not uncommon in other parts of the United Kingdom. This is a convenient and simple piece of banking machinery which was invented in Scotland nearly two hundred years ago. The business man who puts up with a bank's sureties or securities on the promise that he will do all his business with the said bank draws upon that bank, from time to time, for such money as he needs, not exceeding the amount for which he has furnished guarantees, and is, of course, charged interest only upon what he draws.

Bankers in England will not open an account with a married woman without the consent of her husband; and, in case of the marriage of a female customer, the signature of her husband is necessary in order to draw the money.

Bank of England notes, five pounds and upwards, are a legal tender in all England and Wales, except at the Bank of England and its branches; but not in Scotland or Ireland, where coin only is legal tender. As the Bank of England notes are never issued a second time, they are made upon much thinner paper than is used by the banks of Scotland, which keep in circulation a large issue of one-pound notes, and which apply to them no such a rule as the Bank of England regulation I have named.

In most English banks the clerks are not allowed to made erasures upon the books. I have known American banks which have set up this English rule, and I believe the idea to be a good one. Erasing has helped along large bank defalcations.

I found in some large London banks an "arrival book." This was kept where each officer could handily put down his name when coming in in the morning. The banks of London keep open from nine till four, except on Saturdays, when they close at three. After nine a black line is drawn across the page of the open arrival book, and those coming after nine must write their names below the prompt line.

* * *

A very large part of the work which would naturally fall upon London collecting clerks is done through the great London Clearing House located in Lombard Street, and managed by a committee of most active London bankers. The hours for morning clearing are from 10.30 to 12; for the country clearing, 12 to 2.15; afternoon clearing, 2.30 to 4. The regular city bank clearing is just like ours.

Although the London Clearing House was set up more than a hundred years ago, it was at first, and for a very long time, confined in its uses exclusively to private bankers. It was not till 1854 that the joint-stock banks of London were admitted to its settlements. In 1855 the work of clearing country checks was added to its mission. At the date of the admission of the joint-stock banks, a rule was made that all the banks and bankers that were members of the London Clearing House should keep accounts with the Bank of England, and settle their clearing differences by checks on that bank, and I found that this was the present rule.

With the introduction of the country check in the London Clearing House came of necessity the rule that country banks, wishing to enter this clearing, must have in London agents, either banks or bankers, who were members of the London Clearing House. And upon the checks drawn upon these country banks by their depositors is always printed conspicuously the name of the London Clearing House agent.

When country checks of this class are deposited in London banks they are at once charged in through clearing to the London banks which are their agents. But, though sent in daily, pay is not received for them until the morning of the third day after they have been sent in. As the clearing for country checks does not take place till 2.15 P.M., and as it is an iron rule in London banks that all country checks must be sent home for collection the very afternoon of the day they are deposited, it follows that the corresponding clerks of the London banks must do a deal of late-in-the-day work. All checks that are returned from the country unpaid for any cause must be returned to the city bank owing them before 12.30 o'clock of the third day after their entry into the clearing house. This method of clearing country checks by a London clearing necessitates the keeping of credit balances by the country banks at their London agencies, for overdrawing is not a common feature of banking in England.

I was struck by the fact that the mail facilities of the kingdom seemed to be of the most perfect character; and, in the application of these facilities to the collection, for London accounts, of checks drawn upon all parts of the United Kingdom, a rapidity and promptness is obtained that eclipses us.

In conversations with London bankers I compared notes on this point, and I had to concede that American collecting methods and machinery were far behind theirs, and, in getting my own drafts on London cashed in Scotland, and in various parts of England, I had practical demonstration of the perfection of English collection systems. Great use is made of the wires in this business. London banks are quite in the habit of making their depositors no charge on country collections; and, where any charges are made, they are light. It should, of course, be remembered that the collecting area of England is strikingly limited compared with ours, and that in this little territory of theirs they have thirty-four hundred banks, while we have, in all the United States, only about two thousand national banks. Nevertheless, English banking methods are most admirable, most progressive, and contain many features which we should at once copy. They laughed at me in English banking circles, when I told them we made all drawers of checks identify themselves, and said they never could get through a day's business in London banking if the same identification rule was there applied; and they wondered how we could get along without crossed checks, and commissions on small deposit accounts.

* *
*

There is one sort of examination of banks in London which is a regular thing, though it is not known at all here, and which we trust does really amount to something. The chartered accountants of London are professional auditors, and, as such, they are regularly employed to make what are supposed to be most thorough examinations of the banks, doing this as representatives of the shareholders. We have no profession in America corresponding to this one, though our professional experts in accounts come the nearest to it. The English chartered accountant is educated exclusively for the profession which he is to follow, graduating from the "Institute of Chartered Accountants in England and Wales," whose head offices are in Copthall Buildings, London, E. C., where stated preliminary, intermediate and final examinations of candidates are made, and certificates of graduation issued.

I found it quite common in London for these chartered accountants to do business as firms consisting of several members; and some of these concerns are of ancient and very high standing, and transact a large and most responsible business. One of the leading items of work attended to by this profession is that of the examination and general overhauling of the books of great bankrupt concerns. When great failures occur in London, it is the usual custom to place all the books at once in the hands of a firm of chartered accountants, and little else is done in settlement of the affairs of the bankrupts until these accountants have made a full report to creditors.

It has appeared to me that there was room for such a profession in our American cities, since much of the work of examination of assets and liabilities of bankrupt houses, which is now put into the hands of attorneys who often have not been specially educated for such business, could be profitably given to special and recognized accountants of position and authority.

* *
*

Rates of interest upon solid London investments, though low, are not in such surprising contrast with the income from the same class of securities here as they once were, since the monetary world has, during the last decade or two, been brought near to a dead level of interest by well-understood influences.

Both in London and New York I found three per cent net readily accepted by an immense class of investors who wished their means to be where they would be as secure as in the Bank of England, and also where the amounts invested would take on an annuity form, or, at least, something approaching that.

The class of investors in the United States who willingly buy a three per cent United States bond, with the hope it will never be called, is in London represented by a class which pays a slight premium for English consols, a security which is about as good as our government bond. I found I had not exactly understood what these consols were, and, as there is a possibility that others may not have comprehended their exact nature, I venture on a note of explanation. Every one understands, of course, that the term consols is used for consolidated three per cents.

Consolidated three per cents stand for the funded debt of England, which, starting two hundred years ago, when some extravagant king borrowed one million sterling, has now reached seven hundred and thirty millions sterling. Now when my reader next takes up his English monetary reports, he will find quotations of this character: Consols, 102; reduced three per cents, 101½; new, 101. These three quotations all apply to consols, and the reason for the different names is found in the fact that they are different issues, and the reason for the variation in price is that the interest upon them is payable at different times. Consols are always quoted *flat*, and some carry more accrued interest than others.

The interest upon most of the consols is payable quarterly; but purchasers can obtain stock with interest payable annually, and some do this. I have mentioned that the present rate of English income tax is fivepence in the pound. But from time to time this rate is raised or lowered, as the needs of the treasury may dictate.

Incomes under one hundred and fifty pounds are not taxed at all, and there is a partial exemption where incomes are under four hundred pounds. There is no income tax levied upon government pensioners.

The purchaser of consols receives a certificate which states that he is a holder in the funds; and, when the interest is due, he either goes, or sends by attorney, to the Bank of England, and collects his regular interest. Under the income tax, which is at present fivepence in the pound, a deduction is made of this tax from the gross interest collected. The three per cents are the most popular security in England. They are favorites because they are considered so solid, and also because they are so convenient. There are two sayings current among English investors which embody the popular view of them. One is, "Blest is the man who is content to put his pounds in three per cents;" and the other, "The sweet simplicity of the three per cents." Many United States investors hold this stock, believing it as good as the United

States bonds, and are led to this by the idea that it is not wise to put all their eggs into one American basket. On the other hand, United States bonds are very popular in England, because Englishmen consider them good, and also because they pay a fair rate of interest.

The interest upon consols proper, or the old issue, is payable January 5 and July 5. The "reduced" and "new" three per cents interest is paid April 5 and October 5; and, as these securities are always sold flat, this varying time of their interest maturities accounts for the variations in their quotations. One of our best informed financial writers has just been saying to me, that it is a curious fact there are no certificates of consol proprietorship, but that the owner of property in the public funds has his name registered, and the sum he owns recorded on the English treasury books, these records being all there is to show his ownership. I have noticed that this is the general impression in American financial circles. Our friends have never seen an English government bond, and really don't believe there is any such thing. But there is, nevertheless; and they are in small as well as large denominations. Any person who wishes can go to any post-office in England that has a savings-bank attached and put in from twenty to one hundred pounds, and in a short time receive, through the same postal savings-bank, a certificate of consol stock.

To fill these postal orders, the general post-office in London employs brokers who go into the market and buy the government stock on the best terms they can. Heavier investors in British governments do not patronize the post-office. They buy direct through their own brokers. The English postal banks also make a business of collecting the maturing government interest for the small investors. In the English stock and bond markets there are what are termed settling-days, for the settlement of all purchases of bonds and shares, as well as for the settlement of transactions in sterling exchange. The settlement days in the share and bond market are usually the first and the middle of the month. A "bought," or contract note, bridges over the transactions. It is a fact, novel to American shareholders, that English railway companies charge 2s 6d for making a transfer. All transfers are also subject to a government transfer stamp.

* * *

London capitalists are cosmopolitan in their investments. At the London Stock Exchange the daily movements in bonds and shares call up the names of companies and kingdoms located in almost every corner of the habitable world. British capital and British financial enterprise follow the beat of England's drum in its circuit around the belted globe. I hastily summarize the regular plan of "The Times's" reports of the money market.

This London money article first gives the city rates for time and call loans, and the prices for foreign bills of exchange. Then follows a statement of the Bank of England, with a glance at the leading features of its regular return, if one has just been published. "Funds" are then quoted, "funds" being English government bonds. Other monetary points follow in this order: The home railway market, the Canadian railway market, the American (United States) railway market; the foreign bond and share market, embracing a field stretching through every country owning a railway or issuing a bond, from the Argentine Confederation to Patagonia and New Zealand.

These reports are supplemented by a *résumé* of the condition of the money market in all the leading cities of the world, and the state of the local markets for wheat, provisions, cotton, cloth, etc., in all the principal cities and towns of the kingdom. This is indeed a "financial" with a sweep, and the facts in it are generally presented in a clear and able manner, without the waste of a word or a figure. The English merchants and bankers who work the great financial and business engine, whose vibrations are noted in this money article, are an active, progressive set of men, ready to grasp at every new business idea and method, and there is in their methods and machinery a dash and expertness which commanded my admiration, though I had come to England with the idea that London bankers and merchants were a slow and old-fashioned set.

It is very true that some of their modes of doing business are precisely the same as they were two or three hundred years ago. But it by no means follows that all the old ways in these premises were clumsy and undesirable, or that they should be discarded simply because they are old-fashioned.

This is a point that was entirely overlooked by some lively banking friends of mine from the West who, on the deck of our returning steamer, spent a deal of time in denouncing all the English business methods and machinery they had come in contact with, ending with the stereotyped charge that "those fellers" were clinging to customs as old as the foundation of the Bank of England. A banker myself, I do not hesitate to say that in the matter of banking very many of our best modes of procedure are direct importations from England, and that there are in force there to-day many practices and methods in "banking and broking" that we could adopt at once with great advantage, and we are the "old fogies" because we do not do so. We are, for instance, behind the age in not establishing the use of crossed checks, clearance systems for country checks, and many other desirable English money methods. In illustrating the "dash" of London banking methods, I recall a conversation I have had with a gentleman long an active member of a great London banking-house. Said he, "You have an idea we are slow and mighty careful, yet, in some points, we are far less so than are you New York and Boston bankers. For instance, we have a custom of turning every day all our foreign exchange into the hands of dealers who give their special attention to such drafts. There is a reguular settling day for all these bills (mostly Continental), and we do not receive our pay for them until, some days after, we pass them over to the bill broker. Yet we never have a thing — not a scrap of a receipt, or voucher — for them, and we do not hear from them till we get our money." Such is London business conservatism.

* * *

It is becoming more and more the custom of both the London joint-stock banks and the private banks to allow interest upon all deposits. But, in the case of the first-named institutions, the practice is to gauge the rate of interest allowed by the official minimum of the Bank of England, the current rate it has set for discounting bills, placing their rate on deposits just one per cent below the Bank of England's discount rate. There are serious objections to this long-established custom, and many London bankers are in favor of breaking it up. The principal objection is found in the fact that the Bank of England's minimum is not by any means in steady harmony with the current outside rate for discount of bills. It was remarked by one thoroughly conversant with this matter, that the Bank of England's minimum was, in fact, the market rate for bills for only certain periods of the year, and under normal circumstances, and that it was often very much above the outside rates. The private bankers, who regulate their interest rates upon deposits entirely independent of the action of the Bank of England, are much more advantageously situated in this matter than are the joint stock banks. One feature of their management of this business is the habit of changing their rates of interest much oftener than the Bank of England. With the single exception of the Bank of England, which pays no interest upon deposits, all the banks and bankers of London are great borrowers of money.

* * *

The Bank of England is a sort of regulator of English rates for loans upon first-class security. But there is a class of "banks" in London, and in other leading English cities, that have a style of their own for doing business.

I have preserved an advertisement of a specimen London institution of this class which I saw in a north of England paper, in which it had been inserted for the purpose of picking up trade among the needy ones in the country districts. It termed itself "The Charing Cross Deposit Bank," with a capital of one hundred and fifty thousand pounds, and announced its readiness to lend money without sureties. It also offered to advance upon furniture, trade and farm stock, plant crops, etc. "Easy payments. Strictly private. Call, or write."

* *
*

London rates of interest are generally low, viewed from a Western stand-point, yet even in London extremely high rates crop out in the advertisements in the newspapers, and in the court-rooms. I have in mind a London money-lending case, which was brought before Mr. Justice Chitty, where Messrs. Morris & Benjamin had charged a borrower of twenty thousand pounds at the rate of sixty per cent.

The tempting rates offered for loans through the columns of the London journals — rates ranging from eight per cent upwards — indicate that adventurers there, as well as here, are endeavoring to induce men with means to embark in schemes of a very doubtful character. There is probably no city where there are so many swindling financial and business schemes thrust before the public as in London. Companies for every imaginable object, of all dimensions, are steadily before the investing public with the most seductive prospectuses, many of which are as big swindles as can be conceived. I recall one of these frauds which came to the surface while I was in England, where a ring of adventurers had actually succeeded in inducing honest investors to take shares in a bank they were setting up in Manitoba, with a claimed capital of thirty-five million dollars; and in other companies connected with this banking scheme which were just about as gigantic and fraudulent.

* * *

I noticed, in visits to various London banks, that the counter arrangements were about the same as ours. We have copied the English bankers' methods and machinery in these and in very many other points. There, as here, the tellers stand behind the bars and hold money intercourse with the dealer through a low-down hole in the wall; and there, as here, thieves lie in wait to steal in between.

* * *

LONDON BANK DIVIDENDS.

HERE are some specimen figures of good proportions: The Union Bank of London has paid at the rate of fifteen per cent per annum the last three and one-half years, and its last dividend is at the same rate. From eighty to a hundred thousand dollars a year has been added to this reserve fund for many years. What we term surplus fund is in England styled a bank's "rest." It is laid aside for the avowed purpose of using as a dividend resource when earnings fall off, or are reduced by losses. The Union Bank carries a loan of fifty million dollars, and its "rest" now amounts to a very large sum, while its deposits foot up about seventy-five million dollars. The last dividend of the Alliance Bank was at the rate of seven per cent, and it has a rest amounting to one million two hundred thousand dollars. The Adelphi has just paid at rate of eight per cent; the National Discount Company, at the rate of thirteen per cent per annum.

* * *

The English banks and bankers have a rule that their employés shall not speculate in stocks, and Rule 56 of the London Stock Exchange House somewhat vaguely forbids, or, rather, cautions, members against dealing with clerks in public and private establishments without the knowledge of their employers. London bankers are demanding that for this mild rule shall be substituted one peremptorily expelling from the London Stock Exchange any broker carrying on the business last named.

I have known of instances in the United States, and have heard of them in London, Paris and

Liverpool, where brokers have gone on for years doing a losing business for bank officers, and where the losses were by the hundred thousand on salaries of a few thousand a year. It is for the correction of such crimes as these that London proposes to rule brokers guilty who take part in them.

Not long ago the London Stock Board discovered that one of their number had been dealing for an employé in the well-known house of Baring Brothers & Co. The board at once promptly suspended him for four years; and a leading London journal, in commending this action, said it could not fail of having good results.

* * *

I have elsewhere spoken of the fact that it is a very common custom to pay directors in English corporations for prompt attendance at board meetings, and that this fact made many of the nobility and gentry more than willing to serve on as many boards as they could find time to attend. But, though this practice of feeing directors is coming into vogue with us, another English custom, which is still maintained there, is not as common with our banks as it once was. I can remember when it was the general habit with the American banks to have a "director for the week," who was, during his week, to attend specially to the management of his bank.

The method of selection was just like that in

gue in London to-day. A *rota*, or roll, of the directors was made, showing the order in which the individual directors should be taken in turn. In some London banks the term of office of this director is fourteen days, and I observed that the duties of the London director for the week were by no means nominal. One part of his duties was to go each morning to the safes in the "strong room," and take out and place in the hands of the subordinates of the bank such cash and securities as might be wanted for current use during the day. At the close of business he would bring up to the strong room the money and securities not used, initializing the entries showing what disposition had been made of those used. There is a deal of system and red tape in the administration of some of the London banks.

Fault is sometimes found with the way bank directors in American cities examine the banks under their management; but it seems to me they do the work fully as well as the average of London directors. I have known of an instance in London where in court, after a tremendous defalcation of a leading officer in a London bank, it was proved that at the directors' examination only the wrappers of the securities were looked at, that brown paper might easily have been passed off on them for Egyptian bonds, that securities were shifted while directors' backs were turned, and that London bank directors were quite frequently in the habit of simply looking at labels and wrappers when they made their periodical examinations.

I have had considerable experience in the matter of examinations of our banks, both by national bank examiners and bank directors, and can testify that I never knew of an instance where such loose inspections as this one just described were indulged in.

Those financial students who have an idea that failures in business are not quite as frequent in England, and not of such disastrous character as in the newer and more progressive countries, should read the bankruptcy columns of "The London Times." Here are to be found records of some of the most scandalous explosions, — failures for hundreds of thousand pounds, with the smallest assets.

I picked up some English statistics relative to bankruptcies in the United Kingdom which are rather unique. In a series of eight recent years, it was found that Scotch bankrupts paid an average of nine shillings the pound; Irish, seven shillings and seven pence; English, six shillings and a half-penny; Welsh, five shillings and a half-penny.

While wandering about London, and looking upon financial names which had long been familiar to me, I saw the name "London and Westminster Bank" over the entrance of its stately central office, and fell in with its great branches in various parts of the kingdom. A few points of the history of the rise and progress of the famous London and Westminster are of peculiar value, for they well illustrate the way of life of many of England's most famous banks. They have generally had what I may term an individual origin. The London Westminster was formerly Jones, Lloyd & Co.; and Jones, Lloyd & Co. was, to the modern financial English and American world, simply that wonderful individual tower of moneyed sagacity, strength, prudence and honesty, Lord Overstone, who half retired from public view a quarter of a century ago, although he has only recently been borne to his grave at the age of nearly ninety. It used to be said of one of Boston's ablest merchants that he had, by nature, fitness for the Church; and that, if he had entered it, he would surely have been a very solid doctor of divinity. Lord Overstone, who lived and died a devout Christian man, always said that he would have liked the Church, and would surely have entered it, had he followed the inclinations of his boyhood. His father was in early life a clergyman, but, marrying the daughter of a Mr. Jones, who was a Manchester banker and manufacturer, he gave up his clerical profession, and went into partnership with his father-in-law in the establishment of the house of Jones, Lloyd & Co. of London. Lord Overstone succeeded to the business of his father in 1844, which business he conducted with the highest success, the house under his headship becoming one of the soundest and largest private banking concerns in the world. But Lord Overstone's widest fame was attained by the far-reaching sagacity of his discussions in and out of Parliament, and his many papers upon theoretical finance. He became the leading financial authority of the realm, and for a long life was the "consulting engineer" of England's banking and treasury department.

Experience has convinced me that the best business men are those who are not completely absorbed by their trade, and Lord Overstone's career is an apt illustration of the truth of this philosophy. He was a man of many hobbies foreign to the banking business, among which were passions for making art collections, and for literary pursuits. And let me here put on record the noble Christian sermon written long ago by Lord Overstone. His father used to say of him, "Sam has no rubbish in his head." There is certainly no rubbish in these, his own words, on his religious belief:—

"I am, like yourself, a religionist and a Christian, upon full and careful consideration. My decision was formed with a full knowledge that sceptical theories had obtained in past times, and will again spring up around us. But to these I pay no attention. My decision has been formed with the best use of the faculties with which I am endowed, and in it I have the concurrence, not unanimous, but of an overwhelming majority, of human intellect in every successive age. I therefore stand by that decision with all its consequences, and will not consent that the question should be continually reopened. I refuse any attention to the disturbing theories of the present hour. They are mutable : they are not consistent with each other, and experience of the past teaches us that they will be evanescent."

Turning from ethics to finance, I note that our great banker was a famous hard money man. He believed in paper money, but only in paper money that had the gold behind it, and he had much to do with framing legislation that was intended to keep the Bank of England strongly fortified with gold reserves. He believed in that precious gold metal, every ounce of which, as some one has graphically said, costs an ounce of gold in labor and material to gather it from its far-scattered hiding-places.

Only once in Overstone's day did the old bank fail to respond with gold when pressed to redeem its issues. The only issue of a "Sunday London Times" took place in 1847, when, in the midst of a great panic, a Sunday slip from "The Times" office announced to the world that the Bank of England had secured from the Chancellor of the Exchequer the suspension of a provision of its charter, — had, in fact, temporarily suspended payment.

Bankers under the national system of the United States will be particularly interested in the fact that this great London banker, Lord Overstone, was the originator of the system of making regular public returns of the amount of bullion on hand in banks of circulation. Before his time, the Bank of England had always gone on the policy of maintaining the utmost secrecy in this regard.

Lord Overstone's life shows how a man, inheriting great wealth, and the management of a most far-reaching business which demanded the closest attention, may, at the same time, be a public-spirited citizen, a statesman, a Christian philanthropist, and a patron of art and literature. I have in mind a banker in this country whose career has shown him to be, in many points, like Overstone, though he is not yet, by any means, so old a man as was the London banker.

By his generous patronage of good causes, his aid to schemes for developing art in this country, and by his generosity to those who have helped him make his fortune, he has shown himself, perhaps without knowing it, to be a disciple of the head of the old London banking-house of Jones, Lloyd & Co.

* * *

In collecting payments upon a letter of credit, signatures alone satisfy bankers in England that the payments are being made to the right person. But their customs in these premises are best illustrated by a chapter from my own experience with a letter of credit. Every traveller's letter of credit has attached to it a long list of banks and bankers where it may be presented and advances obtained. In the case of the bill I carried, this list stretched from Halifax to Jerusalem. But few travellers are aware that this list is, to a great extent, merely suggestive. The fact is, it is to be understood that the bill can be presented, and payments negotiated, with almost any banker of standing in any country named on the bill. And it is hard to imagine any civilized country on the face of the globe that is not glad to purchase of you a reliable sterling draft on London. Such drafts should sell at a premium almost anywhere. A shrewd American friend, just returned from a tour around the world, says he almost always got a premium when he drew on his letter of credit from points away from London.

* * *

The London Institute for Bankers holds its meetings in Finsbury-circus. Its president is

Richard Martin, M.P., and its membership is made up of the best bankers and general business men in London. At its gatherings, which are held monthly, the members discuss a wide variety of banking and business questions; and experts from all countries appear, from time to time, before the Institute with specially prepared papers on banking and finance. At one meeting we find the president opening the exercises with a presentation of his views upon the subject of the liability of banks and bankers for special deposits left with them by their customers, which address is supplemented by a discussion of this topic in which many members participate. Then the chairman introduces an eminent Frenchmen who has, by invitation, run over from Paris to give the Institute a paper on the history and practice of banking in France, which will include an explanantion of the methods and machinery of the Bank of France, an institution which transacts business for the public in one hundred and fifty-six different towns, besides having a head office and eight district offices in Paris. And the French financier also tells them, in an incidental way, about the methods of the Bank of France in its great safe deposit business, which it has carried on so well, that no securities have ever been stolen from its strong room.

On another evening the Institute may give its attention to recent Continental changes in laws relative to bills of exchange and notes, discussing the new Commercial Bill Act of the three Scandinavian kingdoms of Denmark, Sweden, and Norway, a law which has set the United States a good example by abolishing days of grace.

These are specimens of the topics that come before the Finsbury Institute, and suffice to show the wide and profitable range of their discussions, and the need there is for the establishment of institutions of a similar character in America.

* * *

Purchasers — consumers — in London, whatever may be the class of supplies upon which they are drawing, depend more upon brokers, commissioners, and agents of that sort, than we do in the United States.

An illustration from one department of London trade illustrates this. The commission merchants of the city depend almost exclusively upon brokers in disposing of their merchandise to the consumers. This is a custom that is upon the increase here, and is a practice that we have been and are still copying from London. In the transaction of the immense business of London there arises, of course, a necessity for a large class of these negotiators, and many of them have a standing and responsibility that is unquestioned. Yet I was surprised to note the independence of action that was allowed these broking concerns, particularly in the stock and exchange market, and the way funds and securities were by custom, and even law, allowed to remain unaccounted for in their hands till that special London institution, "settlement day," came around.

Readers accustomed to glancing at London market reports must have noticed that there are settlement days for all sorts of stock, exchange, and general trade operations.

My friend in Bishopgate Street, who receives in the way of trade all sorts of Continental exchange, passes the same over to his broker, gets no voucher at all from him, and awaits in a confidence supported by custom till settlement day for exchange comes around with the money for his bills. The law fully recognizes these methods and customs. A guardian wished to invest for his ward fifteen thousand pounds sterling in Continental securities. His broker said he had purchased them on settlement day, and gave his principal a "bought note," a regular London institution in the memorandum line. The broker had not bought the bonds, and ultimately absconded with the money. The court of appeals and the House of Lords acquitted the guardian when he was sued by his ward, saying that custom and law authorized the bought-note method.

* *
*

Since 1870, when the national school system of

England was established, a common school education is placed within the reach of every child in the kingdom. English parents, of the artisan class, who have had schooling experiences in both old and New England, have assured me that their children made better progress in their studies in England than in the United States. And they furthermore claim that the allotment of studies is more satisfactory in England than here to the parents of children who wish their boys and girls to acquire a practical education, — an education adapted to their position and prospects in life. I found that reading, writing, arithmetic and history were taught in the common schools of the kingdom, while other branches of education were left almost entirely to schools of another class. The national schools were met, at their start, by a decided opposition from the Established Church. And even to this day they are under the ban of this church.

Quite recently a prominent Church of England divine openly expressed his alarm and his regret over the fact that the education of the children of England had so largely fallen into the hands of a school system which considered it no part of its duty to teach the pupils the religion of the Established Church of England. The "high" wing of the English Church is particularly hostile to the national schools. The leading men in this branch of the Church loudly lament what they term the encroachments of infidelity and scepticism through the influence of the secular teaching of the national schools.

But these opponents of England's national schools have a school system of their own which is entirely after their heart. Their pet schools are established under their National Society for promoting the education of the children of the kingdom in the principles of the Established Church; and, in the schools under this organization, more pupils are to-day being taught in the kingdom than in the national schools.

The national Church schools have in charge 2,385,374 pupils; the national board schools, 1,298,-746; the Roman Catholic schools, 269,231; the Wesleyan, 200,909. There is one fact, relative to this school question, which seemed novel to me. I visited in England common schools of the various classes, and often met with their teachers and the pupils out of school. I also gave no little time to the study of the educational system of the country. I found that these common, nominally free schools, which have been in many points modelled after the common schools of the United States, are almost entirely patronized by the children of the humble classes of the country, — by the very poor, by the agricultural laborers, and by the artisans. The kingdom is full of private schools which are supported by the patronage of the classes other than those I have named, and vast numbers of children are sent to private schools on the Continent, single lists of which, to the extent of five thousand, I have seen advertised in London papers.

I have spoken of the national, Church and other common schools of England, which are mainly filled by the children of the humbler classes, as being modelled after our own free schools. But it ought to be stated that the children are charged a small school-fee. This, although a penny or two a week, becomes quite a burden to a poor man, having, as is so commonly the case with England's poor, a large number of school-needing children. This fee is remitted, to be sure, when parents are willing to say they cannot pay it, but England's poor laborers are proud, and, therefore, very reluctant to acknowledge themselves paupers; for the claim for the return of the school-fee amounts to this. I observed that the school boards often found themselves placed in a singular position in this matter of school-fees. They were obliged to instruct teachers to send pupils home whose school-fees were not paid. And, at the same time, if the parent is found not keeping his children in school, he is liable to be summoned into the police court.

I was interested in seeing the throngs of little children, all of the poorer classes, tramping along the London sidewalks, books in hand, on their way to the board schools, which are what we should term the common schools of the city. Yet they differ from our common or free schools in several points, one of which is the practice just mentioned, of making a small tuition charge against each pupil.

A little note about one of these board schools will be interesting as illustrating the methods and machinery of all of them. It stands in the heart of one of the poorest districts of London, and its buildings, made of stone and brick, have cost seventy-five thousand dollars, and will accommodate twelve hundred children, each of whom pay four pence a week tuition. Opposition to this tuition-fee often crops out most decidedly, and many of the parents say they wish they had the ragged schools again, for those cost them nothing.

At the time I was in London, the metropolis was going through with elections of members of the school board, and the exciting discussions over the question of the merits of the various persons who presented themselves as candidates for these positions incidentally led to an active canvass of the whole board school question. I noticed that one of the charges oftenest made against the board schools was that they did not pay sufficient attention to instruction of a technical character, an objection which had a decidedly home-like flavor. Candidates for positions on the board adopted the style of appealing to electors through advertisements in the leading papers.

The London school board is a triennial one, and election takes place November 1. It has been in existence twelve years, and consists of fifty-two members. Once every three years a struggle, which has been termed a heterogeneous scramble, takes place for positions on this board.

Only a small proportion of the expense of running the common schools of England is paid by the school-fees. The London school board pays, for instance, a million and a quarter sterling annually for the expenses of its schools, and of this amount it receives only about one hundred thousand pounds sterling in the way of annual school-fees. The school-teachers of both sexes in these schools are paid very small wages, and occupy a much more humble position socially than the same class in the United States. I found them quite often bearing the appearances of overwork, close confinement, and not over-generous living. I could not but notice the significance of an incident or two bearing upon this question of the social position of the common-school teacher in England. In one case, I heard that one of these teachers, who had for thirty years been an instructor in a parochial school, which had been rotated out of existence by the establishment of national schools, had taken to the road as a beggar, and had been arrested for asking alms. In another case which I happened to hear of, a male school-teacher got into court through marrying in haste, and somewhat irregularly, a tap-room bar-maid.

England's school-teachers are very much better paid than formerly, yet in some portions of the kingdom their remuneration seems small to an American. There, as here, the best salaries are paid to teachers in the largest cities and towns, and London heads the line. Its board schools divide their teachers into six classes, made up of the trained and untrained. The salaries of the male teachers range from sixty to one hundred and fifty-five pounds a year, and of the women from fifty to one hundred and twenty-five pounds. It will be observed that there are no such discrepancies between the male and female teachers as exist with us.

Many Londoners grumble over what they term the exorbitant salaries paid the city school-teachers, and at the meetings of the London school board speeches are made, sounding much like those we hear in our school boards, denouncing the extravagance of paying school-teachers so much more than hard-working shopkeepers' assistants are able to earn. I think the teachers in the London board schools work very hard, — much harder than teachers here. The scholars are almost entirely children of the humblest classes. Many of them come to school in a ragged and half-starved condition. I have known of instances where the board school-rooms were thrown open at an early hour in order to give destitute children food, warmth and shelter. Lunches are, in many cases, provided at school for the poor children at public expense. It will readily be inferred from these facts that the teachers must have to do a deal of disagreeable "police" work.

In Scotland the teachers in the Presbyterian schools receive, on an average, sixty-nine pounds a year; in Wales, seventy-eight pounds. In Denmark school-teachers' salaries range from eighty-six to one hundred and thirty-five pounds; in Ireland, the average is forty-five pounds; in Berlin, the lowest salaries paid male teachers is sixty-three pounds; in Alsace-Lorraine, forty-eight to sixty pounds.

These figures are curious, since they show how low rates of wages for so-called instructors of the rising generation are running in Britain and on the Continent; yet the real value of the statistics can only be got by accompanying them with a full description of the general character and social status of the teachers of the various countries named. I saw and talked with many country pedagogues in England, and visited some schools on the Continent, and from what I saw and heard, I received the impression that the average European school-master and school-mistress are about up to the standard of ours in the days of our grandfathers, though training-schools are steadily raising the profession.

The village school-master in England has "no sort" of a social position. Another school incident, that came under my observation, illustrated the influential position of the vicar of a parish in the matter of school affairs. One of these clergymen was brought into court in connection with an assault case growing out of his peremptory dismissal of the parish school-master. The vicar and the lord of the manor generally rule in an English village.

In the rude, barn-like school-houses in England's rural districts, I found over-crowding and poor ventilation quite common. Then, again, there, as well as here, the cramping, confining school regulations, necessary in order to attain any approach to successful results from teaching under such unfavorable circumstances, render the situation of the pupil most uncomfortably restricted and entirely unnatural.

As a consequence there was heard, in many quarters, a clamor about overworked scholars, and a deal of talk about various sorts of diseases, and troubles with the eyes, such as chronic weaknesses and near-sightedness. But the more advanced thinkers were found arguing with much force that these school debilities came from causes other than over-study. And, as far as school pressure was concerned, it was proved conclusively that the standard of Great Britain was, age for age, the lowest in Europe. This last is a most interesting fact, since I had been led to look upon England as occupying a foremost position in educational matters. Mismanagement and under-feeding at home are, it is claimed, leading causes of the ill-health of English school-children.

I was much interested in my many visits to rural school-houses by the resemblance of their interiors to the old-fashioned school-rooms of New England. While we have progressed into more convenient and more attractive school-buildings, the English school-houses, having been built of stone and brick, and built to last hundreds of years, often remain just as they were long before the landing of the Pilgrims. The extreme plainness, even roughness, of the finishings and furnishings of these old school-houses surprised me. Yet the associations clustering around these buildings were more interesting than any thing else about them, for the traveller has pointed out to him the very seats — rough benches of oak — upon which once sat and studied men whose names to-day are identified with the literature, the politics, the wars of a time which appears very remote to us.

As an evidence of the age and permanency of

English educational institutions, I recall the fact that quite recently the buildings of the Dorchester (England) Grammar School were found to be in a rather dilapidated condition, and the school commissioners finally concluded to erect new ones in their place. The buildings taken down had been used, without a break in their career, as schoolhouses since 1571, or more than fifty years before Dorchester, Mass., received the emigrants by the Mary and John.

Corporal punishment, once more common in America than at present, was one of those old England notions that we imported, and which is still in high favor in the mother-country. I found the teachers in the national schools quite liberal in the use of the rod. Once in a while I would hear of instances where irate parents prosecuted teachers for what they deemed unwarrantable punishment of their children. In one case, I noticed that a prosecuting parent won his case; not because the child got a very severe whipping, but because the rod was applied by an under-teacher when the head-teacher was the only one legally allowed to do the strapping. In looking over the reports of these cases, I received the impression that the justices were generally inclined to support the whippers.

James Russell Lowell has said of the United States, that it is the most common schooled and least cultivated nation upon the face of the earth. England's national and Church schools, and her compulsory education laws, give her just about as much common schooling as any nation needs. But she is deficient in means for furnishing the children of the middle classes with an education of a grade higher than that furnished by the national schools. This fact is becoming fully recognized by the advanced thinkers of England, and the public demand for this middle class education is greatly upon the increase. There is one feature of the London board schools which particularly pleased me. These schools have a certain number of scholarships, worth from forty to fifty pounds sterling, open to freest competition, the successful candidates being given opportunities to receive two years' education in high class schools, the sums named defraying the *cost*. These scholarships are open to both boys and girls.

On the boards of school inspectors, which correspond very nearly to our board of supervisors, many very eminent men and women do service at salaries which do not seem extravagant. For instance, Matthew Arnold is a school inspector at a salary of three thousand dollars.

* *
*

At the races the little fellows, in the traditional gay toggery of the turf, upon their unique and tiny racing saddles, attracted my attention about as much as any other feature of the course. Such riders as Fred Archer, Tom Cannon (who won with the American horse Iroquois), Charley Wood, and George Fordham are great lions in their circle, light of weight as they are. Their modes of handling horses in a race are something that one who has any taste for the horse cannot easily forget. There is something quite monkey-like, to my way of thinking, in their position and action when in a contest.

They sweep by you, as you watch the running, with the speed of the greyhounds, leaning forwards, as if anxious to even get ahead of the gaunt, clean-limbed thorough-breds beneath them, not forgetting, the meanwhile, to ply the whip most vigorously, and to do something in the way of stimulating the animals by yelling at them.

Turf pictures have done much towards making the appearance of these jockeys familiar to most readers. But one can get little real idea of their most unique points except from actual sight of a "school" of them skimming the field at some great race. Some of these jockeys, who are favorite retainers of the great turf patrons, like the Dukes of Westminster and Hamilton, Sir George Chetwynd and the late Count de Lagrange, make a deal of money, own fine studs of horses, and elegant places in the country. But these jockeys have to make hay while the sun shines. By and by they get stout and can't ride. The minimum weight is under six stone seven pounds; for I heard it stated that it ought to be raised to that amount, since "it was positive cruelty to keep growing lads down by the present scale."

* * *

The Briton's elephant is his magnificent draught-horse, an animal which has been rightly termed the dray-horse of the world. When I first saw specimens of this splendid animal in the streets of London and Liverpool, or saw the stalwart fathers of these Clydesdale giants making their slow jaunts for service through the farming districts, I was surprised, and filled with admiration.

Lincolnshire and Yorkshire have long been specially famous for their breeds of draught-horses; but it is in the great cities that one sees them to their best advantage, for it is there they are to be viewed at their work of drawing, with apparent ease, loads heavier than I have ever before seen behind a single horse. Some of these animals weigh a ton and a half.

String teams and light-weight dray-horses are at a discount in London; for the traffic of this immense city, which is steadily growing heavier and more encumbering, demands the use of single teams of the largest capacity,—teams that require the minimum of human attendance, and the smallest space possible, combined with the largest possible carrying capacity,

We have brought out of England some very fine specimens of these Clydesdale pullers,—a race of animals whose unique pre-eminence has been attained in England within the last twenty years, and largely through the exertions of Mr. Lawrence Drew, agent of the Duke of Hamilton.

The saddle-horses, and the coach-horses of England, in fact, nearly all horses in what may be termed pleasure use, as compared with working use, wear the square "banged" tail.

There is another horse-tail fashion which is, I think going out in England, before the decided opposition of modern individual and society protectors of animals, and that is the practice of "docking," which was at one time more common in this country than it is at present.

The painful and disfiguring operation by which a portion of the bone and flesh of the horse's tail is chopped off is a dangerous proceeding, for death from tetanus sometimes supervenes. Horses are still "nicked" in England; but I am glad to say that this, too, which was quite common in America thirty or forty years ago, has here pretty much gone out of practice. In the English nicking of to-day, the muscles on the under side of the tail are divided by three or four transverse incisions that cut to the bone, and the tail then slung up in pulleys for a while, but this English notion has been rarely adopted here.

But I do not believe that we have ever gone so far as did the English, at one period, in horse brutality, when they had a rage for cutting off the ears of horses close to their heads. From England we have also brought over the fashion of clipping horses. But there, as well as here, a strong sentiment exists against this clipping.

* * *

The finest horses I ever saw, and undoubtedly the finest carriage and saddle horses to be found in the world, can be seen in the London season on the roadways, and in Rotten Row, Hyde Park, London. To see the full tide of silks and satins under the saddle, one must visit Hyde Park during what London terms the morning (10 to 2); to see the driving, go to Hyde Park between the hours of 3 and 8 P.M. I will not describe the magnificence and magnitude of the Hyde Park horse, saddle, and carriage show, for it is a topic upon which most travellers write; but I will note one particular point about the carriage-horse portion of the grand parade-ground which few notice, because most observers are not horsemen. And this point is what is termed the "park action" of London's splendid carriage-horses. Breeding and training aim at the most perfect development of this magnificent "park action," — aim at it through generations of horse-flesh, and are only satisfied when something in the way of a pair of coach-horses is developed that is so high-stepping and dainty, graceful and proud, that the admirer of a good horse who has come from a country where little has been done in this direction stands before such animals lost in admiration of their capacity for proud display.

The French carriage-horses which I watched hour after hour in the Bois de Boulogne, Paris, amount to nothing beside these high-steppers of London; and the best pleasure-horses that are driven in Paris are brought from London. In the great annual horse shows that are held in London, leading prizes are always given for "harness horses of the best shape, with park action;" and the "London Stand Stud Company's" horses are quite apt to carry off the prizes.

The average American, who has not travelled in England, or made a careful study of the habits and characteristics of that country, is quite sure to hold the opinion that England is thoroughly given over to the patronage and support of horse-racing. He gets this idea from perusing a certain class of British novels, and from observing the fact that the leading English newspapers devote column after column to racing matters, and that Parliament adjourns for the Derby, where, in early spring, a million or two spectators cluster on Epsom Downs to witness the most fashionable horse-race of the year. He has also fallen in with stray accounts of English hunting and horse-racing parsons, like Rev. Jack Russell, and has glanced at the cartoons in " Punch," all of which serve to deepen his impression that all classes in England, not excluding the clergy, believe in horse-racing. But there is another side to this question, about which it is quite possible they have heard but little.

It is true that the leading races of England are attended by vast crowds. But the country is so densely populated, and is, at all seasons of the year, the resort of such an immense crowd of visitors from all parts of the Continent, as well as from more distant quarters, that shows of any importance draw immense crowds. But the usual character of the throng in attendance upon English races indicates the status of the sport.

I was present one Saturday in spring at a race at Alexandra, where a couple of hundred thousand spectators were in attendance. I have never anywhere, or "any when," seen such a gathering of roughs of the lowest description, or witnessed so much gambling, betting, fighting and general rowdyism. I was told that the Alexandra races, from their close proximity to London, drew out an unusually "hard crowd;" yet all English races may be depended upon to bring around them a "bad lot."

I was not present at the Derby; but a member

of my family seized his "Gladstone," and joined "all England" in the rush for that famous race. He came out of the racket whole and sound, yet ready to believe the statement made to him by an Englishman that all the rascals at large in the kingdom were at the Derby. "The Times" of next day set the crowd at two millions. A mild estimate, undoubtedly; for London, with its five millions, was what is termed emptied on Derby day.

But though Parliament adjourns, it must be remembered that there is always a strong minority, that is increasing every year, which votes and protests against adjournment, and a host of good citizens who never patronize a horse-race.

To be sure, all London is said to be at the Derby, yet one would not expect to meet Matthew Arnold there, or Mr. Gladstone, or Mr. Tennyson, or Canon Farrar. After all, racing in England has about the same "social standing," if I may use this expression, that it has here, though it is a more prominent institution than it is with us, because English people have more of wealth and leisure to put into it than we, and greater age and experience in the sport. By inheritance, they have taken on a habit of indulging freely in sports of the field, and their present bent in this direction is only a survival of sporting habits which were a necessity as a means of obtaining food in the olden times.

An illustration of the point I have been considering may be found in the fact that no class in England is more heartily despised than those dissipated and extravagant noblemen who have, in so many instances, wasted their substance on the turf. I remember well the bitter contempt with which an intelligent Scotch merchant spoke of the Duke of Hamilton, over whose estates the railway was at that moment bearing us, who had made himself notorious by his racing extravagances, and who, to pay turf losses, had sold and scattered a magnificent library which had been a family heirloom. As still further showing the dislike of racing entertained by many good people in England, I recall the fact, that, when a certain jockey-club not long ago proposed to set up a race-course at Leeds, thirty-five of the Leeds clergy, and many other leading citizens of the place, appeared before the government of the town, asking that the laying-out of the race-course should not be permitted, since its presence would be inimical to the best interests of the place; and the council agreed with the petitioners, and rejected the race-course which had been tendered by the jockey-club, after thanking them for their courtesy.

* * *

Stepping into a neat little restaurant in the very heart of London, I asked the pleasant young women, who seemed to be proprietors of the shop, if the eggs they were serving me were fresh. They assured me they were, and more, that they were very fresh, since they had just been laid by their own hens in the back part of the shop. And, sure enough, there the hens were, right in sight from the table where I was sitting, ready to furnish, in due time, more regular "hand-picked" eggs.

I saw, not long since, placarded in a Boston window, "Fresh Coup Eggs;" and, in passing the sign, kept wondering "what in time" it all meant. Finally I asked the egg-seller for an explanation, and he explained the mystery by saying he had a hen-coop in the back-yard and raised his own eggs. I was satisfied with the explanation, and so waived the matter of the spelling.

In both these last-named cases the hen product offered was certainly more attractive than the raft of limed eggs all the way from Copenhagen and Rotterdam, that have, at some seasons of late, been poured into the New York market, and sold at such prices as to lead the Central Ohio Butter and Egg Packers' Association to loudly denounce the "infernal activity of the pauper hens of Europe."

* *
*

I have never met an Englishman who did not evince surprise to hear that in America the cowslip (marsh marigold) and dandelion were boiled, and eaten as green food. They seemed to think such things should be considered only as fodder for cattle. But it should be borne in mind that the English cowslip, the wild flower found in English pastures and hedge-banks of a color varying from almost white to a deep yellow, is of the order *primita veris*, and altogether different from the American cowslip, which is of the genus *dodecatheon*, and which is found only in the elastic sods of the meadows in which water abounds. Out of the English cowslip is made a wine believed in, in the English nursery, as a wonderful source of strength for weakly children. Though I did not find the dandelion on my English table with the beef, I found plenty of its root (*taraxicum*) in my English coffee.

There is, however, one grass which grows with us and also in England, and which is there eaten by every one, and that is the water-cress, which grows in rivulets, clear ditches and ponds. Its leaves, so pungent in their taste, are flourished so constantly before the plate of the American in England as a salad, that he finally begins to think that John Bull lives mainly on grass. The water-cress is most extensively cultivated in the counties bordering on London, and that city's market seems to be flooded with it.

* * *

General discontent prevails in the rank and file of the British army, and desertions are a very common thing. I heard the causes of this discontent quite fully discussed, and I here allude to some of them. The soldiers are the victims of poor pay and hard work. They are promised, when they enlist, a shilling a day, with food and clothing. They find, when they have enlisted, that they get a net wage of about a sixpence a day; for half of their promised shillings go to make up the deficiencies in their rations and clothes supplies, and in the discharge of various petty regimental dues. They are told, when they enter the army, that their daily labors will be of the lightest description. But when in the service they find themselves, even in times of profound peace, subjected to the most inordinate and, as it seems to them, useless amount of drilling and sentry duty. I found the British soldier on his long and weary watches and guards everywhere in London. I have been informed that some of the Guards' battalions at the West End have hardly two consecutive nights in bed. A great number of sentries are ranged around St. James and Whitehall, sometimes a half-dozen within fifty yards.

Another cause of the British soldier's discontent is found in the fact that the law and custom is to punish him in the most severe manner for trifling offences like the following: Drilled to death by an upstart non-commissioned officer, an awkward and badgered raw recruit from the country "got mad," and made some uncomplimentary remark about the personal appearance of his drill-master. His sentence was two years' imprisonment with hard labor.

There are other reasons why the soldier deems his lot an unhappy and weary one ; and, until some of these sources of discontent are removed, there will remain existing in the British army an element of weakness of no trifling dimensions.

* *
*

The advertising columns of the leading London journals are instructive study for the student of English life and manners, and no American visiting England should neglect this sort of matter-of-fact literature. Here are a few peculiar specimens of the press-matter in question : —

MRS. JONES wants a parlor-maid and a house-maid. Both must be *tall*. Two in family; *no fringe*. Quiet place.

I leave my readers to guess out that "no fringe" business.

Here is an advertisement in the stock-broking line : —

JOHN SHAW, stockbroker, opens speculative accounts with 1 per cent cover. Deals at tape prices. Both tapes in office. Grants options at low rates without "distances." £21, 5s. commands £2,000 stock.

Mr. Shaw is evidently ready for all sorts of speculative accounts.

"Alpha" advertises for an indoor servant. Enclose photograph and address, and state religion, and where last employed. Piety and good looks evidently in demand in this case.

A BREWER, who is the owner of a considerable number of tied trade-houses, and an old established tied-trade, is open to purchase a Brewery. Address, confidential, X. Y. Z.

A gentleman of position and influence advertises his special facilities for getting up limited companies and introducing into their management strong directors.

JAMES, 13 Enkel Street, advertises that he will sell for £500 quarter share of a patent ship that *cannot sink or be burnt.*

Cheap enough! Charles Neville, Brighton, announces :—

DELIGHTFUL Home Employment. Delightful work for willing hands. To pass the idle hours; to gather up the golden sands, that fall in countless showers. Write for full particulars how to make money in spare time.

LE MARS, in Iowa, advertises that he will receive 2 pupils on his farm, for moderate premium.

Le Mars may be depended upon to give those boys something to do on his Iowa farm, upon which, under these "openings for gentlemen's sons" arrangements, they are always expected to pay for the privilege of laboring.

There is in London, and in other English cities, a profession termed law stationers and partnership agents. I found these persons advertising their readiness to arrange new copartnerships, and secure capital for firms wishing to enlarge their business. That law stationers should carry on such a business seems novel to us.

The business of taking on, in large brewing establishments, articled pupils who pay large premiums where opportunities are guaranteed to the pupil of receiving chemical and microscopical instruction in the brewery laboratories, is set forth in many an advertisement in the London papers. This brewery business is a tremendous one in England, and gentlemen's sons are often glad enough to get a chance to see the inside of it, paying therefor these heavy premiums.

The English company director business is often managed in a machine-like way which is not well understood here. Thus, Saxelby & Faulkner, solicitors, advertise that there are openings for two directors of high position who are willing to subscribe not less than five hundred pounds. The men who scramble for such openings as these must expect to get pay for their service in attendance fees and pickings and stealings.

Here is an advertisement of the society class of a type not at all uncommon in the English press:—

A GENTLEMAN and Wife, of large literary experience, educated, and of good position, offer to take management of a household, or to travel as companions and secretaries.

This is one of the notices that remind us what

varied services can be obtained for the money in old England.

* * *

I heard a good deal, while I was in England, of a singular sect of religionists called the "Peculiar People." They have a chapel in London, in the parish of St. George the Martyr, Southwark, and in this chapel they have been in the habit, for forty years, of holding four meetings a day on Sunday, commencing before breakfast, and closing with an evening preaching service. The congregation, as well as the leaders in conducting worship in this chapel, are the humbler class of people. The founder of this society was William Bridges, a block-maker; and men and women of the laboring class were his early co-operators in the movement.

Their method of worship resembles that of the earlier Methodists. Their belief in the matter of the treatment of all the ills that flesh is heir to, except those that are in the line of broken bones, and the like, which they give over to the surgeon, is unlike that of any other existing sect, hence their name of "Peculiar People." They place full reliance on the prayer cure, the scriptural method of the laying on of hands, and anointing with oil, and will not employ medical aid of any sort.. They take the ground that medical assistance may be summoned, and may be made useful where sufferers do not believe in the power of Christ to heal; but, as for the faithful, — as for themselves, — they are above and beyond any need of the services of the doctors. They claim to take the Bible for their sole guide, and point, in support of their views, to the fact, that, throughout the whole of the New Testament, there is no trace of the use of medical skill. There is no authority in Scripture, they say, that God will heal broken limbs; but he has said, "I will heal all manner of sickness and disease." But these peculiar folks think they have a very hard time of it in England, and believe their faith brings upon them unjust persecution.

Their "troubles" come about in this way: Officers of the law drag them into court for allowing their children to suffer from typhoid-fevers, diptheria, and, in fact, from all sorts of illness, without the slightest medical attendance; and, although the authorities might permit these maniacs to neglect themselves to a certain extent, they will not willingly permit their innocent children to suffer through their folly. I was observant of several London cases where the vigorous judges gave these "anointers" lectures of the sharpest character, and fines and imprisonment, all of which they merited. In this country we have a cropping out of the "peculiar" belief, but it has not taken the obnoxious London character.

* *
*

I observed, in England, any quantity of ignorant

"medical prejudices," and these are by no means confined to the Peculiar People. There are, for instance, many intelligent and quite devout people in England, persons within the pale of the Established Church and good society, who will not subject themselves or their children to vaccination. These profess to have conscientious scruples against the practice, founded upon the scriptural fact that the Bible has nothing to say about vaccination, and believe that such an attempt to ward off disease is flying in the face of Providence. There is another class who denounce and resist vaccination because, to use the language of one of them who was arrested under the compulsory vaccination act, "Doctors are now coming round to the opinion that vaccination is a ghastly process, and not only a folly but a crime."

The law — the judge — disposes of such foolish people by ignoring their pleas, and punishing them, as they should be punished, by fines and imprisonments. Dr. Jenner's shade rules England to-day, and vaccination is enforced with rigor.

There is one peculiar fact relative to the prevalence of small-pox in England, in these days, which I could not fail to observe as I wandered about in the country, and that is the presence everywhere of a very much larger number than one sees in this country of persons whose faces show the marks of the ravages of this dread disease. It does not seem to have been stamped out as it should have been, and this may be largely owing to the ignorant opposition to vaccination to which I have alluded,—an opposition fully deserving the denunciation expressed by an English judge before whom one of these vaccination resisters was brought. "Fine him," said the judge, "no matter what may be his defence on the ground of his conscientious scruples, etc. Punish him. An unvaccinated child in a neighborhood is as bad as a mad dog."

* *
*

Most of the land upon which London is built belongs to great landed proprietors, a large proportion of whom are titled men of high degree. Typical holders of this class are the Dukes of Bedford and Westminster, both of whom are proprietors of some of the finest real-estate properties in the metropolis. In my rambles about the city, I had pointed out fine squares and streets in the most central and most fashionable parts of London which were owned by these, and such as these, and also tracts of land belonging to them, and centrally situated, which were covered by the meanest imaginable dens and rookeries, all crowded to suffocation with the most filthy and poverty-stricken tenants. Here was land of great intrinsic value, apparently, half wasted by its occupancy with buildings of the most worthless and tumble-down class.

An explanation of this situation is found in the fact that these lands were under long leases under which sub-letting had gone on indefinitely, until the last leaser had found a rapidly expiring lease upon his hands, the shortness of which would not warrant him in putting up new buildings, since, in a few years, the land, and all upon it, would revert to its ancient lordly proprietors. Many of these great owners will soon find their incomes immensely enhanced by the termination of leases of eighty or a hundred years, that have been running on rents, which are only a trifle compared with the present rentable value of the territories.

* * *

English cities and large towns are a perfect paradise for street-musicians. Only a narrow channel separates England from the Continental home of the needy organ-grinder, the street string-bands and brass-bands, and they float over in strong force.

Stray about town in London, Birmingham, Newcastle, or other English cities at the close of any pleasant day in summer, and you will find a crowd hanging upon the strains of a German band of wind instruments in one street; a string-band sawing their elbows with frantic violence in the next; an organ-grinder vigorously grinding out his cranky music in the next alley; and a species of piano on trucks, played also by turning a wheel, still farther on. The crowds listen, the hat goes its seductive rounds, the half-pennies fly in, the police stand by, and the performers are not ordered to "move on" unless the streets become too much blocked.

The ruling majority goes in for street-music, pays pretty well for it, and stands up for the organ-man and the monkey, the brass-band and the fiddles. A sensitive, nervous minority often sets up a howl of opposition against the wandering melodists; and editors, and other brain-workers of the crowded towns, have been known to work themselves up into an agonized opposition to them.

* *
*

"Walking encyclopædias" can be had in London for the money. I have before me advertisements of various descriptions, wherein are set forth the talents and accomplishments of persons offering themselves as amanuenses, private secretaries, and as helps in all sorts of ways, to persons engaged in literary work, or in public life. And the compensation demanded in England for such service seems small. Short-hand is an accomplishment now quite generally demanded in London of clerks and book-keepers. For one hundred pounds per annum the merchant there often expects to hire a clerk who understands both book-keeping and short-hand writing. It is more common in England than here for young ladies to hold positions of private secretaries. One of the best helps to literary and general work in business and public life that I observed in English cities is the existence, in the heart of the cities, of large, exhaustive reference libraries open to the public, and in charge of very accomplished librarians. London has even taken a step in advance of the reference library idea, by setting up the "Universal Knowledge Society," an organization which has for its scope the work of answering promptly all the literary, political, art and science queries that are likely to come up. Its methods and machinery have, so far, been most successful in their results; and authors, cabinet ministers and members of Parliament are loud in its praises. The society has vast capabilities from a public point of view.

* * *

New opportunities are being constantly afforded in England for women to work at remunerative and not uncongenial occupations, and there is no other city which has so large a class as London of men and women of high social positions and ample means who are constantly devising new schemes for giving the right sort of work to the girls of the kingdom. One of the most successful experiments in the direction in question has been made at Lambeth, where the Doultons employ three hundred women in their art potteries.

These girls commence at three and four shillings a week, and range upwards in wages till the skilled among them readily command twenty-five shillings, with the exceptional cases where women of rare talent earn as high as five guineas a week.

The advance in the wages of these pottery girls is graduated by their marks at South Kensington examinations. I note here, as a curious fact, that the Doultons have flatly stated that their greatest difficulty with their girls lies in the absence in them of *any ambition*. They are, say the employers, patient, neat, accurate, satisfactory in morals, but *without a spark of ambition;* and, withal, rendered less persistent by the fact that the possible husband is always looming in the distance. I have nothing to say regarding this blunt testimony. The successful Doultons, with their three hundred well-paid girls, must be held responsible for this verdict.

Not long ago, noble London women determined that young women should have improved opportunities to qualify themselves to serve as merchants' clerks and book-keepers; and so they have set up free commercial schools for young women, where they are being instructed in the same manner that our young men are here taught in private commercial academies.

* *
*

In the border counties of Scotland I found

large numbers of women at work in the farmers' fields, often doing rough and heavy labor. I have lingered by the roadside and talked with these women. They seemed strong and healthful, but coarse, and far from neat in their appearance. They wore short dresses, heavy shoes, or none, and were oftener than otherwise without any head-covering. In the streets of Ayr, and elsewhere, I have often seen a large party of the female farm-laborers going to, or returning from, their work, driving along rapidly, at a sort of dog-trot gait, barefooted and bareheaded.

These gangs of workers made long, hard days of it, weeding turnips, hoeing potatoes, "paddling" wheat, etc. These women were the wives and daughters of the agricultural laborers. These latter are called hinds in those border counties, just as they are termed in old English literature. And the "bondager" system, which we read of as having existed in England long ago, still prevails in some of the districts of which I am writing. Under the bondager arrangement the hind bound himself, on renting a cottage of a farmer, to allow his wife or daughter to work four weeks in time of harvest without pay, as an equivalent for rent.

* *
*

In Scotch and English cities I found educated doctors charging, in their practice among the laboring classes, two shillings a visit. Apothecaries' prescriptions, written upon the same system as with us, are put up on a much lower tariff. In walking over English country roads, I often had pointed out to me the country doctor, as he flew over the hedged-lined, smooth roads in the inevitable dog-cart or gig, — the doctor's "trap," as the people termed it, — always open, and generally equipped with a large carriage umbrella and a mackintosh.

But while the charges are thus small in laboring circles of practice, the regular fee of an accomplished medical attendant in fashionable circles is a guinea a visit, medicines extra. Many of my American friends, who have had the misfortune to fall ill in London, are ready to testify to the kindly skill and heavy bills of London practitioners.

* * *

There is no city in the world that has a more prolific press than London; no city where you can purchase at a low price such an abundance of good reading; and no city more cheaply supplied with books, papers and periodicals of a most wretched character. I found on sale, at all the book-stores, fair editions of the standard English novels at sixpence a volume, and a poorer edition at threepence. There are excellent newspapers in London that are sold at a penny, — standard journals, printed on good paper, containing leading articles of a high character, and a fair *résumé* of the news of the day. "The London Times" still clings to its old-time price of threepence, which is a reduction from its still older time higher price of sixpence.

In all parts of the kingdom newspapers of a large size, but of a very low standard, as far as literary pretensions and tone are concerned, are published and sold at a penny; in some instances, at half a penny. I had an idea, before I travelled in England, that it was a country where only what are termed the better class bought and read the first-class journals, and that second-hand copies of the leading London daily journals were deemed good enough for the middle and lower classes.

I remember talking over this point with the landlord of the little "Wheat Sheaf" inn, near Shenley, a dozen or fifteen miles out of London; and he told me how, fifty years ago, when he was a boy, and when stage-coaches from London rolled by his door, papers were scarce and high, "The London Times" costing about three times its present price. Then his father was glad to buy or borrow a two or three days' old London paper. Now I found, with breakfast chops at the "Wheat Sheaf," and on the morning tables at little inns far away from London, the morning's editions of "The Times," "Telegraph," "Chronicle," etc.

In the cheapest workingmen's eating-houses in London, where the carpet was sawdust, and a cup of coffee a penny or less, and where I have seen a crowd of workingmen gathered at six in the morning eating their breakfast of bread and cold meat brought from their homes in their handkerchiefs, and only spending a penny for hot coffee or tea to wash it down, I have seen hung over the back of the rude stalls the leading London daily papers.

And in the cottages of the poor papers were generally plenty. Going into the little one-roomed cottage of an old Scotchman, who had been a farm-laborer, but who was now too old to work, and was a pensioner upon Lord Somebody's estates, I saw the old man eating his dinner of bread and tea, and doing his own simple cooking. Yet I found the postman stopping at his door, and leaving regularly an Edinburgh paper neatly done up and addressed to him.

But I observed, however, a class of periodicals, largely taken in and read by the humbler classes, which were as objectionable as they could be without being open to the charge of flagrant indecency. These were printed on mean paper, filled with mean illustrations, while their letter-press was of the most sensational character, being made up of "continued love stories" of an extravagant and unnatural type from the pens of a school of writers, whose names are, unfortunately, not unfamiliar this side of the water, of whom G. W. M. Reynolds and W. H. Ainsworth may be said to be the leaders. I have now before me one of these cheap, and, I am almost ready to say, nasty magazines. It is about the size of "Harper's Young People," contains twenty-five pages of closest print, a large number of hideous woodcuts, is made up on the poorest paper, and is retailed at a half-penny. It has an immense circulation, and has reached its twentieth volume. The titles of the continued love stories in the number before me will clearly indicate the character of this magazine.

We have here "The Defeated Detective;" "Wagner, the Wehr-Wolf," a romantic story by G. W. M. Reynolds; and "The Miser's Money, or the Chamber of Death."

* * *

Street-retiring houses, where the stranger in London, or the Londoner a long way from his home, may step in, and get a chance for a wash, etc., for a penny, are a great social convenience, and it is a pity its thronged streets are not better supplied with them. In Paris, and other Continental towns, these places are numerous. In London, some of these houses have been put up by a company known as the Swiss Chalet Company, Limited; and its buildings, which are very neat in appearance and of an attractive style of architecture, are increasing in numbers, and it is an interesting fact that many of London's poorest will go into these *chalets* and pay a penny for a wash.

* * *

It seems to me that I have never, in any city in the United States, or in Europe, found the streets so clean and so well paved as in London. Not only are the leading avenues thoroughly paved, but every side street, and every little back street, appeared to be just about as handsomely and substantially paved as the great main streets.

I am confident that London streets are kept in a far smoother and cleaner condition than are the streets of Boston and New York, notwithstanding the enormous traffic and travel that encumbers them. Very many London streets are paved with wood, mainly with plain, rectangular blocks of Swedish deal. It was at one time quite a common practice to creosote these blocks. But the paving authorities have finally concluded that creosoting does not add to durability, and now the wooden blocks are put down in their natural condition.

Out of London's two thousand miles of streets, over fifty miles are paved with wood, mainly with pitch-pine wood, though some oak, elm and larch are used. Here are the statistics for the remainder: Macadam, five hundred and seventy miles; granite blocks, two hundred and eighty miles; asphalt, fourteen miles; eight hundred miles of flints or gravel; the remaining portion, with pavement of miscellaneous character.

The management of the paving, cleaning and lighting the streets of the city of London is still in the hands of the inhabitants of the parishes.

The wide streets, which are the leading thoroughfares, are so full of the traffic of the great city that it is exceedingly difficult for a pedestrian to get safely across them. To aid him in his dash over them, small raised places of retreat are often placed in the centre of them around a lamp-post,—little islands, as it were, of stone and brick, which a venerable London acquaintance, who used often to walk the streets with me, termed "cities of refuge."

The asphalt paved streets of London are exceedingly slippery, especially when the weather is wet. The horses, donkeys and ponies which are flying over them in such crowds, and with such rapidity, are continually slipping down. I noticed many of these falls, as I wandered around London, and was much interested in noticing the way they helped up the fallen animals.

It was a little thing, showing the perfection of system upon which most every thing is conducted in London, that, at regular intervals, along the street, there were placed near the sidewalks small piles of sand. Whenever an animal slipped, and fell upon the slippery pavement, there seemed a man ready to seize a shovel, and run with a lot of this gravel and scatter it under the horse, so as to give him a footing in his struggles to regain his erect position. The use of the gravel in this way seemed to be highly successful.

In the Strand, as well as in the other popular thoroughfares of London, and the other great cities of England, the great crowd of pedestrians pouring through the streets do not, as with us, keep to the sidewalks. They make the most free use of the pave, and seem to take to it naturally, as if it belonged quite as much to them as to those who move about on wheels and in the saddle. In fact, it soon became quite evident to me, as I watched the tide of humanity which surged through the avenues of these old cities in the busy hours of the day, that the sidewalks were by no means large enough for their accommodation.

There is another feature of London street management which I have never seen elsewhere. This is a force of street workers in London, under city pay, of boys of the age of fourteen to sixteen years, who are termed "street slippers" in the local vocabulary of the town. These little fellows, who are about the age and general style of the London boot-blacks, are paid wages of a ninepence a day or so; and their special duty is to keep the streets clear of the filth made by the horses. Each boy carries in his hand a small broom and a small box; and the rapid, lively manner in which they dart among the flying teams and saddle-horses, and whisk into their boxes the manure of the street, rightly entitles them to the name of "slippers." The contents of the little boxes are emptied into larger boxes that are placed at regular intervals along the streets. These large boxes are daily emptied of their contents by city wagons which unload in a city yard. From these city yards the street-sweepings are sold to the farmers, who take them by boat, railway and road to their lands. I was told in London that the sales of the manure thus gathered far more than compensated for its collection. Thus the streets of London are kept clear of one sort of filth at a profit to the city.

* * *

A great problem in London is how to dispose successfully of the sewage of that immense section of outer London which lies for miles along the Thames. This portion, swarming with population, derives no benefit from the drainage system of London proper, which sends its sewage to Barking, and is forbidden by law to drain into the Thames. Having consulted the highest sanitary authorities, it is now believed to be best to carry all its sewage to a spot on the banks of the Thames at Mortlake, where it is to be at first treated by chemicals till a fluid, claimed to be but pure water, is allowed to run into the river. The sludge remaining is, by the aid of canvas bags and an immense pressure, to be made into solid cakes, and sold to farmers for fertilizers.

A little way out of London, near Epping Forest, is one of those suburban villages which is one of a large number that have sprung up suddenly about London, and the growth of which has been very rapid. This one, about which I have rambled quite extensively, is called Leyton. Here are being adopted some of the most advanced sewage methods. The town originally poured all its sewage without hesitation into the river Lea. But the influence of England's river purification society, and other incentives, have led Leyton, Essex, to adopt the method of separating the solids of its sewage from its liquids by mechanical and chemical processes of the most ingenious and scientific character; and its methods have been perfectly successful. The water left, after passing through the manipulations named, pours itself into the Lea in a clearer condition than the river water with which it unites; and the sludge, which has been precipitated in the processes, is sold to farmers at seven to eight dollars a ton. And all these sewage manipulations near Ruckholt farm, Leyton, are conducted in such an inoffensive manner that not the slightest odor is detected from the works; and house-lots are in good demand along them.

* *
*

The fire-insurance business, like that of life-insurance, is claimed to be a product of English ingenuity. In London it has grown to enormous proportions. There is not a civilized country on the belted globe that has not become stamping ground for the agents of these London fire offices. By English energy the business of these offices has been carried to the ends of the earth. It is estimated that the London companies alone cover fire risks amounting to over five hundred millions sterling. There are London fire-insurance companies whose yearly premium receipts amount to a million sterling. The old Alliance (fire and life) has a paid-up capital of twenty-five million dollars, —that grand old Hebrew, the late Sir Moses Montefiore, was its president; and Rothschilds, Cavendishes and Grosvenors are on its board. This company has been running since 1824. The London Assurance Corporation, with funds in hand to the amount of sixteen million dollars, was organized in 1720. The Westminster Fire-Insurance Company in 1717. Many of the London insurance companies occupy the finest buildings on the finest business sites in the city. The first insurance company set up in Great Britain was organized in 1696, and now exists under the name of the Hand in Hand Insurance Company. The present reach of the business of the London fire-insurance companies is immense. Not long ago their returns showed, that, in London alone, the total value of property covered by them amounted to £488,500,000.

Notwithstanding the age, magnitude, and far-reaching character of the English fire-insurance business, it is claimed by those English writers upon the fire-insurance interest, who have made it a matter of the most careful study, that it is not always conducted upon a system that is satisfactory. Competition for business has taken on such an active character, that the various leading companies indulge in the most indiscreet cutting of rates, both at home and abroad. Shrewd and heavy applicants for insurance have only to practise a little sharpness in the way of playing off one company against another, in order to get what they want at really less than cost.

The endless variety of London's insurance schemes interested me very much. Into whatever business there enter elements of chance, danger, or uncertainty, insurance of some sort or other stretches its hand. As extreme illustrations of this point, I recall the fact of the existence in London of a rent-insurance company,—a company which, for premiums paid, guarantees the payment of rents due, and incidentally manages estates large and small, and superintends the erection of buildings; and of an insurance company which insures transmission of articles by the general post-office parcel posts, since the post-office disclaims all responsibility for the custody of their travelling parcels.

I was, of course, interested in the workings of the Bankers' Trust and Guarantee Fund. One section includes English banks; the other, foreign banks.

Fidelity insurance is, in London, the general bond-giver for officers holding places of trust in banks. In London the fidelity of bank clerks and bank managers is never insured beyond five thousand pounds each, and only in the sum of two thousand pounds unless in exceptional cases.

* * *

London gas-companies are immense corporations. In wandering about the city, I saw many of their enormous works, whose tall chimneys and vast piles of buildings of stone and brick, about which would be piled mountains of coke, formed marked features in the scenery of the great capital. While in the great coal-producing regions of Lancashire, where the bulk of the coking coals used for gas-making purposes in England are produced, I had occasion to hear much about the terrible dangers of coal-mining, arising from the liability to explosions of fire-damps and foul-damps, — those destructive gases evolved by the coal-beds. In London, a city whose custom is to turn night, to a very great extent, into day, I could hardly fail to remember that the ability of the city to light up o' nights in this brilliant manner came from the discovery that the coal-gas, which drove out the miners, could be utilized above ground as an illuminator. In the hundred years that elapsed between 1650 and 1750, the attention of leading men of science in England was repeatedly called to the possibility of piping and using the inflammable gases that were blazing at the mouths of the exploded mines; but it was not till 1792 that gas-lights came into full existence. To-day, London has ten great gas-companies, with an aggregate capital of $50,000,000; and in all England, outside of London, there are over five hundred gas-companies. The "London Gas-Light and Coke Company" is the largest gas-company in the world. Its receipts last year were £2,663,508. The average London rate for gas is three shillings per one thousand cubic feet. The financial position of all the companies is strong, the lowest dividends paid on the ordinary stock being ten per cent, the London Gas-Light and Coke Company being the only one of the gas-companies whose dividends are limited.

In all the hotels in rural England, and in many of those in the cities, candles were served for bed-lights; and I was often told by hotel-keepers that none of their English customers would tolerate for a night in their sleeping chambers the gas-lights so common in all our public houses. They deemed them unhealthy, and could not for a moment think of sleeping in the same room with gas-pipes.

Many of the baronial halls are lighted by electricity. Hatfield House, the home of Lord Salisbury, I found well equipped with the electric light. Still, the universal cheapness of gas in England leads to an enormous consumption of it. Many of the English cities manufacture their own gas. Manchester is among the number, and I found that city charging its consumers two shillings eightpence per one thousand feet, and making out of the business twenty-five thousand pounds per annum, and free light for its own streets. Liverpool charges its consumers two shillings tenpence per one thousand feet. London, not having what is termed a municipality, is debarred from the advantage of running its own gas-works.

* * *

The telegraphic wires of England, now in the hands of the Government under the postal system, were over me or under me wherever I travelled in England. I seldom entered a village or hamlet where I did not find a postal wire ready to report me to my family at London at the rate of twenty words for a shilling; and twenty words, to one who had long been accustomed to the habit of endeavoring to tell all his wire stories in ten words, seemed a luxury of language.

I found the telegraphic accommodations everywhere arranged upon a well-nigh perfect system, and the operators in charge patient, intelligent, and most courteous. There is a loud demand in England for what is there termed sixpenny telegraphy, — a reduction of the twenty words tariff from a shilling to a sixpence, — and this demand the Government will before long acquiesce in.

This call for an inland rate of a sixpence has been before Parliament since 1868, and financial expediency has been the only cause of its having so far been received with deaf ears. The assumption by the Government of the wire net-work saddled it with a debt of ten millions sterling; and it is only quite recently that the profits of its telegraphic business have been sufficient to even pay the interest upon this telegraphic debt. But under the new *regime* the use of the wires has increased enormously. I found all classes using them with a frequency and commonness that surprised me.

There are six thousand telegraph offices open in the United Kingdom. Previous to the adoption of the postal system, six million messages a year was the highest number reached; last year thirty-one million were sent. I heard a new and apparently practical telegraphic idea suggested in England. It was that two rates should be established. The higher for prompt, rapid telegrams, which should have precedence; the lower for the wired words that should travel less fast, — express lightning, and lightning that travels slowly and stops at all way-stations.

I asked an Englishman why telegraph and telephone poles seemed so few to me as I walked over England, or dashed through it on the railways, and he replied that they were certainly thicker there than he had ever seen them in America; but that they were always so neatly finished and well painted as not to obtrude themselves at all on the traveller's sight; and if they were seen by me, I had probably taken them for something else, all of which I now remember to have been true. Certainly in England it is not easy to get far away from telegraph-wires.

There, as well as in America, strenuous exertions are being made by crowded towns to drive the wires into an underground position. But in this matter there seems to be a conflict of authorities. Citizens petition the post-office department to refuse to grant licenses for the erection of new wires, unless coupled with the condition that the wires be set underground. The postmaster-general replies that he has not authority to take this stand, but that the local powers, the vestries, etc., must regulate this matter. These latter reply that they can do nothing, and so the work of darkening London's skies with a net-work of wires goes on unchecked. I have never anywhere seen such a vast number of wires over my head as I have seen in parts of London. In Leadenhall Street alone, a short street, fourteen hundred wires may be seen cutting the air above you. Nervous London people are getting so alarmed over the dangers from falling wires that they will not ride outside the omnibuses.

* * *

The organization known as the London Corps of Commissionaires was the model from which our soldiers' messenger corps was organized, and it is in a most satisfactory position. It is doing a noble work, inasmuch as it serves the public well, and at the same time provides for the maintenance of a worthy set of men who have done the State military service without any appeal to the Government for assistance. I found these neatly uniformed commissionaires standing at nearly every corner, in the most central districts of London, clad in tasteful half-military uniform, oftener than not wearing upon their breast a variety of medals and decorations, testifying to the heroic service they had performed in almost every quarter of the globe around which the arms of the British have been carried, — standing there patiently, ready to serve as guides, or run of errands, on a most reasonable tariff of compensation, and also ready, and guaranteed by the organization which manages them, to perform in the most trustworthy manner duties of delicacy and responsibility. American travellers are, I observed, fond of employing these military messengers.

This corps was founded by Captain Walker of the Regular Army, and the Regular Army is proposing to raise a fund to present to the captain some testimonial in honor of his services in organizing the commissionaires, and to aid in the endowment of the corps. This movement finds favor among the rank and file of England's soldiery, because the plan of Capt. Walker helps recruiting greatly, since the broken-down and honorably discharged soldier has so often found remunerative occupation in the commissionaire corps. It is pleasant to record the fact that the demand in the streets of London for commissionaires far exceeds the supply, so well have their honest and skilful services been appreciated. New branches of the corps are constantly being added.

* * *

The flowers of England are of almost infinite variety and beauty. I was especially struck with the abundance and exquisite loveliness of the wild-flowers which abounded on every hand in the spring-time; and I often visited the flower-markets of London, Liverpool, and other large English cities. The vast stores of flowers here on sale were in the hands of women dealers, as is also the case in the flower-markets of Paris; and every variety of flower, from the most costly to the poor man's, — the wall-flower, — could be seen as one travelled, in early morning, up and down the lanes of these great flower-marts. On the open streets of London, I found the active retail trade in flowers in the hands of about as ragged, dirty and disagreeable crowds of women as I have ever met in trade anywhere. There was something very incongruous in this fact that the lovely flowers of the meadows, fields and gardens of England were in the dirty hands of a gang of flower women and girls who were ready to chaff each other in the most rude, and often indecent, manner, and ready, also, to abuse and cheat the traveller who lingered among them in search of a supply of the treasures of joy and beauty in which they dealt.

Vast quantities of flowers are constantly brought into England from the south of Europe, and sold in the flower-marts of London and other cities at prices which seem very low to an American. I have observed in "The Times," "Pall Mall Gazette," and other papers, advertisements which are a curious illustration of the status of the English flower supply. Flower growers in Italy, and other countries of the far south of Europe, advertise their readiness to send by mail, packed securely and "preservatively," rose-buds, tuberoses, pinks, etc., on receipt of the very low prices named, to any address in England. And the mails are often weighted with these sweet invoices passing in this rapid and convenient manner from sunny Italy to the less favored kingdoms of the far North.

The internationalism of business is vividly shown by the custom of the flower-dealers of Russia, and other cold European lands, scouring the shores of the Mediterranean for flowers whenever great social events in those northern lands, like a coronation or a princely wedding, create an overwhelming demand for flowers. At such times great refrigerator cars whirl over the long routes of the rail their fragrant and lovely burden of the products of the vast flower-gardens of the South. The international flower trade of Europe is becoming one of its most lively industries. There is one English flower custom which I observed with a deal of pleasure as I lingered among the busy merchants on change in the great cities of London and Liverpool, or sauntered through the streets and parks when business men were resting from their daily routine of work, and walking for exercise and recreation as they are so much in the habit of doing in city and town,—and that was the custom of wearing something in the flower line in the way of a button-hole bouquet. Very staid, conservative men of business—men whose ships were on every sea, and whose transactions on change were of magnificent proportions, merchant princes who were no longer in the primrose paths of life, but whose heads were silvered with advancing age—could be seen wearing button-hole bouquets of so huge a size as to astonish and perhaps, at first, amuse an American not accustomed to see such profuse floral adornments of the masculine figure. But the custom in question is so general in England as to pass without observation.

On the 19th of April, while walking in Hyde Park, London, I observed a very wide use of the primrose as an adornment. The beautiful English girls, who galloped by me in Rotten Row upon their fine thorough-breds, their graceful forms elegantly clothed in glove-fitting riding-habits which displayed to the best advantage their fascinating proportions, wore upon their breasts large bunches of primroses; and the "fair women and brave men" who rolled by me in their coaches also blossomed in the same style. Primroses were all about me, on foot as well as on wheels and in the saddle.

This 19th of April is the anniversary of the death of Beaconsfield; and the primrose, which had been his favorite flower, has been adopted as the badge of Toryism, and is held sacred to the memory of the great Conservative leader. On the first anniversary of Lord Beaconsfield's death, the wearing of this lovely pale yellow flower — the *prima rosa* of England is of this hue — was generally held to be a demonstration of Conservative sympathy; and so it continues to the present year, and is likely to live in future years. Grave objections to what some term a rather novel and theatrical exhibition of hero worship are urged in some quarters; and I have read the inevitable letter to "The London Times," signed by the remonstrants against the practice, wherein it is urged "that, if every good Conservative and Liberal is, in future, to wear or place on his table a visible token of the faith that is in him, a new element of friction and discomfort will be introduced into our daily life."

But by a large class of living English men and women the memory of Beaconsfield is intensely idolized. Pilgrimages are made to the manor of Hughenden, where he lived and died, and flowers, especially primroses, are strewn upon his grave. Through the entire year his grave is kept covered with flowers. Some have asked what Disraeli himself would have thought of such proceedings, since he was not given to the use of flowers in such connection, and would not permit a single flower to grow above the grave of his wife. Many admirers of Beaconsfield journey to Hughenden in the season of primroses, for the sake of gathering them there, and carrying them away to treasure as mementos of their dead leader. These flowers are not, however, very abundant in the locality. But the speculative urchins about the place grub far and near for them; and then, no matter where they have gathered them, offer them to visitors as having been gathered in Beaconfield's favorite paths, while the buyers seem to have faith in these statements.

Said a huge flunkey to me in the lobby of the House of Commons, "Gladstone is no sort of a man for the times. Lord Beaconsfield was the chap. He was a hornament to the nation." It is a curious fact that the whole army of hangers-on to Parliament, of the doorkeeper and general flunkey class, seem to be proud of their Toryism.

But this tendency towards an idolization of Disraeli is widespread in aristocratic England; and there is a secret political society, known as the Primrose League, the members of which have bound themselves to be faithful to the memory of Disraeli, and, in political matters, to be ruled by his precepts.

Yellow is now the Conservative color; and, at grand rallies of that party, ladies and gentlemen are quite apt to display not only primroses and yellow favors, but the gorgeous sunflower. This last floral ornament seems somewhat out of place when used as a button-hole bouquet by an English Tory, since, unlike the primrose, which is really a typical British flower, it is a native American, pure and simple, though it has long been cultivated in Europe, where, particularly in southern Europe, it grows most luxuriantly, and is used for fuel, as food for cattle and poultry, for oil-making, and even for making bread, as it was once used by the American Indians.

But certainly the soft, delicate, solitary flowered, perennial primrose — that sweet ornament of the groves and meadows of England, and which is a native of Europe — seems quite in place when worn upon the breast of a beautiful English girl. The primroses I found in English gardens, and growing wild in English fields and meadows. I doubt not their sweetness and beauty have led to their cultivation from the very beginning of English floriculture. They are one of the earliest flowers of an English spring, and their name was given them because of their early coming. Wherever I wandered in England in April I found them growing in abundance, and I have been told they are to be found in abundance in the mountainous regions of the far north of the kingdom.

* * *

An English loaf of bread is close-grained, solid, but sweet, and of a very nourishing character. In England wheat-loaves are hardly deemed fit for table till they are at least a day old. In my visits to English bakeries, I was struck by the prevailing neatness of the establishments, though I found there was an outcry going on about the filthy condition of some of the bakeries in the great cities. I often tried to find out from English bread-makers why their wheat-bread was entirely unlike ours, and I finally came to the conclusion that it arose mainly from the character of the yeast they used, and from the thorough kneading. Bread from the public bakeries is almost universally used in cities and populous towns, and is more and more generally used in the rural districts. One of the most frequent sights I met with, on quiet back country roads, was that of the bread man, in his open gig, moving rapidly from one laborer's cottage to another.

In many of the smaller towns and villages some of the artisans and agricultural laborers are in the habit of taking their provisions to the public bakery to be cooked. This is a very ancient custom. The housewife mixes her bread, and then takes it in a cloth to the bakery, when she kneads and shapes it, and sees it placed in the hot oven. For a penny she gets, said a Bedford man to me, a half a peck — six or seven pounds — of bread well baked. The Sunday dinner, which is made a deal of in England, and which usually consists of a piece of meat resting on or in a pudding made of a batter formed of flour, eggs and milk, is apt to be taken to the baker on the way to church, and called for on the return. And the charge for this baking is only a penny. It must be remembered that I am here writing only of the home customs of the humbler classes.

Wheat-bread is the main staff of life with England's laborers. Butter is eaten with it either very sparingly or not at all; but beer must, if possible, always be at hand to wash it down, and by many is deemed a greater necessity than the loaf. An English loaf of wheat-bread is something that makes an impression upon the American traveller in England. In fact, it is capable of making an impression upon anybody or any thing, for I found the standard article in this line to be solid enough to bombard a city. Yet I am ready to confess that I am very fond of the English loaf of wheat-bread, and to testify that I never fell in with an American consumer of the article who was not a liker of it.

To-day, in England, public bakeries do almost all the bread-baking, and the product they turn out is not in the least like our baker's bread, for it is close-grained, solid, and sweet with the flavor of the wheat of which it is made. All Englishmen say English wheat-flour is better than the American. I am not expert enough in the premises to pronounce upon the correctness of their judgment. But this I do know, that I found everywhere in England the use of American flour the rule rather than the exception, and all were willing to concede its excellence, claiming, at the same time, that it is now much better than it was formerly, and saying that it once had the taste of onions, from the fact that the Americans then took no pains to rid their wheat of charlock seed.

* *
*

Co-operation is a great success in England. The leaders in this business were the "pioneers" of Rochdale, who were working people. To-day the Army and Navy Co-operative stores in Victoria Street, London, constitute one of the most interesting lions in the city, and I was deeply interested by the inspection I made of them. After passing through all the departments of this immense establishment, I came to the conclusion that they had there on sale every thing a man could possibly need in running a complete family establishment. And co-operation, which began among the humble laborers of Rochdale, has culminated in the case of these co-operative society stores in an establishment patronized by the wealthy and fashionable.

The streets in the vicinity of these shops were filled with the waiting equipages of the nobility and gentry who were inside buying. On benches at the entrances were long lines of flunkies, waiting for the return of their masters and mistresses; while inside, around the thronged counters, was to be found a crowd made up of lords and ladies, eminent soldiers, and, in fact, a large representation of what London terms its best society.

The Co-operative Wholesale Society of the United Kingdom has six hundred and thirty-nine stores, situated in all parts of the country, whose sales foot up five million dollars a quarter. There are, in England, seven hundred and eighty-two retail co-operative societies, whose yearly sales are immense. But the most interesting co-operative movement that I have observed in England is one that has been made by the junior clerks of London, the shop-keepers' assistants, as they are there termed. The custom of the great establishments of providing residence accommodations for all their employés which, down to a late date, was almost universal, is rapidly going out of date. And now the hard-worked and lightly-paid clerks of London are forming a mutual society for providing themselves with food, lodgings, clothing, and, in fact, all the necessaries of their lives.

* * *

The retail stores of London, on what one would term the good streets, I found neat and attractive in their exterior, filled with the choicest and most substantial goods, and attended by intelligent and courteous clerks. All this as a general rule; but in London, as everywhere else, all rules have their exceptions. One noticeable feature of London stores, particularly those devoted to the sale of gentlemen's furnishing goods and small wares, is the custom of keeping a large proportion of the goods compactly done up in wrappers and strings, and packed away on shelves and in drawers. The amount of unpacking and packing the polite shop-keeper would sometimes have to go through with in order to get at the right sized gloves or hose for me when shopping would make me feel that I was putting him to a deal of trouble, though he would not appear to consider it in that light.

London shop-keepers and London clerks look upon their Christmas and other stated holidays as something very sacred, and not to be encroached upon except in cases of extreme necessity. Thus, where a well-known large retail mourning house advertised that a few clerks would be in attendance on Christmas Day to meet the necessities of customers who had to make sudden preparations for funerals, they also advertised, in concession to the prevailing sentiment, that such a holiday should be duly regarded; that the clerks in special attendance, as mentioned, would have given them, subsequently, any day they might select as a compensation for the one taken from them to accommodate patrons.

* *
*

The Bluecoat Boys of Christ's Hospital, London, who number about seven hundred and fifty, and who seemed to me to be running about the streets in all parts of the city, at all times of the day, bareheaded, are certainly a personal novelty, particularly in the eyes of Americans. Like the Shakers of the United States, they are dressed in a quaint costume, belonging to ancient days, which the rules of their order do not allow them to change. In the case of these little boys of the bare poll and picturesque long, blue frock, down would go their Christ's Hospital, which gives them food, shelter and education, if their unique spencers were shortened, or the colors of their knee-breeches changed one iota; for the large fund of their foundation rests upon an ancient will, the breaking of which would relegate the Bluecoat Boys to poverty. There are many curious customs connected with this venerable charity, whose home is right in the heart of London,—a home which I explored and examined with a deal of interest. One of these is connected with Easter, at which season the boys all go in procession to the Mansion House of the Lord Mayor of London. As the boys pass the Lord Mayor, each receives a gift in new coin fresh from the mint, the thirteen Grecians receiving a guinea each; eleven junior Grecians, half a guinea; forty-two monitors, half a crown; and six hundred and seventy-five of the rank and file of the school, a shilling each. As they leave, they are given each a couple of plum-buns, and a glass of wine or lemonade. After the ceremony, the Lord Mayor and sheriffs go in state to Christ Church, Newgate Street, where the spital sermon is preached by the Bishop of Rochester.

* * *

The largest school in the world is the Jews' Free

School of London, an institution which has been helped forward by such eminent Hebrews as the Rothschilds and the Montefiores, and which is to-day in a most flourishing condition. Here may be seen children of all nations, as far as extraction is concerned; and children, too, speaking nearly all languages, but who are of one blood and race. There are thirty-two hundred children on the register of this great school, and the average attendance is thirty-one hundred.

I have often heard it said that there are more Jews in London than in Jerusalem. However this may be, statistics clearly show, that, out of the five millions of Jews assigned to the entire world, at least three and one-half millions are to-day in Europe. A Jew is a leading director in the Bank of England, into which position he was finally lifted after a financial and social battle which has become historical, and everywhere in London one finds evidences of the wealth and power of a race which, centuries ago, was driven from England by an infuriated rabble, leaving behind, in the hands of the king, "all their property, debts, obligations and mortgages."

To-day, in England, the Jews are foremost in matters of education; and the average attendance at their schools is larger than that of any other class. And it has lately been stated that there are two classes in Great Britain who have never asked that the standard of education be lowered, — the Scotsman and the Hebrew. Old Hebrew writers said the world could only be saved by the breath of school-children, and uttered the maxim, "First build schools, then the temple, then the synagogues."

* * *

The economical method by which the ashes and soot are collected and disposed of in London is worthy of notice. The ashes are, of course, soft-coal ashes, as soft coal is the fuel of London, and the vast quantity of London soot comes from chimneys swept about once a month to clear them from the accumulations caused by these soft-coal fires. The dust-men of London traverse the streets of that city, collecting in their wagons all the ashes made. Their collections are taken to a large city yard, where they are sifted by city men, who, by the sifting, separate from the ashes every particle of unconsumed coal, and all material that has found its way into the dust-barrel which has any possible junk value. The cinders saved accumulate in vast piles, and are sold to the poor at low rates for fuel, and the old junk is disposed of by the city in the most profitable manner.

The city of London allows nothing to be wasted. The coal-ashes thus gleaned are used for filling purposes. But the uses of soot were novel to me.

Not only in London, but all over the United Kingdom, all the soot gathered from the chimneys and flues is carefully saved, put into bags holding about a couple of bushels, and sold to the farmers and gardeners, who prize it very highly as a fertilizer. In wandering about the farming districts of Great Britain, I often saw wide fields of grasslands upon which the very black bags containing soot had been placed in regular order all over the land preparatory to being scattered broadcast over the fields, and, at first, I thought these black objects were sheep or dogs lying upon the grass. Many of the farmers of England were loud in their praises of the value of soot as a fertilizer.

* * *

PRÆDIAL, MIXED, AND PERSONAL.

This mysterious combination of words applies to various classes of church-tithes which still have an existence in England. To attempt to describe the precise characteristics of these various tithes would be going beyond the province of these practical notes. An accurate acquaintance with the complicated tithe-system of England would betoken a liberal legal education, for this system is the result of a series of statutes extending over a very long period.

It may, in a word, be said that the tithe situation in England to-day may be described as a substitution of a money-rent charge, varying on a scale regulated by the average price of corn for seven years, for all the other forms of payment that have heretofore existed. Those of my readers who may have had an idea that tithes no longer really oppressed the people of England will read with interest and surprise the following incident, — an incident of English church-life of to-day : —

He lived in Bleak House, Langley. He had refused to pay £29 8s 8d due as "extraordinary" tithes upon fruit and hops. The Rev. W. B. Pusey had levied upon his two cows; and Mr. Anscombe, the auctioneer, in the midst of a great crowd, among which were many members of the Anti-Extraordinary Tithe Movement, mounted a block in the Bleak House farm-yard, and began to sell the two church-captured cows. The first bid was five pounds; and, in the midst of a deal of excitement and threats of boycotting the auctioneer, this bid was run up to thirty-eight pounds, the amount of the tithe claim and expenses; and so the other cow was released from the clutches of the Established Church. After the sale, an indignation meeting was held, at which the tithe system and the cow sale were vigorously denounced. But the cow had, nevertheless, been sold and driven off, and rector Pusey paid.

* * *

Many Englishmen think they see signs of the decline of fox-hunting, while others deny that it is decaying. Some famous keepers of hounds have, within a year or two, given up their packs, — Lord Radnor and Mr. Combe, for instance, — and there are certainly indications that fox-hunting is upon the wane in some districts. There are a few easily understood reasons for the opposition which exists to hunting. The farmers of England are low-spirited and cross over the agricultural prospects. They find but little money in wheat-growing, and their impatience over the rough fox-hunting riding over their growing corn is upon the increase.

It was prophesied in the early days of railroads that they would destroy fox-hunting. But the first result of their establishment was an increase of the sport, for the rail gave a chance for quick rallies from distant points at hunting centres. Now the opportunities the trains give for these gatherings is developing renewed opposition from the farmers, for in the trains comes a motley crowd that joins in the chase, many of whom pay nothing to the subscription fund which goes to compensate the farmers for crop-hurting damages. Another reason for the growing unpopularity of fox-hunting in some farming localities comes from the fact that hunting areas have become very much circumscribed, thereby resulting in more frequent ridings over those that remain. A limited acreage for the sport now means a more frequent and more inconvenient hunting use of it. The one great argument in favor of fox-hunting that is most frequently urged in the rural districts is, that it keeps the gentlemen on their estates, and makes things lively there, and trade good round about them at a season when these estates would be otherwise abandoned.

* * *

London streets seemed full of poor children. Ragged and destitute little boys and girls, presenting a more woe-begone appearance than any children I had ever before seen, swarmed about me wherever I wandered about the streets of mighty London. Often children of the most tender age were dragged before the courts on charges of crimes indicating a maturity of wickedness that was absolutely appalling. They have a law in England permitting these youthful criminals to be peremptorily punished with the birch, and dismissed, instead of sentencing them to confinement, where the companionship of more hardened criminals would complete their ruin. But London is full of individuals and organizations laboring to rescue and aid the poor juvenile delinquents. The ragged-schools of the city are one of its most useful institutions.

We have, in our great cities, summer excursions for poor children. This is a good English notion which we have closely copied. In London these excursions are termed garden-parties for the poor children. In a term of eight years one hundred and fifty-two thousand of the ragged little ones of London have been sent on these excursions, and the expenses per head have only been about a half-penny. They have, in London, a wonderfully economical system of furnishing entertainments for the poor.

* * *

I have often heard it argued that the children in the poor localities in large cities got along just as well, as far as health was concerned, and grew up as tough and strong, as the children of the better classes. Statistics upset such a theory as this. In parts of Whitechapel, London, which have a birth rate of forty per thousand, the death rate is twenty-six per thousand against twelve per thousand in Hampstead. Paris, Lyons and Marseilles furnish similar distressing figures. Liverpool is undoubtedly worse than London in this regard.

I have before me a statement made by the Liverpool Insanitary Property Committee, which is to the effect that there are in that city fifteen thousand houses unfit to be inhabited by human beings, which dwellings are now the only homes of a population of sixty thousand people. My own personal explorations of Liverpool have fully prepared me to accept this statement. Liverpool philanthropists are convinced that the cottage system must there be abandoned, since its population is so rapidly increasing, and its territory is so limited, and that the flat system must be universally adopted. I saw, in Liverpool, blocks of flats recently erected for the laboring classes which were real curiosities on account of their great ground extent and immense height. Liverpool says it must have such homes furnished at a cost of a shilling per week for each room.

Here is a reliable table relative to rents, wages, etc., of the class of families we are writing about. It will be seen that about a quarter of the wages go for rent. The district is Finsbury, London:—

Occupation.	No. of rooms occupied.	No. of child'n in family.	Wages when fully employed.	Rent.
Moulder.	1	4	18s 0d	4s 6d
Porter	1	2	18s 0d	5s 6d
Laborer.	1	5	20s 0d	3s 6d
Printer	1	0	25s 0d	6s 0d
Bootmender	1	7	17s 6d	6s 0d
Painter	2	5	20s 0d	6s 6d
Laborer.	2	6	20s 0d	5s 6d
"	1	6	20s 0d	4s 6d
Riveter	1	6	?	2s 9d

On the Thames, near London, I have seen an institution which might, I think, be copied on our waters. I refer to the floating house-boat. Some of these homes upon the water are fitted up quite finely, and contain, in some instances, living and sleeping accommodations for a dozen persons. Lines of them may be seen in some places on the river, forming regular marine villages. Many of the river abutters look upon these house-boats as perfect nuisances, since their house-keeping machinery, and its results, pollute the river, and their tenants rob the shores of that seclusion of which Englishmen are so fond. Proprietors of riparian Thames rights, under a so far unsettled claim that they own the bed of the river half-way across, and many other rights in the river, such as control of the fishing, and the right to cut the valuable crops of reeds in the river, have made the most strenuous exertions to clear the stream of these house-boats; but, so far, the boats have had it pretty much their own way, and are steadily increasing in number and size. Although these boats are mainly built to sleep quietly at moorings, they usually have some go in them. From a house-boat that has floated up and down the Thames, a distinguished artist has taken quite a gallery of fine sketches; and I have seen one of the Thames house-boats advertised for sale with the statement that it had crossed the Channel.

* * *

I don't know how many times I visited St. Paul's, or how many hours I may have spent in its ancient two-acre church-yard, standing so near a thoroughfare thronged by a host of the busiest shops of London; but this I do know, the American in London finds this stately cathedral one of the most interesting sights in London, and does not feel that he has "done" the city unless he has attended church-service there on at least one Sunday. The congregation he there meets is as remarkable as is the cathedral; for St. Paul's has no parochial charge, and the immense throng of worshippers he there finds around him, listening to the most eminent of England's preachers, are gathered from every corner of the civilized globe.

And now just a few words about St. Paul's methods of worship and varied ministrations.

In the first place, this magnificent old cathedral is open every day in the week for religious services. And every day in the week there are several different services. To detail just what and when these are would be tedious; but I must mention that it holds every morning a celebration of the Holy Communion, a plain service at 8 A.M., a short daily service at about 1 P.M., and many evening services. At St. Paul's, as in all the great English cathedrals, a very strong point is made of its music, and very strong and sweet music it has, as I can testify. Doctors of music of high degree preside over the grand organs of the cathedrals. Some of these are paid large sums for their services. I happened to notice that the accomplished organist at York Minster was given a salary of four thousand dollars a year, a large wage in England. But in these cathedrals almost all their workers are entitled to a pension at a certain age, and present incumbents are often heavily taxed to support the pension fund. In our home churches fault is often found because singers are neither devotional in their manners, their spirit, or in their outside surroundings or antecedents.

At St. Paul's, the eighteen men who worship with song, and who form a portion of its great choir, are all communicants of the church. They hold their situations for life, being entitled to a pension at sixty. The thirty or forty boy choristers of St. Paul's are schooled, boarded, clothed and generally cared for by the cathedral. So it seems that the pure and soul-stirring music of this great spiritual centre comes from voices that are really in spiritual harmony with the Church of England.

But, after all, the outside work of St. Paul's is of the most interesting character. It has lectures upon literary, social and scientific subjects, classes for the pursuits of various studies, including the study of Shakespeare, associations for recreation, *soirées*, and societies for mutual improvement. It has also an ecclesiological club, one of whose features is a weekly (Saturday) excursion to interesting churches in and about London, for the purpose of studying their construction ; and these parties, which are generally put in charge of some distinguished architect, afford a deal of instruction and pleasant recreation. The architects deliver regular lectures to the parties, as they explore the old churches, having about them, as they walk and talk, illustrations, in wood, stone and brick, of the points upon which they are dwelling.

I have spoken of its cosmopolitan Sunday congregation. But, though I found it thronged well-nigh to suffocation with an audience largely made up of strangers in London, there was evidently present quite a sprinkling of Londoners. These admire its service, and are justifiably proud of the general attractions of their great cathedral.

Though I have, in England, enjoyed the worship of the Established Church, I cannot help noting here that I found the sermons generally dull and unsatisfactory. The preaching seemed highly evangelical, but it was usually upon texts and topics not calculated to touch the human heart.

It was in serious earnest not long ago suggested by an English churchman that the sermon be done away with. In a press discussion that followed this recommendation, a gentleman wrote to a leading London paper that he favored this abolition, for he had never heard any sermons in his church that interested him; and that, during a long course of sermon-hearing, he could remember hearing no topics of the class which he longed for: those of a stirring nature, and sure to command the attention of men, such as life and death, and all the tender relations of human beings to one another, — "noble, tender, pathetic, solemn, uplifting to noble endeavor, or rebuking for shortcomings." During a long course of sermons, he could solemnly declare he could recollect no such choice of topics as these, but he could recall a few subjects which were the only ones that had fixed themselves upon his memory, and these were, —

1. The character of Saul.
2. The proper limits of veneration to the Virgin Mary.
3. The offence of Simon Magnus.
4. The necessity of attending church more than once on Sunday.

We have been hearing, in these modern days, a deal about the bitter outcry of the poor of London, who can find no homes in London for themselves. I should term this wail, which I have just quoted, an outcry over a spiritual destitution there existing on account of the death in life in the sermons of her Established Church. But if the sermons are poor, they are very short, and occupy a minor position in the grand service of English cathedral worship. And nowhere in England did I find this worship more impressive than in venerable St. Paul's.

* * *

I found many curious old customs and laws, with which English story and history had made me familiar, still in working order in old England. My morning "London Times," in its voluminous court reports, would, for instance, have all the details of a lawsuit which had resulted in the imprisonment of a young captain in the army for marrying, without consent of the chancery court, a ward in chancery. Nothing whatever was adduced against the character of the soldier. His only crime was that of successfully making love to, and finally capturing, the fair ward, which crime the judge pronounced one of the most flagrant character; for the young man had not, in advance, obtained the consent of the court. In this particular case which came under my observation, the offender, who had been languishing in prison for some time, petitioned for release, on the ground that his health was giving way under the confinement. But release was peremptorily refused. He had sinned greatly, and in prison he must remain.

These young women who are thus hedged about by the court are minors, with property and without natural guardians. The chancery appoints guardians, whom it supervises. And even the guardians cannot issue a permit to the ward to marry without first obtaining consent of the chancery court.

When a forbidden alliance has taken place, the

husband in prison for contempt of court is quite sure to be kept there till he consents to such a settlement of the property of the ward as the court orders, which settlement is always to the effect that the husband shall never have any interest in the property of his wife. In the particular case in question, the terrible offender had the misfortune to be forty years old, and not rich, while the ward was twenty, with one thousand pounds a year.

Another of the English institutions we read of, and which is still existing, is the custom, at any session held by a judge of the superior court, to present a pair of white gloves to the judge if the session turns out to be what is termed a maiden assize; that is, a session of the court to which no criminal business presents itself. I noted that several of these opportunities for going through the very old form of the white-glove donation came up within a few months, as, in the discharge of their duties, the judges moved around the country. In the conduct of court business, a deal of what may be termed old-fashioned pomp and ceremony is still gone through with in England. Take, for illustration, a glance at the "show" witnessed at an opening of the Worcestershire winter assizes, for venerable Worcestershire clings fondly to all her old forms and ceremonies. His Lordship Baron Huddlestone, who is to sit at this assize, is met at the station by high sheriff, under sheriff, sheriff's chaplain, and a large detachment of the county police. This procession escorts the judge to the shire hall, where he is presented with a large bouquet. On Sunday the judge is driven to the great cathedral in the splendidly appointed carriage of the high sheriff, under escort of a crowd of officials, made up of the city government, — sheriffs, chaplains and constables; and in the old cathedral a sermon is preached by the high sheriff's chaplain specially appropriate to the occasion. In fact, a court-opening in old Worcester is a very imposing and interesting affair.

A quaint old performance, which is every year gone through with in London, is a vivid reminder of the curious tenure upon which some English lands are held. On a certain fixed day the solicitor and high sheriff of London, with other representatives of the corporation, present themselves before the Queen's Remembrancer, an officer of the Government whose duty it is to look after the papers, deeds, etc., of the sovereign, at which time two proclamations are made.

"Tenants and occupiers of a piece of waste ground called the Moors in the County Salop come forth and do your service" is the first proclamation made on behalf of the Queen. The London solicitor then steps forward and cuts one fagot with a hatchet and another with a bill-hook.

Then the Queen's Remembrancer proclaims, "Tenants and occupiers of a certain tenement called the Forge in the parish of St. Clement Danes, in the county of Middlesex, come forth to do your service." Then the London representatives count out and pass over six horseshoes and 10 nails, the Queen's Remembrancer saying, "Good number." Thus is discharged an ancient *feu* which was payable in work, and the title to I know not how many millions sterling worth of land in London "nailed."

The lawsuits of the English courts of to-day are constantly settling questions which intertwine with times antecedent to the settlement of New England. A whale stranded upon the shores of an old baronial estate was captured by some fishermen. Their claim to it was disputed by the landed proprietor; and, on his proving that as far back as 1592 the lord of the manor had held on to all whales on his shore, the courts sustained the proprietor and ousted the fishermen. An easement upon an estate in the shape of the right of the poor people to take stones from it was reaffirmed, though said easement bore the date of the sixteenth century.

* *
*

There are no betterment laws in England, nor, in fact, in Europe. The idea of assessing estates for improvements made in their vicinity, which have increased the value of those estates, is a genuine American notion; and the use of the word in the sense I have just named was first introduced into Vermont statutes, and then copied by New Hampshire, from which State it was imported into Massachusetts, where it has had an active career. In many parts of London open spaces for recreation have been recently set apart at great expense, yet the city has never levied a dollar of the costs of these parks upon adjoining estates, though in many cases their value has been enormously enhanced by the public improvements. And in many instances the authorities have entirely renovated whole neighborhoods occupied by dwellings of the poorest classes, thereby largely increasing the value of adjoining estates, and yet have overlooked the American betterment idea. But, not long since, a member of Parliament, Mr. Cohen, while speaking upon the necessity of London's doing more to improve the dwellings of the poor, endeavored to convince his listeners that the United States plan of assessing for neighborhood improvements ought to be introduced into England.

* * *

There is probably no country in the world where the government and the laws watch more closely over the individual rights of the people than in England. Our own country might copy, with signal advantage, many of the laws which have been enacted in England for the protection of its citizens from the encroachments of those whose greed would lead them to a disregard of the health and felicity of others. Dr. Carpenter, not long ago, delivered an address entitled, "Happiness through Sanitation." England seems determined, as a general thing, that its people shall not be subject to what may be termed the assaults of wilful insanitation.

A single illustration must serve to point this paragraph. About seven miles from Liverpool is a great paper manufactory, and near it a large garden belonging to a florist and nurseryman. The man of plants and flowers suddenly found them withering under what he declared were the noxious vapors from the paper-mills, and he entered suit to recover damages for the nuisance. In the Queen's Bench, before Baron Pollock and a jury, quick work was made of this case. The plaintiff was awarded heavy damages. But it should be stated here that when the defendant's counsel asked for a stay of the execution, that Baron Pollock granted it, saying that meanwhile perhaps the plaintiff will consider whether he had not better grow his roses elsewhere.

* * *

I was told that I must surely see London by mounting its omnibuses, and riding as far as they went in any direction I happened to find them going. I did not do this to the extent I had been advised for two reasons,—one was, they moved so very slowly that I had not the patience to wait the movements of their great three-abreast, overworked horses, and so often walked ahead of them; the other was, that in the spring of the year, the season that found me in London, I could not mount to an outside seat in my walking suit without suffering from the cold, while to ride inside, in these close coaches, was the perfection of discomfort from the want of ventilation and opportunities to see the street sights. Still, I rode on them, and observed them sufficiently to become well acquainted with them. The vehicles themselves are more heavily built than our own, and the horses larger and more powerful. The drivers and conductors are a shrewd, sharp set of fellows well up in all the slang and tricks of London street life, and full to overflowing with the chaff of the sauciest and most broadly witty character, which comes out freely in their frequent encounters with street life. "Talking back," when they stir up a cabman, or other driver, is an accomplishment they seem to be proud of.

The drivers are paid well for London. They work seven days in a week, receiving a hundred pounds (five hundred dollars) a year. I take the story of one driver as a fair illustration of a London omnibus-driver's life: His route, seven and one-half miles long; to run his single omnibus, eight horses required. Eight days out of eleven these horses make their sixty-five miles. The 'bus and driver make sixty miles a day seven days in a week. The driver finds his own clothes, gloves, etc., and his whip. A good whip costs him about two dollars, and soon wears out. He is liable for one-third of the costs of his blamable accidents. They are poorly off in the matter of holidays; but their occupation is a healthy one, and I found that many had driven a good many years without having a sick day.

To be a good omnibus-driver in the thronged streets of London requires great skill. If you doubt it, ride on the seat with them, and watch with breathless trepidation on your part the work that is required of them in order to navigate in safety through the packed streets of the heart of London.

* * *

LONDON GUILDS.

THESE number about ninety, have a membership made up of 10,000 "freemen," 7,319 "liverymen," and 1,500 making up what are termed the "courts" or governing body. It is exceedingly hard for an American to understand just what these guilds and liverymen are, they are so entirely unlike any thing we have in this country. And well they may be, for they had their origin so long ago that they had a history in the thirteenth century, and were based at the start upon a feudal conception of society. They have passed through many changes, but have never been reformed. Like the House of Lords, they are just about the same as they were five hundred years ago. Consequently, like the House of Lords, they are entirely out of sympathy with modern England, and, like the House of Lords, will have to bend or go under. These guilds are, in a word, incorporated municipal committees of trade and manufactures.

The names of the leading guilds are Mercers, Grocers, Drapers, Fishmongers, Goldsmiths, Skinners, Merchant Taylors, Haberdashers, Salters, Ironmongers, Vintners, Clothworkers. They have property which gives them an income of eight hundred thousand pounds a year. Vast sums have, from time to time, been bequeathed to them in trust for special charities. Out of their income, which is not under orders from these ancient trusts, they have about four hundred and twenty-five thousand pounds, which they expend in this way: One hundred thousand pounds for elaborate dinners for themselves, one hundred and seventy-five thousand pounds for what they term maintenance of their organization, and one hundred and fifty thousand pounds which they spend in benevolence. The disproportionally small expenditure for charity has gradually made them a scandal in the eyes of many thoughtful Londoners, and Parliament is pressed to take them in hand and investigate and right them, as Parliament did with the Oxford and Cambridge foundations.

There is little doubt that in a short time these rusty old closely co-operating guilds will have to show their hand, use their enormous incomes as they ought to be used, and gracefully yield some of the absurd old rights and privileges given to them by a feudal age. Few things about them seem more absurd than the names they bear, when one takes into account their wealth, their costly entertainments and generally high pretensions; for it must be borne in mind that these monopolizing proprietors of some of the finest real estate in London still call themselves fishmongers, skinners, salters, clothworkers, etc. The London Fruiterers' Company has for its arms the tree of Paradise, environed with the serpent between Adam and Eve; and for their motto, "*Deus dat incrementum.*" And one of their curious customs is to present to the Lord Mayor of London, every year, an assortment of all the choice fruits in their season; and, in return, the Lord Mayor gives the fruiterers an annual dinner.

* *
*

It does seem to me that the men and women of

England's higher classes are more given to works of charity, philanthropy, and the labor of improving the general condition of those below them in the social scale than are their similarly situated brothers and sisters on this side of the water. Some English writer has said that the difference between an English nobleman of large estate and a working man, as far as the point of daily hard labor is concerned, is that the former is obliged, by a sense of duty, and a due regard to the responsibilities of his position, to work harder than the man who is simply laboring because he feels obliged to do so in order to support himself and his family.

Without doubt some of the greatest workers in the United Kingdom are men in the highest social position, who give nights as well as days to wearing labors for the improvement of the masses of England. Among the many modes of work common with this class, and which have been made more or less familiar to social reformers in America, I recall two of rather a novel character which might well be copied here.

In London, ladies and gentlemen belonging to the nobility and gentry make a special point of using their finest accomplishments in furnishing amusements,—entertainments for the poor. They have instituted concerts, readings, dramatic entertainments, and so forth, where all the performances are given by these high-class amateurs, and where the charge for admission is merely nominal. It can easily be believed that these entertainments are some of the finest that can be furnished. Even the household of the Queen lends a frequent hand here.

In illustration of the general habit of the better portion of the best classes of both sexes to do gratuitous and noble work among the lowly is the practice I have observed in England of young ladies of refinement and culture giving themselves enthusiastically to the work of instructing classes of poor children in the accomplishments they themselves possess, such as painting and drawing, music, and various other high and useful branches of education. This is certainly an English notion that we might here copy with advantage.

Some of London's great scientists and social reformers are organizing what they term "Guilds of Good Life," for the good of working men and women. These are societies which propose to hold regular meetings for the purpose of presenting lecturers and engaging in discussions upon such topics as: The Care of the Young, or How to bring up Healthy Children; Health and Happiness; Cleanliness, or Wash and be Clean; Description of a Healthy House and Home; Food and Feeding; Drink and Drinking.

* *
*

Among the most interesting and most curious places I visited in England were her law courts. I saw various kinds of them under full blast. Judges, juries, lawyers, spectators, made up an amusing and most novel study for me. The most of my readers have seen the trial of Mr. Pickwick on the American stage, either behind the footlights of the theatre, or as presented in a less elaborate style on the amateur boards. They have laughed over the scenes of such presentations; and have, very likely, like myself, supposed them broad caricatures of the real thing seen in an English court-room. But I do assure my reader that the "real thing," as I saw it in English court-rooms, seemed funnier to me than Dickens's so-called travesty. I did not, of course, hear English lawyers arguing in the chops-and-tomato-sauce style, nor English judges making points after the manner of the judge in the Pickwick case. But judge and jury, lawyers and spectators, all carried themselves in the genuine Pickwickian style; and I could hardly divest myself of the idea that I was witnessing a trial scene in a comedy, instead of a suit in actual progress in a real English court-room.

The judge wore a big wig and a voluminous gown, and flourished a long quill pen with which he rapidly noted down the testimony given before him. He could write fast; yet, ever and anon, he would ejaculate, "Stay, stay!" to the voluble witness, who was swamping him with words. Then, as the witness stayed, and allowed the judge to overtake him, the judge would balmily say, "Now proceed, and tell us what you did or said next." The lawyers were prompt, spicy, learned and "sassy;" and, when the judge would remonstrate, would say, "M'lud!" smile serenely, and go on sinning as before.

The jury, the culprits on trial, and the audience that watched the proceedings, each had features which made a study of interest for me, — features purely English in their characteristics. The term "lawyer" is used in England, as it is with us, to denote a class engaged upon the law. But there are, in England, sub-divisions of the legal profession which are entirely unlike any thing known here. The old term "attorney," coming from the Latin *attornatus*, one who takes the place, or turn, of another, is applied in England to those lawyers who act for clients in studying up and putting their law cases in shape for action.

The attorney in England does not go into court and make pleas. This latter work is done by barristers. The term "barrister" comes from *bar.* They advocate and plead at the bar. In old times, the name was spelt barraster; and at one time their English title was "apprentices of the law." These barristers, as I saw them in action in the

English courts, presented the traditional stagey appearance in their gowns, wigs and bands,—a plain stuff gown and a short wig. In English parlance these barristers are termed "utter barristers," or "junior counsel." Next above them come the sergeants-at-law, who are distinguished by the *coif;* and, when in forensic dress, a violet colored robe and a scarlet hood. The barrister gets his commission from the Crown. It sets him apart from and above the plain barristers. Next above the sergeants-at-law come the Queen's counsel. These are selected from both the lower grades of the profession. They are the leaders of the bar, having peculiar privileges and rights of precedence which it would be tedious to detail. These wear silk gowns and full buttoned wigs.

* *
*

The poor-box of the English courts is a great institution, and it would be a good thing if we had something of the sort here. Its use is to aid people whom the law has oppressed; and the judges, who in the English courts interfere in trials in a way that would never be tolerated here, seem to take a deal of pleasure in drawing on this poor-box in aid of prisoners whose situation has excited their sympathy. Two little incidents of court-room life will illustrate this: A poor servant girl who had been summoned from a distant part of the kingdom to give her testimony in a case, and who had paid her own railway fares and the expenses attendant upon her detention as a witness, found that there was no money coming from the court to reimburse her, since the person under arrest against whom she had testified had not been convicted, but was discharged as not guilty. The judge was indignant over the situation in which the poor girl was left by the workings of law and red tape, and ordered twelve shillings and sixpence, the amount justly due her, to be paid out of the poor-box.

A poor woman was brought into court for not sending her son to school, having been arrested under the compulsory education act. On looking into her case, the judge discovered that she was a very destitute widow, and that she put her son at some work, when the law required him to be in school, in order to save them both from starvation. When these facts leaked out in the course of the trial, the kind-hearted judge growled over the case, and excitedly asked the officer making the arrest why he had not told him all this before; and he not only gave her money out of the poor-box to meet the fine which the law forced him to levy on the woman, but he gave her more money from the same box to relieve her destitution.

The money in this court-room poor-box comes from the voluntary contributions of generous people who fully recognize its usefulness, and from deposits in it of unclaimed witness-fees.

WHAT LAND SELLS FOR IN ENGLAND.

I FOUND it somewhat hard to get at an answer to this question, as I wandered about in town and country in England. If I asked it of a laborer upon the land, as I would often do as I leaned upon the wall by the roadside, and talked with him as he rested upon his hoe, he would invariably reply that its value was, say, five pounds, or four pounds, or something in that vicinity, where the land referred to was of the finest quality, and near to some great business or manufacturing centre, or materially less where it was poorer, and less favorably situated.

I soon discovered that these figures simply referred to the leasable price of the land, and not to its freehold value. These poor workers, who had never owned a rood of land, and whose fathers and grandfathers had been just as landless, had, in all probability, no idea at all of the salable price of the fields and plantations about them. Once in a while, to be sure, the great estates upon which they and their ancestors had been laboring for generations changed hands. But such sales were great business operations, negotiated, likely enough, through London lawyers and land agents, with which they would have no acquaintance, and could not understand, if they had heard about them. Still, I managed to get at a few interesting points in these premises by extending my investigations in other directions.

Land in old England is cheaper in the heart and suburbs of her large cities than in corresponding situations in New England and New York. For instance, I found in "larger London," twelve miles from the Bank of England, one of the finest estates in England, consisting of nineteen hundred acres, with excellent home buildings upon the same, — an estate consisting of a splendid park, vast plantations of oak, beech, larch, fir, etc., and good farms, — which was offered to me at a thousand dollars an acre, — $1,900,000. There were, on every side, most perfect and exceedingly cheap steam connections with London "city."

Land relatively so situated in the suburbs of Boston and New York is often held at twenty-five cents a foot, or $10,000 an acre. I heard of a sale of forty-eight acres of land on the borders of Herts and Middlesex, near London on the north, for £23,000, — $115,000.

* *
*

I always made it a practice, in my wanderings about the United Kingdom and the Continent, to visit, very early in the morning, the fish and meat markets, and the flower, fruit and vegetable markets, of the cities and large towns in which I might be lingering. To make such excursions nearly always required of me a very long walk before breakfast; but this was amply compensated for by the lively, novel and instructive sights furnished by these early trips.

But the most novel and interesting of the market sights I met with in Europe came under my notice in the great fish-markets of London and Liverpool, where a large share of several branches of the trade was entirely in the hands of some of the most vigorous women of business I have ever seen. The Billingsgate Fish-Market of London, named after one of the ancient great water-gates of the city, and which covers about an acre of land, was a surprise to me, for I had entered it expecting to hear some of the "lingo" which had made the name of the market a synonyme for blackguardism the world over, but I heard nothing of the sort. A trade of the most lively character was at high tide at 5.30 A.M., when I walked into Billingsgate, for it was the hour given over to the wholesale traffic; and a trade of a still more active description was going on, as I walked out of the great fish-mart at about eight o'clock, when the market was given over to the retailers. This market opens daily at 5 A.M., Sundays excepted, summer and winter.

The London fish-markets receive in a year one hundred and fifty thousand tons of salt-water fish, —a supply which gives about a quarter of a pound a day for each of its inhabitants. The London supply of fresh-water fish is quite limited, and should be, since the rivers of England are mainly sewers. Yet, after all, the English, as compared with Americans, are very light fish eaters. This is the universal testimony of those who have travelled in both countries, and is confirmed by statistics. I found fish but little in use on such tables of London as came under my observation, and it was the general testimony of Englishmen with whom I talked on this subject that the laboring classes of England would seldom eat fish if they could get beef or mutton. The English are inclined to consume more meat than Americans, and they look upon fish as a light and unsubstantial diet.

* *
*

I was never weary of sauntering through the London streets, and looking in the shop-windows upon the endless variety of wares there exposed for sale. It is quite a peculiarity of the city stores, that those of very contracted interiors, and quite limited supply of shelf goods, will manage to flare out with a show in their windows of an astonishing brilliancy, only to be equalled by the poverty of display within.

I have sometimes entered one of these pretentious fronts to find within a shop so small, that the ambitious keeper seemed to have hardly room to turn himself round therein, and very small space to dispose of his stock in trade. If the shop windows in the thronged and brilliant streets devoted to mighty London's immense fashionable retail trade presented studies of marvellous richness and enchanting beauty, the stores in the narrow and dingy streets of the lower portions of London interested me by their window shows of an equally novel though less pretentious character.

I found streets crowded with shops for the sale of second-hand goods, where would be displayed in their windows, or projected in stands upon the sidewalk, tremendous stocks of well polished boots and shoes with a history, — boots and shoes that have certainly been well broken in, if not entirely broken up, and long black ranks of the Englishman's inevitable, indispensable high hat, dignified and polished in their decline, and to be had for a few shillings apiece, though they often looked as if they might have topped out noble lords in their earlier days. Second-hand military and naval uniforms were also an attractive feature in some shops, and their former ownership was often volubly expatiated upon by the Hebrew proprietor.

While wandering among the avenues devoted to trade in articles that had seen hard service, yet had not quite given up hopes of still further usefulness in an humble way, I remember stumbling upon a little shop, kept by a pleasant old lady, which revelled in a window display of second-hand goods of the most unique character, among which I noted second-hand false teeth and human skulls, both of which articles bore marks of having seen hard service.

The lady offered to sell me a good skull, with a pedigree (for she had it labelled with its name and outline biography), for ten shillings. I did not buy for two reasons, — one, that I did not know what the home export duty was on old skulls; and the other, that I could not think of any use to which I could put a skull if I did ship it home. As for the false teeth, I had no desire to add the old grinders to my collection of bric-à-brac.

* * *

I turned away from venerable Stratford, a town without an equal in its attractions for the traveller from the United States, with deep reluctance; for I was nearing the end of my travels in Europe, and might never see the old town again. A few miles from the place, in the midst of the most charming rural scenery, and near where stands the magnificent country home of a great Manchester cotton lord, I had occasion to call at the house of a cottager. The laborer was at work in the fields, but his wife received me kindly, and answered my inquiries most intelligently. Before I turned to leave, her curiosity about me seemed to be excited; and, looking at me over her spectacles in the most kindly manner, she said, "Be you the nuisance from Stratford? For if you be the nuisance from Stratford, I can only say that old Lucy is a mean landlord, and won't do a thing about my drains; and if things haint right about my place, he is the only one to blame."

This, and more of the same sort, soon made it quite clear that the good woman had been alarmed by my call, thinking I was a Stratford health-officer, come to inspect and condemn the sanitary condition of her house and grounds, which was undoubtedly faulty, and the subject of previous complaint. A tenant upon the estate of the Lucy's, she had, I doubt not, a good opportunity of understanding the character of the present representative of that family. But very likely she let her feelings run away with her when, in talking upon the conflicts she was having with Lucy on the matter of rent and repairs, she was even more severe upon him than was Mr. William Shakespeare upon the Lucy of the old time in his lousy Lucy squib.

* * *

Sir Joseph Paxton, made a knight by Victoria in recognition of his work at Chatsworth, Sydenham, and elsewhere, sleeps at Edensor in the lovely little church-yard that overlooks the Duke of Devonshire's model village of Endensor and his magnificent Chatsworth estate. After a long walk across country, among the peaks of Derbyshire, along the banks of the Derwent, and over the grounds of noble Chatsworth, I turned aside and sought for the newly made grave of the latest member of the Devonshire family, who had been laid at rest in the family burial place under the shadows of Endensor Church, — Lord Frederick Cavendish, the Phœnix Park victim.

While searching for his grave, I came upon the grave of the sixth Duke of Devonshire's head gardener, the yeoman's son, Joseph Paxton. A very simple monument with a simple inscription marks the spot. But earls, dukes and lords who lie buried around him have just as simple memorials above them. Yet the head gardener of Chatsworth and the builder of the Crystal Palace of Sydenham, upon whose beautiful proportions I had so recently been gazing with so much interest and admiration, has little need of a monument, —

"Needs but a simple tomb-stone with birth and death carved neatly
And no hollow sounding praises of him whose work is past.
His monument is elsewhere — in the Chatsworth gardens stately,
In the far-off Crystal Palace where the world looked on him last."

Lord Beaconsfield once said that the lowliest born boy in England might, if he had talents and persistency, rise to the highest position but one. But, after all, very few boys in England do get out of the plough-ruts in which they were born.

Generation after generation they plod along in the same tracks of lowly labor, accepting their humble status in life as an inheritance from which there is no delivery except at the grave.

Joseph Paxton was born in 1803, and was buried in 1865 on this hillside upon which I was standing. In his comparatively short lifetime he did a work and won a fame which proved to the world that, even in England, the son of a serf of the soil might win the right to sit among the noblest in the land. He was but a gardener; and all about me the flowers and trees he had planted and watered were blossoming and putting forth their spring-time leaves, while the artificial waterfalls and fountains he had planned were sparkling like silver in the morning air. Yet he had sat for ten years in Parliament, and had written volumes upon horticulture, architecture, and landscape-gardening which had become standard authorities in England and the United States.

He was but a gardener, and I was looking down upon the gardener's house, at the gate of the stately Chatsworth, which had been his home. Yet the name of the gardener of the Duke of Devonshire's show place in Derbyshire has overshadowed that of his master.

I have said I saw the gardener's house in which Sir Joseph Paxton lived at Chatsworth. I ought to add that the noble duke treated his brilliant gardener most generously, for the house at the gate where the gardener lived had conservatories, stables and gardens of its own, and was, perhaps, as fine a place as I have ever seen in the States occupied as the home of a gentleman. England excels all other lands in the beauty of its landscape-gardening. For hundreds of years workers in this department, like Uvedale Price, and others whose names are familiar to students in this sphere of labor, have toiled with hand and brain upon the homes and public parks of England with such magnificent success that travellers from all lands who ramble, as I have rambled, through lovely England in the spring-time of the year, turn from it with but one expression on their lips, — the declaration that this little island is the garden of the world.

* * *

I had always heard of the enormous consumption of beer and ale in England, but the half had not been told me. When I say that everybody drinks beer in England, I do not make a statement of precise accuracy, but I come very near it. Said an Englishman to us, just as we were sailing for England, "Be sure, all of you, to learn to love good honest English beer, and to drink largely of it, before you come back." He could not think of any more judicious and more friendly parting advice to give us.

The consumption of beer by the laboring classes of England is perfectly enormous, and is not upon the decrease, as statistics show.

In 1831 the annual "drink bill" of England was estimated at about seventy millions sterling; in 1881 it reached one hundred and twenty millions. In 1831 the average sum spent by the English citizen for intoxicating drinks was about three pounds; in 1881 it was four pounds. In 1831 there were, in England and Wales, fifty thousand licenses for the sale of spirits; now there are one hundred and fifty thousand. Then there was one license for every two hundred and sixty persons; now, one for every one hundred and seventy. In 1881 174,481 persons were arrested for being drunk, or drunk and disorderly, — an increase of one hundred per cent on the figures of 1860.

I am fully convinced, by personal observation, and by the testimony of others, that drunkenness is on the increase in Scotland. I happened to notice, while travelling in Scotland, that Scotch whiskey and other fiery drinks were as openly and freely sold in the stations on the railroads as soda and lemonade are sold in similar places in the United States.

English statisticians say there are only sixty thousand licensed drinking places in England. It seems to me they must be wrong in their estimates. I talked this matter over a good deal in

England, and with intelligent Englishmen on the steamer in which I returned from Europe, and also looked into the subject for myself, and I came to the conclusion that there were in rural England alone just three million beer-shops. They line all the highways, and I seldom found any by-way so narrow and secluded as not to demand a beer-shop. Beer, beer, everywhere! There is one verse of old English literature that the traveller in England is sure to get by heart, for it seems to be written on about every other door-post in rural England. It is this: "Licensed to sell beer at retail to be drunk on the premises."

The common language of the street of any country is apt to be quite direct. This, which I have never seen in print, is a common yet rather grim saying among beer-drinking workmen: "Bread is the staff of life, but beer is life itself; give me the beer." Beer is the bane of the British workmen. Many fully realize this. Said one of them to me, jumping from his seat where he sat sixteen hours a day: "Write it down, and don't you forget; and don't soften it at all. Beer is the English laborer's greatest curse."

There are, I found, two kinds of temperance reformers in England; one class preaching moderation in the use of beer, etc., the other contending for total abstinence, — teetotalism. In the county of Herts, I stopped to talk with a farmer, who was cutting down his tall, handsome hay-rick, and loading the hay for the London market. He was a lively, progressive sort of a man, who had been an emigrant to Australia, and after long residence there had again returned to the home-farm; and, like many others who had lived years away from England, he had returned with many broad ideas in his mind.

Speaking with him of the bad beer-drinking habits of the English laborers, he said the great trouble was they would not use the beer in moderation. A moderate use of beer he thought might be beneficial to them. I asked him to tell me what was his idea of moderation in this regard. He replied that, in haying-time, which is a period when the farm-hand is expected to work unusually hard, a laboring man ought to be able to get along on a gallon of beer a day!

If the men would put up with about that quantity, beer would not hurt them. These very astonishing "temperance" views I afterwards heard advanced by other quite intelligent English farmers.

The wages of an agricultural laborer in England range from thirteen to eighteen shillings a week. I gave this matter of wages a good deal of attention, and found that the best farm-laborers generally received but fifteen shillings a week, boarding themselves, and supporting families. Out of these fifteen shillings the laborer, who hardly ever owns a foot of land or any sort of a tenement, pays two shillings and twopence a week rent; and for beer, which is an injury to him, he pays, as a general thing, more than he pays for rent. Beer is a comparatively expensive article, even in England. A half-pint pot of beer costs, in the cheapest pot-house, a penny, or two cents; a quart pot, eight cents. The temperance man who said the farm-laborer ought to be content with a gallon of beer a day, in haying, would therefore set aside thirty-two cents a day for the haymaker's beer.

I found that many English laborers seemed to live almost entirely on beer. A very little bread and a large amount of beer seemed to make up their daily sustenance. I remember seeing an English laborer, who had himself abandoned its use, holding up before me a very small loaf of bread, — a loaf about the size of a coffee-cup, — and exclaiming, "See this! One of our hard workers will make a day's food out of this if you will give him beer enough to go with it." I used frequently to see these beer-drinkers sitting in the tap-rooms at all times of the day, but they swarmed into these places at night. It is often the custom for a little clique of British workmen to sit down around the plain, pine table in the beer-house, and begin the evening by ordering a quart pewter pot of beer between them. They pass this around from mouth to mouth, with a "drink, mate," chatting the while. When the mug is exhausted, it is, "Here, Missus, another pot of beer;" and so they keep it up till the evening is over.

There are some very curious laws in England for the regulation of their beer-houses and inns. One of these peculiar laws relates to their Sunday management. It provides that they must be closed on Sunday except between 12.30 or 1 P.M. and 2.30 or 3 P.M., and between 6 and 10 or 11 P.M. Local authorities have power to vary these regulations a little. A set time for opening and closing is also prescribed for secular days. But travellers and lodgers are, as a general thing, exempt from these rules.

I note here an explanation of the use of terms which I had at first a difficulty in understanding in England. A beer-house is a place simply licensed to sell beer; an ale-house is a place where all sorts of intoxicating liquors are sold. The term "public," or "public house," is generally applied to the ale-house. Public houses which are in readiness to entertain travellers with bed and board, beer, etc., included, are in England, as with us, termed inns, hotels, or taverns.

The use of the word "public," as applied to an ale or beer-house, at first led me into several mistakes in England. For instance, when, early in my rambles in England, I asked regarding the accommodations on the road before me, I supposed inns or taverns were referred to if I was told there were several publics in the village or hamlet I was approaching; and so I often came to them expecting an opportunity to get a supper or a night's lodging. I soon found, to my disappointment, that, as I have before mentioned, a public in England meant nothing more than a beer-shop.

All England employs women to keep its hotels, and to retail its beer. Wherever I travelled, in city or country, I found women, generally young women, standing ready to receive me if I entered an inn, and, in the inns, serving as clerks, book-keepers, and bar-tenders. I heard general regret expressed by thoughtful English people that the business of tending in tap-rooms had been so universally delegated to the young women of England. It was by them rightly deemed most unfortunate that girls should be obliged to serve in positions where they must, of necessity, be brought in contact with rough men in their roughest moods, and be compelled to listen to all sorts of low chaff and conversation from men who were not to be frowned upon, because they paid well for the beer upon which the profits of the house so largely depended. I have seen, in a local English paper, a significant communication from a lady, who signed herself, "A soldier's sister," which said, among other things, "that women will never meet with proper respect in England while they continue to serve out drink to any man who calls for it." The poor girls who are expected to appear to enjoy all the inane drivel which any fool or fop may address them across a pewter counter, are as much to be commiserated as any portion of the community.

As a class, the English girls who serve as barmaids, particularly those who are to be found in the rural portions of England, are neat in their appearance, quiet and intelligent in their conversation, and self-respectful in their deportment. Many of them are really attractive and capable. I remember meeting, at a little inn in an old market town near Oxford, a young lady who was the only representative of that house that I saw while staying for an early breakfast, who was graceful and beautiful, dignified and "competent to keep a hotel;" yet she was working for wages far less than we pay our servant girls, and seemed to be ready to do all work, from making out my bill to drawing a pot of beer for any "chaw-bacon" who might summon her.

I was at some pains to get at the following authentic statement of methods of beer adulteration. A member of London's committee on sewers — an eminent scientist — puts forth the declaration that "It is well known that the publicans, almost without exception, reduce their liquors with water after they are received from the brewer. The proportion in which this is added to the beer at the better class of houses is nine gallons per puncheon, and in second-rate establishments the quantity of water is doubled. This must be compensated for by the addition of ingredients which give the appearance of strength, and a mixture is openly sold for the purpose. The composition of it varies in different cases, for each expert has his own particular nostrum. The chief ingredients, however, are a saccharine body, as foots and licorice to sweeten it; a bitter principle, as gentian, quassia, sumach, and terra japonica, to give astringency; a thickening material, as linseed, to give body; a coloring matter, as burnt sugar, to darken it; cocculus indicus, to give a false strength; and common salt, capsicum, copperas, and Dantzic spruce, to produce a head, as well as to impart certain refinements of flavor. In the case of ale, its apparent strength is restored with bitters and sugar-candy."

One of the means taken by them to secure the purity of the national beverage has been the organization and equipment of a powerful society known as the Anti-Beer Adulteration Society, an institution often heard of in Parliament and on the general platform. Beer from hops, and nothing but hops, is the war-cry of this society; and it wages a sharp war upon the sugar-beer makers, and all other "tamperers" with the so-called national hop-drink. But it is a curious fact, that few are aware of, that the time was in England, and that not so very long ago, when it was deemed quite an outrage for any beer-maker to introduce into his "good beere" that noxious weed the hop, which was sure to be the "spoyling" of it.

I noticed that drinking of beer in inordinate quantities seemed to have different effects upon different English beer-drinkers. Some would show their intoxication by unseemly and excessive merriment,—a "market merry," as they term it in England; or, the beer had the effect of making the drinker unnaturally talkative and hilarious. More are, however, made excessively heavy and stupid by much beer-drinking. In English country taverns I have seen workmen sit and drink beer by the hour, until they had drugged themselves into a well-nigh unconscious state. Some, under the influence of beer, will become perfect raving maniacs, often so full of fight as to be with difficulty controllable. I found many Englishmen who were firm in the idea that such effects as I have described as coming from beer came mainly from drinking *poor* beer. They said *good* beer — beer made by the most reputable makers — would not have such bad effects.

I doubt not beer in England varies very much in intoxicating qualities, and in what may be termed general quality, or "merit." It is claimed that in small beer there is only one per cent of alcohol; in ale and porter for home use, about six per cent; in East India pale ale, ten per cent; in beer which is made in England for shipment to the United States, which is often termed "dry beer," ten per cent of alcohol.

I have had occasion to allude so frequently to the beer-drinking habits of the laboring classes, that there is danger of my conveying the impression that the consumption of beer is mainly confined to these classes. On the contrary, it seemed to me that beer was a universal household beverage in England. In many families it was on the table at lunch, dinner and supper. Its household use is shown in the advertisements of servants, and places for servants wanted, in London papers. In "The London Times" now before me, I find many of these significant notices.

Advertiser wants plain cook, offering twenty pounds a year, all found but beer. This means that board, including tea, coffee and sugar, will be supplied, but *not* beer. If the cook wishes beer, she must buy it. Tea, coffee, sugar and beer are generally considered, in English households, as luxuries, as far as the help are concerned, and are not supplied, unless "all found" is named as part of the contract. Here is another advertisement of parlor-maid wanted, wages sixteen pounds and all found; another of house-maid wanted, Church of England, wages twenty pounds, all found but beer; another of a coachman who wants a place, married, no family, *abstainer*—a teetotaler; but he will be sure to want the money in lieu of the beer usually supplied. Every person doing work for you in England seems to have an eye on that beer perquisite. A Londoner is having his coal put in. The man bringing the sacks is an abstainer, yet he asks for the beer money. In the rural districts, I found this practice of giving beer money in lieu of beer was followed by many farmers who were themselves abstainers. Yet some of these teetotal employers expressed their belief that farmers who furnished a liberal supply of beer to their laborers got more work out of their men than they did,—got more work for their beer than they did for their money. Some farmers supply their workers with malt at about four shillings the bushel, and let them brew their own beer at haysel and harvest. This home-brewed ale is cheap, mild, and, in the opinion of most Englishmen, very refreshing and wholesome. It takes a very large quantity of this cottage-brewed beer to intoxicate; therefore, some argue that its use conduces to temperance.

In my wanderings in England I was seldom where beer was not a much more accessible beverage than good drinking-water. But accustomed as I was to the well-nigh universal beer-drinking habits of the kingdom, I hardly expected to find it flowing directly into a place of worship of the Established Church. Yet, at Hampton Lucy, in Warwickshire, the rector "runs" the only public house in the village, and actually pays the salary of his organist out of the profits of the tap-room. There is a deal of talk in England at the present time about adulterations of beer, but the rector in question guarantees his to be pure.

* *
*

England's parliamentary and other orators generally "take a hall" when they go on the stump for the purpose of addressing a constituency. England is a great place for large halls. I saw an audience of five thousand persons crammed into Exeter Hall, London, when Lord Shaftesbury was to preside at an anniversary meeting of the Young Men's Christian Associations of England. In all the large towns and cities of England, halls holding three or four thousand are common. St. Andrew's Hall in Edinburgh accommodates an audience of four thousand. On the rostrum, with so great an audience before him, the political orator of the times has a very trying position. The largest latitude is allowed those who are supposed to listen, and that meeting is a dull and tame one which does not bring out a good quantity of wordy and witty combats between the speaker and his audience. The widest latitude is allowed in the matter of interruption; and nobody is "put out," either literally or figuratively, until the limits of decency are overstepped by some fool or "half jolly" man (to use a Lancashire expression), and then the police step in and turn out the offenders in double-quick time. It is quite the thing for a candidate to formally announce himself ready to answer all questions, making this announcement after he has made his opening harangue, and then standing, as it were, with folded arms, to receive the hot shot from a promiscuous audience, which has been requested to "fire away."

Little encouragement is needed to induce them to "talk back." All, from Hodge the laborer, and Tim the "chaw-bacon" in the smock frock, to the tenant farmer, the street preacher or labor reformer, "want to know, you know," all sorts of things, from the speaker's views on the question of marrying a deceased wife's sister, to his sentiments on great Church and State matters, and whether or no he did on a certain occasion speak or vote in a certain manner; and if not, why not, etc.

* * *

Before starting for Europe, I fell in with a friend who had just returned from a tour in England in company with his brother, one of the most able and prominent citizens of New England. I said to him, "You must have received great profit and pleasure from having had in London the advantage of the company of a distinguished American who was sure to be known and to receive a good deal of attention abroad." My friend smiled at my remarks; and, being a frank, honest man, he said that my ideas showed that I did not know much about London; for, said he, we were at once lost in that immense city. Two or three professional friends gave my brother some little attention; but, with that exception, we were permitted to wander about England as unknown and as unnoticed as the humblest travellers.

We read in our own newspapers a deal of gossip relative to American travellers and American colonies in London and Paris, but what sort of an impression does one imagine that the comparatively few travellers from the United States make upon that city of five million inhabitants, with a tide of travel from the Continent, which I have heard estimated as high as sixty thousand a day, pouring through its thronged thoroughfares. For a reply, reverse the picture, and tell me how much of an impression on New York all the pleasure tourists from the whole of Europe make upon that city at any given time. Any thoughtful man, who has been abroad, will tell you that the most significant lesson there learned was that which taught him how little of a ripple he was born to make on the great surface of existing life. The loneliness, the isolation, the loss of individuality one experiences when he wanders as a stranger through the teeming thoroughfares of London, is what I have experienced, but am incapable of fitly picturing.

In connection with this matter, there comes to mind the recollection of an idea that used to crop out in the old-fashioned Fourth-of-July oratory. When the orator came to speak of the wonderful growth of the commerce of the Christian world, he might be depended upon to say that "its sails whitened every sea." Now I have sailed for many days in the great lanes of the commerce of the seas without meeting a sail, and have known friends who have voyaged from Boston harbor to the equator without seeing a ship. Every ocean traveller is impressed with the solitude of the sea. And this figure about ships whitening the ocean is just as false as many ideas that prevail regarding the impress of American travel on the old world.

* *
*

In the course of my rambles in rural England, I one day became lost when striking out upon some specially planned route across country, and wandered on over cross-roads and through green lanes, and even over private fields and on by-paths for three-fourths of a day without really "getting ahead" a mile. I made no unfortunate mistake, for I saw many a rural scene which comes to me now, as I write, like the memory of a delightful dream, — views of halls and parks, lawns and farms, hedges and green pastures, which I should not have seen that day had I not been lost, and which, as likely as not, were nobler and sweeter than those I should have seen had I gone straight ahead. It sometimes takes a stranger in a country to find out and appreciate its real beauty.

While staying at the inn at Edensor, right under the shadow of Chatsworth, I climbed a beautiful hill near by, from whose top I obtained such indescribably lovely views of England's finest estate, and the romantic fields, forests, waters and peaks of Derbyshire, amid which Chatsworth stands, that I had to tell my new-found friends in the inn, who had always lived in the town in which Chatsworth is located, all about the magnificent prospect I had obtained. To my surprise, they said they had never been on that hill, though they had often thought of visiting it, and had always imagined there must be a fine view up there.

The last inquiring the way I did in England was to inquire the way home. I often regretted that there was only one way to get there, and that a way across the stormy, ice-clad North Atlantic. Particularly was it ice-clad at the time I was turning my face homeward, for the cable was daily bringing me reports of how the ocean liners were being wedged in and blocked by icebergs and ice-floes. And when, away in the heart of England and Scotland, I would go to rest at some little inn among strangers, my mind would often pensively turn, as I sought sleep, to thoughts of home and children three thousand miles across the water; and I would fall to wishing that there was a way to walk home, for I seemed to feel that that would be the only safe and sure way of getting there.

THE END.

INDEX.

ADAM SMITH, ideas of, expressed by an artisan, 68.
Advertisements, curious specimens of, 237–239, 327.
Agriculture the leading English interest, 37.
Agricultural laborer, ignorance of, 78; shoes of, 127, 128; wages of, 320.
American oak used in English car-building, 85.
Ancient law precedents, 295.
Ancient rights of way, 13–15. (See *Knole Park*.)
Apprentices, hardships of, 67–69.
Apprentice laws, injustice of, 67, 68.
Army, discontent in, 236; perpetual drilling in, 236.
Arnold, Matthew, a school inspector, 225.
Arrival book, use of, in London banks, 187, 188.
Articled pupils, 239.
Artisans out of work, talks with, 65.
Artisans, travelling expenses of, 24.
Athletics at Oxford, rage for, 126.
Attorney, English application of term, 305.

Bachelor Fellows, nature of, as a class, 27; travelling and living expenses of, 27.
Bank dividends, specimen figures of, 202, 203.
Bankers, courtesy of, 182, 183; English bankers men of cultivation, 183; not as conservative as supposed, 197–199.
Banking terms, unfamiliar nature of English, 184.

INDEX.

Bank of England, assorting-room of, 162; chief accountant in, 159, 177; coin-tester, 165, 166; date of charter, 176; deposits, 200; directors' meeting of, 166–169, 171, 172; debate at meeting, 169, 171, 172; directors' room, arrangements of, 166; employés' arrival, 175; employés' vacations, 176; employés' residence, 176; extent and situation of, 158; hours for business, 175; holidays of, 176; lunch-room, 160, 161; notes of, their aggregate circulation, 161; their cancellation, 162; their manufacture, 161; original capital of, 176; original projector of, 176; physician employed, 176; rigid rule of, 174; rotunda of, 160; salaries, 172, 176; specie reserves, 163, 164; weighing machine, 165; yearly election, 173.

Bank president, term not used in England, 185.
Bank's "rest," a, explanation of term, 203.
Bankruptcies, 206.
Bar-maids, great numbers of, 323, 324; intelligent appearance of, 324.
Barristers formerly known as apprentices of the law, 305.
Beaconsfield, national adoration of, 269–271; primrose worn in memory of, 269–271; visits to grave of, 270.
Bee-keeping, common in England, 75; novel practice in, 76.
Beer, adulteration of, 324, 325; effects of, upon consumers, 326; great amount consumed by laborers, 318–322, 326, 327; organist's salary paid from sale of, 329; statistics concerning consumption of, 318; universal use of, 317, 319, 327, 328.
Bees, beer fed to, with boiled sugar, 77.
Betterment laws, none in England, 295, 296.
Bluecoat Boys, costume of, 277, 278; Easter visit of, to the Lord Mayor, 278; number of, 277.
Bread, character of loaves of, 272, 274; chief food of laborers, 273; commonly sent to public bakeries to be baked, 273.
Brick-setter, a, 116.
Brigstock, oppression of its inhabitants by landed proprietors, 3.
British Bee-keepers' Association, exhibition of, 76.
Broad arrow, the, 129, 130.

Canals, very numerous in England, 73; number of miles of, 74.

INDEX. 337

Canal-boats, ignorance of persons employed upon, 73; number of, 73; registration of, 73.
Carlisle, hiring fair at, 119–121.
Carriage horses, "park action" of, 229, 230.
Cash credits, of Scotch origin, 186; popular in Scotland, 186.
Caste in trades, 69.
Chancery case, a singular, 292.
Charing Cross Deposit Bank, 201.
Chartered accountants, duties of, 191; institute of, 191, 192.
Chatsworth, gardens at, 316; Sir Joseph Paxton's work at, 316. (See *Paxton*.)
Cheshire, length and breadth of, 101; cheese production of, 102; salt mines in, 102. (See *Nantwich*.)
Chimes, great numbers of, in England, 97.
Chiming-matches, 97.
Church tithes, incidents relating to, 282; prædial, mixed, and personal, 281.
Coal, consumption of, in London in 1882, 60; dealers in, obliged to carry weighing apparatus, 65; sack delivery of, 64, 65.
Cocoa-rooms, great numbers of, 25; bill at cocoa-room at Waltham Cross, 25, 26. (See *Waltham Cross*.)
Coffins, American, not liked in England, 89; elm wood generally used in making, 87; wicker, 92–94.
Commission merchants, dependence upon brokers, 213, 214.
Composition foods for cattle much used by English farmers, 44.
Consols, explanation of term, 192; interest on, when payable, 193; popularity of, 194, 195.
Co-operation, success of, 275.
Co-operative Wholesale Society, number of stores belonging to, 275.
County agricultural shows, popularity of, 45; times of holding, 45.
Cow-keeper an unfamiliar term, 116.
Cowslip wine, supposed virtues of, 235.
Cruelty to children, testimony regarding, 81.

Directors' bank examinations, an incident of, 205, 206.
Directors for the week, an English bank custom, 185, 204; once a common American custom, 204.

Donkeys, ill treatment of, 113, 114.
Dorchester, age and condition of grammar schools in, 224.
Draught-horses, great size of, 227.
Drunkenness in Scotland, increase of, 318.
Durham Cathedral, curious facts from registers of, 115, 116.

Economical travelling, 27. (See *Bachelor Fellows*.)
Electric light, use of, in noblemen's residences, 262.
Elihu Burritt, singular portrait of, 6, 7; little gained from his book, 7.
England, pedestrianism in, 7–9; rivers, polluted character of, 123; spring climate of, 1; villages, absolute quiet of many, 3; "Without and Within," a pleasant volume, not a guide-book, 6.
English boys, physique of, 8, 9.
Erasures not allowed in English banks, 187.

Farming machinery much used in, 39; thoroughness of, in England, 41–43.
Fiction much read in manufacturing towns, 142, 143.
Fidelity insurance a general bond giver, 260.
Filtration, 124.
Financial report, summary of a, 197.
Fire-insurance companies: Alliance, 258; Hand in Hand, 258; London Assurance, 258; Westminster, 258; competition in, 259; wide extent of business, 258, 259.
Fires, increasing number of, 153. (See *London Fire-Department*.)
Fish, English use of, less than the American, 311.
Fishing in the Wye, 16, 17; incident relating to, 16, 17.
Flint, abundance of, in England, 122.
Flint-lock guns still made in Birmingham, 122.
Flowers, abundance of, in England, 266; customs concerning, 268–271 (see *Beaconsfield*); trade in, 266–268, 270.
Forests, growth of, in Scotland, 83; growth of, in India, 83; small amount of, in Ireland, 83.
Forestry, great attention paid to, 81, 82.
Fox-hunting, opposition of farmers to, 283; principal argument in favor of, 284; relation of railways to, 283.
"Fresh Coup Eggs," 234.

Gas, prejudice against, in sleeping-rooms, 261. (See *London, Liverpool, Manchester.*)
Goose-clubs, object of, 133.
Guide-posts, peculiar kind of, 9, 10.
Guilds of Good Life, scope of, 303.
Grain, duty on, devoted to purchase of public parks, 84, 146.
Ground rents, 243, 244.
Gypsies, baptisms among, 17, 18; often met with in the country, 17; weddings among, 18, 19.

Haddon Hall, morning walk to, 15.
Hay usually stacked in the fields, 44; "spice" used upon, 44.
Hens in a restaurant, 234.
Hides, importation into England, 70, 71.
Home, thoughts of, 334.
Horses' tails, banging, 228; docking, 228; nicking, 228.
Hospital Saturday, contributions, how collected, 148.
Hospital Sunday, collections taken in churches, 149.
House-boats, numbers of, 287; opposition to, 287; use of, 286, 287.

Imbecile asylums, great size of, 79; very large one at Watford, 79. (See *Watford.*)
Individual rights carefully guarded in England, 296, 297; incident relating to, 297.
Inns, description of, 21, 22; numbers of, in the country, 21.
Inquiring the way, incident concerning, 20.
Insurance boards, titled members of, 155-157; value of services performed by such members, 155-157.
Intensive farming, application of term, 43; comparison of, with "extensive farming," 43; illustration of, 43.
Interest, occasional high rates offered, 201.

Jews' Free School, largest school in the world, 278; number of pupils, 279.
Jews, numbers of, in London, 279; prominent promoters of education, 279.
Jockeys, characteristics of, 225, 226; minimum weight of, 227.

Joint-stock banks, none in England, except Bank of England, over fifty years old, 185.

Kenilworth, tan yards at, 70.
Knole Park, right of way in, 14, 15.

Land, selling price difficult to ascertain, 308.
Lath-render, material used by, 117; meaning of term, 117.
Law courts, amusing features of, 304, 305.
Letters of credit, collections upon, 311; signatures, 311.
Leyton, present disposition of its sewage, 257; situation, 257.
Lich-gate, origin of term, 94; sometimes shut against dissenters, 94, 95.
Limed eggs, importation into America, 234.
Limited Liability Act, date of, 186; provision of, 186.
Liverpool: gas rates, 262; great number of dwellings unfit for habitation, 285; new homes for laboring classes, 286; port charges, 109; rapid increase of population, 286.
London: ashes and soot collected and disposed of, 280, 281; Bankers' Institute, location of, 211; range of discussion, 212, 213; churches, small congregations in, 98, 99; Clearing House, business hours of, 188; location of, 188; regulations respecting country checks, 188, 189; climate warmer than that of the country, 145; co-operative stores, location of, 275; popularity of, 275; corps of commissionaires, by whom founded, 266; popularity of, 265, 266; trustworthiness, 265; East End, degradation of, 147; "hell without the fire," 147; enormous increase of population, alarm concerning, 144; suggestions in regard to, 144; Fire Department, fire towers, 154; effective organization, 153; gas companies, financial strength, 261; number of, 261; rates, 261; generosity, illustrations of, 147–150; guilds, expenditures, 300; motto and arms of Fruiterers', 301; income, 300; names of leading, 300; number and membership, 299; hospitals, support of, 149, 150; omnibuses, slow movement of, 298; omnibus drivers, life of, 299; long hours, 299; payment of, 298; poor children, birth rate in Whitechapel, 285; death rate, 285; depravity, 284; garden parties for, 285; rent and wages table, 286; retail shops, 276, 277;

sewage, plan for disposition, 256; shop clerks' holidays, 277; slight impression made by American tourists, 331, 332; steady growth, 143; Stock Exchange, Rule 56, 203; streets, annual number of miles added, 143; cleanliness, 253; how paved, 253, 254; miles of pavement, 253; street "slippers," duties, 255, 256; transit in business portions, 146; yearly number of houses built, 154.
London and Northwestern Railway, best trains, 29; block system, 30; length, 29; number of employés, 29; tunnels, 32.
London and Westminster Bank, origin of, 207. (See *Overstone*.)
Lord's Day Observance Society, activity of, 100; advertisement of, 101.

Manchester, gas rates, 262; hospitals, 106, 107; population, 105; prominent industries, 105; proposed ship canal from, to the sea, 110; water supply, whence derived, 33, 34.
Maps, excellence of English, 19, 20.
Market terms, unfamiliar nature of, 45, 46.
Married women, bank accounts with, not opened except by consent of husband, 187.
Messingham, calling a congregation in, 97, 98.
Middleborough, abundance of iron near, 103; rapid growth, 103; steel rails made at, 104.
Milk, adulteration of, 50, 51; incident relating to, 50, 51; wooden vessels for holding, 49.
Miners, their prejudice against American pick-handles, 86.
Mines, boys in, 56; heat unendurable below four thousand feet, 60; horses in, 57, 58; rapid descent into, 58; shifts, extent of, 57; women laborers not now allowed in, 56.
Mole-catcher, death of a, 133.
Mole-catching, occupation of, 134, 135.
Moss litter, great use of in British army, 45.

Nantwich, salt mines at, 102.
National schools, attended by children of poorer classes, 216, 217; church opposition to, 215, 216; compulsory attendance, 217; corporal punishment in, 224; lunches provided, 221; number of pupils, 216; number of pupils in national church schools,

216; school-fees, amount of, 217-219; opposition to, 217, 218; scholarships, 225; teachers' salaries, 220.
Newcastle, Springman of, 117, 118; "Thirty days hath September" written in, 118.
Newspapers, cheapness of, 249, 250; generally read, 250, 251; objectionable character of some, 249-251.

Oats, large crops of, 45.
Osier, ancient use of, 93, 94; cutting and preparation of, 91; use of in coffin making, 92-94.
Osier-holts, 90.
Out-tellers, duties of, 184, 185.
Overstone, Lord, a leading financial authority, 208; his confidence in hard money, 209; his religious belief, 208, 209; lessons drawn from life of, 210. (See *London and Westminster Bank*.)

Paxton, Sir Joseph, grave of, 314-316; home of, 316; labors of, 315, 316.
"Peculiar People," customs of, 240, 241; founder of, 240; mode of worship, 240; treatment of disease, 240, 241; troubles of, 241.
Philanthropy, higher classes much given to, 302, 303.
Physicians, charges to laboring classes, 248, 249; charges to higher classes, 249.
Pigeon-flying, common in North of England, 54; description of, 55.
Pineapples, grown in tanbark, 53; perfection of, 53.
Political orators questioned by audiences, 329, 330.
Polytechnic Young Men's Christian Institute, founder of, 152; membership, 151; wide scope of, 151, 152.
Poor-box, a feature in English courts, 306; incidents relating to, 306, 307.
Primroses, abundance of, 272; badge of Toryism, 269, 270; favorite flower of Beaconsfield, 269. (See *Beaconsfield*.)
Public halls very common in English cities and towns, 329.
Public libraries, great numbers of, 142.

Queen's counsel, costume of, 306; rights and privileges of, 329.

Queen's Remembrancer, duties of, 294; proclamations of, 294, 295.

Racing, clerical opposition to, at Leeds, 233; not universally approved by Englishmen, 232, 233.
Railways, employés a fee-taking class, 34, 35; orders of merit for, 35; social position of, 34; frequency of tunnels, 30–32; sleepers usually of larch, 28; solid nature of road beds, 27, 28.
Red brick a popular building material, 136, 137.
Roman Catholic schools, number of pupils in, 216.
Roman roads, 2.
Round-houses, described, 11, 12; story concerning, 13; use of, 12.
Royal Society for Prevention of Cruelty to Animals, benefits exerted by, 113.
Rural schools, extreme plainness of, 223; over-crowded and poorly ventilated, 222.

Safe deposit company, but one in London, 179. (See *Special deposits.*)
Saw-pits, 86.
St. Paul's Cathedral, choristers in, 289; clubs connected with, 289; congregations, 288, 290; lectures, 289; services, 288.
Scripture readers, anniversary meetings of, 98; dress of, 98.
Sea, solitude of, 332.
Second-hand shops, contents of, 312; teeth for sale in, 313.
Seed farm, a great, 40.
"See London, or die a fool," 67.
Sermons, proposed abolition, 290; topics, 291.
Servant-hiring fairs, terms at, 120; time of, 119–121. (See *Carlisle.*)
Sheep, kept in London parks, 46, 47; number of in United Kingdom in 1882, 46; pens for, in Scotland, 47, 48; washings, 47.
Sheffield, manufactures of, 108; razors, 109; Red-Book, 108; supposed properties of its water, 107.
Shoemaking not considered a high-caste trade, 69.
Sir Walter Scott, funeral procession of, 5, 6.
Slippery pavements, use of gravel on, 254, 255.

Smudgers, a local term, 138.
Society for Preservation of Open Spaces, aided by act of Parliament, 84; work of, 84, 85.
Special deposits, 177–182. (See *Strong room*.)
Stable feed, 23.
Steeple-jack, explanation of term, 95; mode of working, 95, 96.
Stone roofing, 139.
Stone stable floors, 22.
Stoves little used in rural England, 138.
Strawberries, large size of, 51; served with sugar and lemon, 52; wild variety, 52, 53.
Stratford, amusing incident at, 314; famous for its beer, 75.
Street music, abundance of, in English towns, 244; opposition to, 245.
Street-retiring houses, use of, 252, 253.
Street "slippers," duties of, 255, 256.
Strolling players, exhibitions by, 79, 80; numbers of, 79.
Strong room, 180–182; responsibilities connected with, 178, 179.
Sunday cricket club, a, 99.

Tanning and tanneries, 70–72. (See *Kenilworth*.)
Telegraph, great use made of in banking, 190; number of offices in the United Kingdom, 263; sixpenny rate demanded, 263; unobtrusive style of poles, 264; vast number of wires in London, 264, 265.
"Thirty Days hath September," author of, 118. (See *Newcastle*.)
Thatching, rye straw used for, 141.
Three per cent, a popular rate of interest, 192, 194; current sayings regarding, 194.
Ticket-of-leave system, Australian origin of, 130.

Universal Knowledge Society, scope of, 246.
Urban population, preponderance over suburban, 153.

Vaccination, opposition to, 242, 243.
Ventilation, great attention paid to, 139.

Walker, independence of, 2.

Waltham Cross, cocoa-rooms at, 25; pronunciation of, 25.
Watch-clubs, workings of, 131, 132.
Water little used for drinking in England, 125.
Water-cress, great use of, 235.
Watford, imbecile asylum at, 79.
Watling Street, 2.
Weights, curious table of, 135, 136.
Wesleyan schools, number of pupils in, 216.
Wheat, average production for nineteen years, 38; limit of cultivation, 37.
White glove, a curious legal custom, 293.
Wide horse stalls, 23.
Women, as laborers in Scotland, 248; lack of ambition in Doulton pottery employés, 247; new opportunities for employment of, 246.
Wool centre, London the greatest in the world, 49.
Wooden houses not common in England, 136.
Worcester, court opening ceremonies at, 294.

Yellow a conservative color, 271. (See *Beaconsfield*.)
York Minster, experience in, 112; special annual service held in, 110–112; view from roof, 111.

www.ingramcontent.com/pod-product-compliance
Lightning Source LLC
Chambersburg PA
CBHW030307240426
43673CB00040B/1089